Managing Maintenance Resources

Managing Maintenance Resources

Anthony Kelly

AMSTERDAM • BOSTON • HEIDELBERG • LONDON • OXFORD •
NEW YORK • PARIS • SAN DIEGO • SAN FRANCISCO • SINGAPORE •
SYDNEY • TOKYO

Butterworth-Heinemann is an imprint of Elsevier
Linacre House, Jordan Hill, Oxford OX2 8DP, UK
30 Corporate Drive, Suite 400, Burlington, MA 01803, USA

First edition 2006
Reprinted 2007

Notice
No responsibility is assumed by the publisher for any injury and/or damage to persons
or property as a matter of products liability, negligence or otherwise, or from any use
or operation of any methods, products, instructions or ideas contained in the material
herein. Because of rapid advances in the medical sciences, in particular, independent
verification of diagnoses and drug dosages should be made

British Library Cataloguing in Publication Data
A catalogue record for this book is available from the British Library

Library of Congress Cataloging-in-Publication Data
A catalog record for this book is available from the Library of Congress

ISBN: 978-0-7506-6993-1
ISBN: 978-0-7506-6995-5 (set of three volumes)

For information on all Butterworth-Heinemann publications
visit our website at books.elsevier.com

07 08 09 10 10 9 8 7 6 5 4 3 2

Working together to grow
libraries in developing countries

www.elsevier.com | www.bookaid.org | www.sabre.org

ELSEVIER   BOOK AID
International   Sabre Foundation

Contents

Preface   *xi*
Acknowledgments   *xiii*
Author's biography   *xv*

Part 1 Introductory chapters   **1**

**1 A business-centered approach to maintenance
    organization**   **3**
  1.1   Introduction   4
  1.2   Business-centered maintenance   4
  1.3   An example of the application of BCM: background   5
  1.4   Part A: Audit of the FPP maintenance department   7
        1.4.1   Maintenance objectives   7
        1.4.2   Life plans and preventive schedule   8
        1.4.3   Workload   11
        1.4.4   Maintenance organization   13
        1.4.5   Maintenance work planning   16
        1.4.6   Maintenance control system   18
        1.4.7   Maintenance documentation   19
        1.4.8   Audit summary   21
  1.5   Part B: An alternative maintenance strategy for
        continuous operation   22
  1.6   Part C: A longer-term view of organizational change   23
  1.7   The strategic thought process   23

2 Maintenance organization in outline   **29**
  2.1   Introduction   30
  2.2   Modeling the organization   31
  2.3   Factors influencing the design of the maintenance
        organization   33

3 The maintenance workload   **39**
  3.1   Introduction   40
  3.2   Categorization of the maintenance workload   40
  3.3   Mapping the workload   43
        3.3.1   First line workload   43
        3.3.2   Second-line workload   45
        3.3.3   Third-line workload   46
  3.4   Forecasting the maintenance workload   46
        3.4.1   First-line workload   47
        3.4.2   Second-line workload   47
        3.4.3   Third-line workload   48

3.5   Case studies in categorizing and mapping the maintenance
      workload   49
      3.5.1   Ammonia plant   49
      3.5.2   Chemical plant   49
      3.5.3   Agricultural chemicals   50
      3.5.4   Alumina refining   51

Part 2   Maintenance organizational concepts, trends and mapping   55

4   Maintenance resource structure   57
      4.1   Introduction   58
      4.2   Mapping the resource structure   58
      4.3   Resource characteristics   62
            4.3.1   Manpower   63
            4.3.2   Spare parts   63
            4.3.3   Tools   64
            4.3.4   Information   64
      4.4   A decision model for the design or modification of a
            resource structure   67
      4.5   The key decision-making areas of resource structuring   68
            4.5.1   Contract labor   68
            4.5.2   Trade-force composition   71
            4.5.3   Plant specialization   74
            4.5.4   Trade-force location   74
            4.5.5   Non-daywork maintenance cover   75
            4.5.6   Sizing the trade-force   77
            4.5.7   Locations of spares, tools and information   78
            4.5.8   Logistics   79
      4.6   A systematic procedure for determining a resource structure 79
            4.6.1   For a new plant   79
            4.6.2   For an existing resource structure   81
      4.7   Summary   84

5   Maintenance administrative structure   89
      5.1   Introduction   90
      5.2   Modeling administrative structures   90
      5.3   Traditional views on administrative management and
            some guidelines   91
      5.4   Characteristics of maintenance administrative structures 97
            5.4.1   The maintenance–engineering interface   97
            5.4.2   The maintenance–production interface   99
            5.4.3   Responsibility for spare parts management   103
            5.4.4   Vertical polarization   103
            5.4.5   The relationship between the professional
                    engineer and the maintenance supervisor   104

5.4.6   Major overhaul administration   104
5.4.7   Summary   106
5.5   The design or modification of the administrative structure   107

6 Human factors in maintenance management   111
6.1   Introduction   112
      6.1.1   What are 'human factors' in organizations?   112
6.2   The human relations approach to management:
      a brief review   113
6.3   Maintenance management behavioral characteristics   114
      6.3.1   Individual behavioral characteristics   115
      6.3.2   Group behavioral characteristics   120
6.4   The effect of outsourcing alliances   123
6.5   Auditing maintenance management human factors   124

7 Trends in maintenance organization   127
7.1   Introduction   128
7.2   Traditional maintenance organizations   128
7.3   Centralized resource structures   129
7.4   Introduction of flexible working practices   133
7.5   Plant manufacturing units   136
7.6   Slimming the structure ('downsizing')   139
7.7   The movement toward self-empowered plant-oriented teams   142
7.8   Contracting, outsourcing and alliances   145
7.9   Summary   147

Part 3 Maintenance organization case studies   151

8 Case study 1: Moving with the times   153
8.1   Introduction   154
8.2   Background   154
8.3   Audit of the CMG   156
8.4   Setting up the alliance   162
8.5   Observations   164

9 Case studies 2 and 3: Cautionary tales of organizational
change   169
9.1   Introduction   170
9.2   Case study 2: A bottling plant   170
      9.2.1   Background   170
      9.2.2   The plant maintenance strategy and organization   171
      9.2.3   Organizational change: the way forward   173
      9.2.4   Short-term actions   174
9.3   Case study 3: An aluminum rolling mill   175
      9.3.1   Background   175
      9.3.2   Plant-operating characteristics and objectives   177
      9.3.3   Life plans and preventive schedules   177

9.3.4	An overview of the organization	178
9.3.5	Maintenance systems	181
9.3.6	Observations and recommendations	182

10 Case study 4: Reorganization of a colliery   **185**
10.1   Introduction   186
10.2   Maintenance consultancy at COALCOM – 1994   186
    10.2.1   Background to COALCOM   186
    10.2.2   Equipment and operating characteristics   187
    10.2.3   Production and maintenance objectives   189
    10.2.4   Life plans and preventive schedule   189
    10.2.5   Maintenance organization   191
    10.2.6   Maintenance systems   196
    10.2.7   Recommendations   196
10.3   Progress visit and consultancy – 1997   201
    10.3.1   Introduction   201
    10.3.2   Organization   201
    10.3.3   Life plans and preventive schedule   204
    10.3.4   Recommendations – 1997   204

**11 Case study 5: The do's and don'ts of maintenance
teams**   **209**
11.1   Introduction   210
11.2   Characteristics of teams at Fertec B   210
11.3   Characteristics of teams at Cario   213
11.4   Improving team operation at Fertec B   214
11.5   General comments on maintenance teams   215

**12 Case study 6: Maintenance audit of an agricultural
chemical plant**   **219**
12.1   Introduction   220
12.2   An overview of Fertec A   220
12.3   Objectives   222
    12.3.1   Comments on objectives   222
12.4   Maintenance strategy   224
    12.4.1   Plant-operating characteristics   224
    12.4.2   Ammonia plant maintenance strategy   224
12.5   Maintenance organization   232
    12.5.1   Introduction   232
    12.5.2   The maintenance resource structure   232
    12.5.3   The maintenance administrative structure   236

Part 4 Total productive maintenance   **245**

**13 Total productive maintenance: its uses and
limitations**   **247**
13.1   Introduction   248
13.2   What is TPM?   248

13.3   An early case study   249
13.4   Fundamentals of TPM   253
13.5   European applications by non-Japanese companies   256
13.6   Summary   261

Part 5 Exercises   **267**

14 Course exercises   **269**
14.1   Exercise E14.1: The changing role of the
        maintenance supervisor   269
        14.1.1   Background   269
        14.1.2   Part A: The supervisor's role in a traditional
                 organization   270
        14.1.3   Part B: The role of the supervisor after a
                 'downsizing' exercise   270
        14.1.4   Part C: Introduction of self-empowered
                 work teams   272
14.2   Exercise E14.2: Maintenance reorganization in a food
        processing plant   274
        14.2.1   Background   274
        14.2.2   Company organization and maintenance strategy 276
        14.2.3   The problem   280

Index   *289*

Preface

Managing Maintenance Resources is the second of three companion books covering material which has been developed (and updated) from my 1997 publications *Maintenance Strategy* and *Maintenance Organization and Systems*, which were subsequently expanded and converted into distance-learning units which comprised the first half of a 2-year Masters program offered by an Australia and a UK university.

The main approach adopted throughout all three books, and which determines the direction and content of all the material, is that of business-centered maintenance (BCM), the starting point of which is the identification of the business aims. These are then translated into the maintenance objectives which, in their turn, are used to underpin the formulation firstly of strategy (the subject of Book 1, *Strategic Maintenance Planning*, *viz.*, the *planning* aspects of maintenance management), secondly of the design of the appropriate organization (the subject of this book, *viz.* the *doing* aspects of maintenance management) and finally the creation of the necessary systems (the subject of Book 3, *Maintenance Systems and Documentation*, *viz.* the *controlling* aspects).

Because the material has come from a distance-learning program all three books contain numerous review questions (with answers), exercises and case studies – these last having been selected to ensure coverage of the care of physical assets across a wide range of industries (process, mining, food, power generation and transmission, etc.). In addition, every chapter has its own clearly specified objectives and learning outcomes – as well as a route map which enables the reader to see where the chapter is in relation to the rest of the topics covered.

Although the BCM approach integrates all three books into a unified maintenance management methodology, I have tried to ensure that each one can stand alone, i.e. be studied and understood in isolation from its companion works. It is therefore inevitable that there is some overlap, *viz.*:

- To explain the principles and concepts of BCM, the same case study (of a food processing plant) is used at the beginning of each book.
- To illustrate the linkage between maintenance planning, organization and systems, a full audit of a chemical plant is presented at the end of each book.

The overall aim of each book is to provide managers of physical assets with a better understanding of the operation of the maintenance function, an understanding which will enable them to identify problems within their own organization and prescribe effective solutions. As asserted by Henry Mintzberg (Managers Not MBAs, *Financial Times*, Prentice Hall, 2004):

> *What managers really need from a course or a book is insight – theories or models that enable them to make sense of practice, learn from experience and reach better judgements.*

The provision of such insight is the overriding purpose of these three books.

Managing Maintenance Resources recognizes that engineering, or re-engineering, a maintenance organization is a complex problem involving many interrelated decisions – concerning such matters as whether or not resources should be centralized, contractor alliances should be entered into, flexible working be adopted, and so on – each of which may be influenced by many conflicting factors (trade union relationships, production policy, etc.). The main purpose of this book is therefore to show how to reduce the complexity of organizational design by providing:

- A unique way of mapping or modeling the maintenance–production organization, a way that facilitates the identification of organizational problems.
- Organizational guidelines that can be used to provide solutions to the identified problems.

Chapter 1 is the key section, setting the maintenance organization within the context of BCM (the principles and concepts of which are explained via a case study of a food processing plant). Chapter 2 shows how a maintenance organization can be mapped using a series of interrelated models. Chapter 3 explains how scheduling characteristics may be used to categorize and map the maintenance workload.

Chapters 4 and 5 draw on a comprehensive case study to explain how organizational models can be used to map the maintenance–production relationships of a large and complex industrial company. Those human factors, such as equipment 'ownership', that can affect the operation of the maintenance department are identified in Chapter 6, and the principle maintenance organizational trends that have occurred over the last 40 years are outlined in Chapter 7.

In Chapters 8–12, six case studies – taken from my own consultancy work – illustrate various important aspects of maintenance organization, such as the impacts of organizational change, team working, alliances and auditing. The book concludes with a review of the concepts and ideas of total productive maintenance (in Chapter 13) and two exercises, for the reader to attempt, in the analysis of a maintenance organization (in Chapter 14).

Anthony Kelly
a.kelly99@ntlworld.com

Acknowledgments

Firstly, I wish to acknowledge a special gratitude to John Harris who has edited the complete text. I must also acknowledge Dr. H.S. Riddell who contributed Figure 5.11, Exercise 14.1, and worked as my co-auditor on Case studies 1 and 6.

Thanks also go to the people in industry, most recently: Bill Sugden, Ian Peterson, Gudmunder Bjornason, Leonard Bouwman, Kevin Hardman, Nigel Beard and many others who provided access to their plants and without whose help this book could not have been written.

Finally, I thank Vicky Taylor for typing the text and Denise Jackson for producing the artwork.

Author's biography

Dr. Anthony Kelly served a trade apprenticeship before obtaining a first degree in mechanical engineering from the University of Wales and a Masters Degree (in corrosion engineering) from the University of London. He then held several industrial positions, in which he was responsible for the management of maintenance resources, before joining, in 1969, the University of Manchester, UK, where he specialized in maintenance management, its teaching and research, and obtained his doctorate for a thesis on maintenance organizational design. Dr. Kelly has published numerous technical papers and seven textbooks which have been translated into several languages.

Over the last 15 years Dr. Kelly has run his own consultancy partnership, operating worldwide and carrying out more than 60 major investigations and audits of a wide variety of industrial activities: mining, power generation and distribution, chemical processing, manufacturing, building services, etc. Over the last 15 years he has also held visiting/industrial professorships at Central Queensland University (Australia), University of Stellenbosch (South Africa) and Hogskolen i Stavanger (Norway).

PART 1

Introductory chapters

1 A business-centered approach to maintenance organization

'In strategy it is important to see distant things as if they were close and to take a distanced view of close things.'
Miyamoto Musashi (1646), Japanese Swordsman

Chapter aims and outcomes

To explain the business-centered maintenance (BCM) procedure and then show how it can be used to develop or modify the maintenance strategy for a complex industrial plant.

On completion of this chapter you should be able to:

- understand the methodology of BCM and why it is so called;
- understand that maintenance strategy is concerned with deciding how to maintain the plant, with setting up an appropriate maintenance organization, and with the establishment and use of systems to direct the maintenance effort;
- understand how the BCM methodology can be used to map and model the maintenance department of an industrial plant in order to improve the maintenance organization – the strategic thought process.

Chapter route map

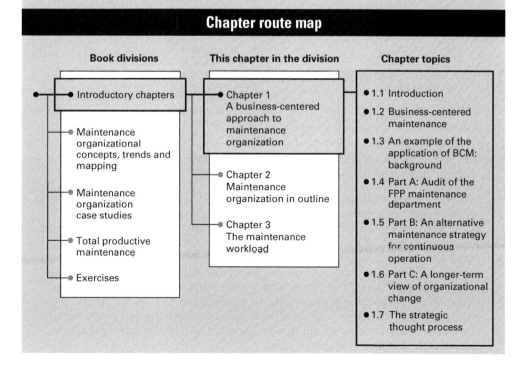

Book divisions	This chapter in the division	Chapter topics
Introductory chapters	Chapter 1 A business-centered approach to maintenance organization	1.1 Introduction 1.2 Business-centered maintenance
Maintenance organizational concepts, trends and mapping		1.3 An example of the application of BCM: background
Maintenance organization case studies	Chapter 2 Maintenance organization in outline	1.4 Part A: Audit of the FPP maintenance department
Total productive maintenance	Chapter 3 The maintenance workload	1.5 Part B: An alternative maintenance strategy for continuous operation
Exercises		1.6 Part C: A longer-term view of organizational change
		1.7 The strategic thought process

Key words

- Business-centered maintenance
- Maintenance organization
- Maintenance auditing
- Strategic thought process
- Business objectives

1.1 Introduction

As explained in the preface, this is the second of three companion books on mainte-nance management. In Book 1, *Strategic Maintenance Planning*, we dealt with the identification of objectives and the formulation of the maintenance strategy. In Book 3, *Maintenance Systems and Documentation*, we dealt with the systems that are needed to support the maintenance effort. Here, in Book 2, we shall examine the organizational aspects of maintenance management. Before doing so, and for the benefit of those who may not have read Book 1 or 3, it is important firstly to recall the overall BCM method-ology, which was described as:

> *. . . a framework of guidelines for deciding maintenance objectives, formulating equipment life plans and plant maintenance schedules (**Maintenance Planning**), designing the maintenance organization (**Maintenance Doing**) and setting up appropriate systems of documentation and control (**Maintenance control**)*

and secondly to outline (via a case study) the concepts, procedures and models of all three of these areas of maintenance management.

1.2 Business-centered maintenance

The structure of a methodology for developing a maintenance strategy – which I call the business-centered maintenance (BCM) approach – is outlined in Figure 1.1. It is based on well-established administrative management principles (see Figure 1.2). It provides a framework for identifying, mapping and then auditing the elements of any maintenance-management system.

> In order to better understand the purpose of Figure 1.1, it is useful to put yourself in the position of a maintenance manager thinking through how he is going to set up a maintenance department for a new plant. Obviously he needs to under-stand the way the plant operates, its relationship with its market and the function of maintenance within this context. Inside the large circle is his strategic thought process starting with the plant maintenance objective (which is subordinate to the business objectives) and proceeding via life plans and organization through to control (this procedure is essentially the same as the basic management pro-cedure of Figure 1.2). From outside of the large circle come the numerous factors (from other departments or from the environment, e.g. industrial relations) that can affect the strategic thought process.

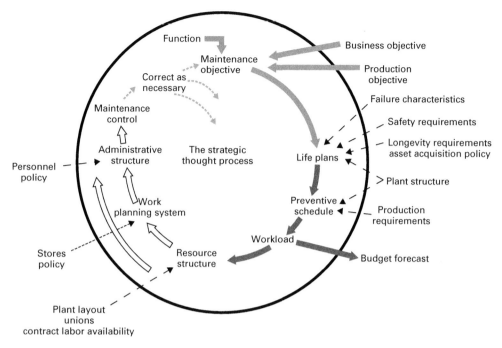

Figure 1.1 A BCM methodology

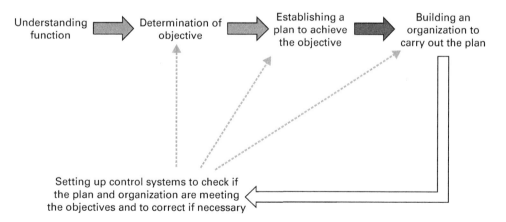

Figure 1.2 Basic steps of the management process

1.3 An example of the application of BCM: background

A more detailed and comprehensive explanation of BCM may be gained by referring to an industrial application, in this case its use in auditing the maintenance department of a food processing plant (FPP).

The plant layout was shown in Figure 1.3, and an outline process flow diagram being shown in Figure 1.4. At the time of the audit the production pattern was three shifts per day, 5 days per week, 50 weeks per year. There was also considerable spare capacity. For example, only three lines out of four (see Figure 1.4) were needed to achieve full capacity. However, each line had its own product mix to satisfy the market demand. Thus, the availability of any given line for maintenance depended on the market demand and the level of finished product stored. Offline maintenance could be carried out in the weekend windows of opportunity or, by exploring spare capacity, during the

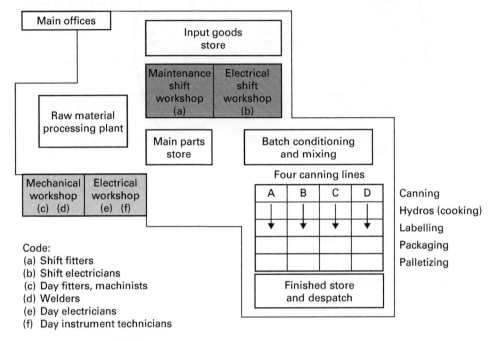

Figure 1.3 Layout of FPP

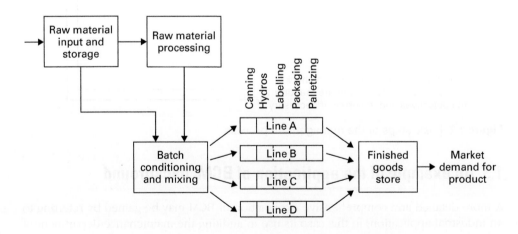

Pattern of operation 50 weeks x 5 days x 3 shifts, Monday/Friday

Figure 1.4 Process flow for FPP

week. In general, the maintenance manager found it easier to carry out most of the offline work during the weekend.

> The relationship between the plant and the market demand for its product (and/or raw material supply) has a considerable influence on maintenance strategy. It governs the way production will use the plant, the plant-operating pattern. This in turn determines the frequency, duration and cost of scheduling the plant for offline maintenance, maintenance windows.
>
> The market demand is different across different industries. For example, baseload power stations (stations that provide the cheapest electricity) are required to operate for as long as possible because of a constant and continuous demand. The FPP of this example is a multi-product company where the demand for each product may well vary with time, often seasonally.

The problem the company faced was that they wanted to increase their output by using the weekends for production and by operating each line for as long as possible. Experience had led to the feeling that each line could operate continuously for about 4 weeks before coming out, for two shifts, for maintenance. The company wanted to know how this was going to affect their maintenance strategy and the following tasks were requested:

A To audit their existing maintenance department in order to compare it to international best practice.
B To propose an alternative maintenance strategy that would facilitate the new mode of continuous operation.
C To provide an organizational vision (via models) of where the company should be heading in the next 5 years.

> The audit of the FPP (task A above) will be used to provide a detailed and comprehensive explanation of BCM. This will include descriptions of each of the main elements of BCM, e.g. objectives, and will also introduce a number of generic models that can be used to map and understand the operation of these elements. You may find it necessary during your progress through the audit to refer back to the master diagram of Figure 1.1. It is important as you progress through the audit that you consider how you would modify the organization to comply with tasks B and C above – the answer to these tasks will be incorporated into this chapter as exercises.

1.4 Part A: Audit of the FPP maintenance department

The audit procedure follows the main elements of the methodology model shown in Figure 1.1.

1.4.1 Maintenance objectives

At plant level this could be stated as being:

> *to achieve the 15-shift operating pattern, product mix and output (cans/week) within the accepted plant condition for longevity and safety requirements, and at minimum resource cost.*

It is the responsibility of the production, safety and engineering departments to specify the plant requirements, and the maintenance department to develop the strategy to achieve these requirements at minimum cost.

If the maintenance department were to develop the 'best way of maintaining the plant' the maintenance objectives needed to be interpreted in a form that is meaningful at a lower level of equipment, the plant unit – a hydro, say, or the cooker (see Figure 1.5). This allowed the maintenance *life plans* for the various units of plant to be established.

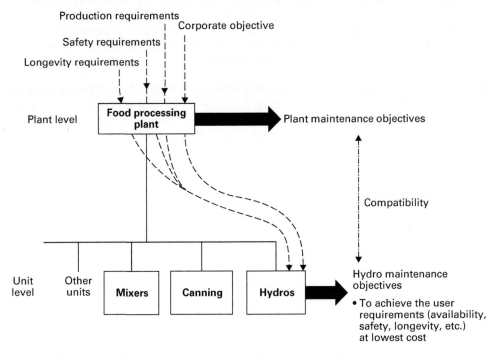

Figure 1.5 Bringing plant maintenance objectives to unit level

The audit established that the FPP were using a management-by-objectives (MBO) procedure. Business objectives were set, and translated into maintenance objectives by the chief engineer. These in turn were translated into key result areas (KRAs) which, rather than being objectives, were a series of future actions to achieve the maintenance objectives. The auditors considered the procedure to be excellent but the KRAs were not well enough directed toward maintenance objectives and were not expressed sufficiently numerical.

1.4.2 Life plans and preventive schedule

A generic model of a life plan for a unit of plant (a hydro, say) is shown in Figure 1.6. Such a plan can be considered as a program of maintenance jobs (lubrication, inspection, repair, replace and carried out at set frequencies) spanning the expected life of the unit. The main decision regarding the life plan is the determination of the preventive policy (replace or repair at fixed-time or fixed-operating periods, or via some form of inspection), which, in its turn, determines the resulting level of corrective work. The life plans should be established, using the well-documented principles of preventive maintenance and should be reviewed periodically to ensure their effectiveness.

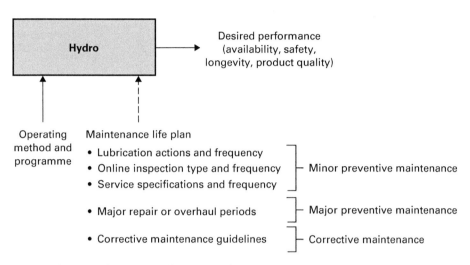

Figure 1.6 Outline of a life plan for a unit of plant

The preventive maintenance schedule for the FPP was assembled from the preventive jobs identified in the life plans (see Figure 1.7). Such a schedule is only one part of the maintenance workload and has to be carried out in conjunction with the corrective work, which has a shorter scheduling horizon – and often higher priority (sometimes restricting the maintenance department's ability to carryout corrective work – an aspect which will be discussed in more detail when we come to work planning).

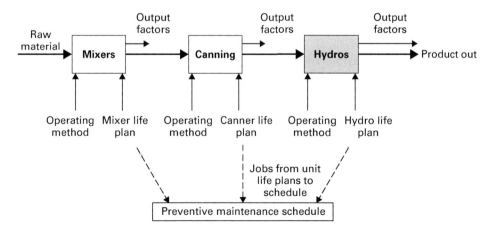

Figure 1.7 Build up of plant preventive schedule from unit life plans

Table 1.1 Outline the hydro life plan

Weekly	Cleaning, check operation of critical parts, lubrication.	4 hours	Minor work
2 weekly/ monthly	Lubrication routine.	4 hours	
3 monthly	Inspection of main drive to include oil analysis.	8 hours	
6 monthly	Inspection of all flights and conveyor drives. Clean hydro internally. Oil analysis of conveyor drives.	3 shifts	
12 monthly	Fixed-time replacement of sprocket bearings. Overhaul drive unit and rewind motors.	1 week	
2 yearly	Replace with speed drive belts.	1 week	
8 yearly	Major rebuild. Exact frequency on condition.	3 weeks	Major work

Table 1.2 Scheduling guidelines for the FPP

	Maintenance philosophy	Work type
Monday to Friday	'Keep the plant going' and 'Keep an eye on its condition'	Reactive maintenance Operator monitoring routines Trade-force line-patrolling routines Condition-based routines
Weekends	'Inspect the plant carefully and repair as necessary in order to keep it going until next weekend'	Schedule corrective jobs by priority Inspect and repair schedule Fixed-time minor job schedule (services, etc.)
Summer shutdown	'Schedule out the major jobs to see us through another year'	Schedule corrective jobs Fixed-time major jobs schedule

The schedule is influenced by the production plan – which itself is a function of the market demand (multi-product fluctuating demand requiring a flexible production plan), operating pattern, plant redundancy, inter-stage and final-stage storage, etc. In the FPP case the important factor was the operating pattern which gave six shift-weekend windows and a 2-week annual window that provided enough time to carry out the necessary preventive (and corrective) work without affecting the production plan.

In spite of the criticism of the objectives the unit life plans investigated were good, e.g. see Table 1.1 for the life plan for the hydro. The work content of the Hydro overhauls (the major maintenance) was based on the monitoring and inspection of its condition. The frequency of overhauls, once every 8 years, was determined only via an experience-based, and approximate, judgment. Nevertheless it did give an indication of the future major workload and its resource scheduling and budgeting. The preventive schedule was based on the scheduling guidelines outlined in Table 1.2. This meant that most of the second-line work was carried out at weekends. Little attempt had been made to schedule this latter work into the weekend, by exploiting spare capacity.

(Life plans and the preventive schedule are covered in depth in *Strategic Maintenance Planning*.)

1.4.3 Workload

The maintenance schedule generates the maintenance workload (see Figure 1.1). The mechanical workload for the FPP is mapped in Figure 1.8 by its scheduling characteristics (the electrical workload can be mapped in the same way). *First-line work* is made up from emergency jobs (which can be defined as work needing to be carried out in the shift of its occurrence) and jobs (corrective or preventive) that are small and do not require detailed planning, they can be 'fitted in'.

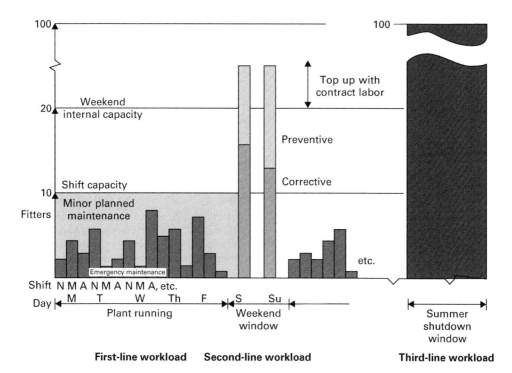

Figure 1.8 Workload profile for fitters

It can be seen that this work is carried out during the shifts over Monday to Friday. Management had manned up the shift resource to ensure all the emergency work received attention during the shift of its occurrence.

Second-line work involves the larger preventive jobs (services, small overhauls, etc.) and corrective jobs that require planning and, via a priority system can be scheduled to be carried out at weekend (or in some other available window).

Table 1.3 Detailed categorization of maintenance workload by organizational characteristics

Main category	Subcategory	Category number	Comments
First line	Corrective emergency	1	Occurs with random incidence and little warning and the job times also vary greatly. A typical emergency workload is shown in Figure 1.8. This is a workload generated by operating plant, the pattern following the production-operating pattern (e.g. 5 days, three shifts per day, etc.). Requires urgent attention due to economic or safety imperatives. Planning limited to resource cover and some job instructions or decision guidelines. Can be offline or online (*in-situ* corrective techniques). In some industries (e.g. power generation) failures can generate major work, these are usually infrequent but cause large work peaks.
	Corrective deferred minor	2	Occurs in the same way as emergency corrective work but does not require urgent attention; it can be deferred until time and maintenance resources are available (it can be planned and scheduled). During plant operation some small jobs can be fitted into an emergency workload such as that of Figure 1.8 (smoothing).
	Preventive routines	3	Short periodicity work, normally involving inspections and/or lubrication and/or minor replacements. Usually online and carried out by specialists or used to smooth an emergency workload such as that of Figure 1.8.
Second line	Corrective deferred major	4	Same characteristics as (2) but of longer duration and requiring major planning and scheduling.
	Preventive services	5	Involves minor offline work carried out at short- or medium-length intervals. Scheduled with time tolerances for slotting and work smoothing purposes. Some work can be carried out online although most is carried out online during weekend or other shutdown windows.
	Corrective reconditioning and fabrication	6	Similar to deferred work but is carried out away from the plant (second-line maintenance) and usually by a separate trade-force.
Third line	Preventive major work (overhauls, etc.)	7	Involves overhauls of plant, plant sections of major units. Work is offline and carried out at medium- or long-term intervals. Such a workload varies in the long term as shown in Figure 1.8. The shutdown schedule for large multi-plant companies can be designed to smooth the company shutdown workload.
	Modifications	8	Can be planned and scheduled some time ahead. The modification workload (often 'capital work') tends to rise to a peak at the end of the company financial year. This work can also be used to smooth the shutdown workload.

When the weekend workload exceeded the internal weekend resource (two of the four shift-groups – 20 fitters) contract labor was used to cover the excess.

Third-line work involves major plant (or parts of the plant) overhauls. It requires the plant to be offline for considerable periods and is carried out at medium- or long-term intervals, in the FPP case in the annual 2-week windows. The planning lead time for such work can be many months.

A more detailed categorization of a maintenance workload is shown in Table 1.3.

The audit revealed a 50% over-manning on the mid-week shifts, caused by lack of clear definition of emergency work – much of which could have been carried out at the weekends as planned second-line work.

1.4.4 Maintenance organization

The workload is the biggest single influence in the size and shape of the maintenance organization. At the FPP the first-line emergency work required shift cover and the yearly shutdown peak required contract labor. Designing the organization requires many inter-related decisions to be made (where to locate manpower, how to extend inter-trade flexibility, who should be responsible for spare parts, how to decide the responsibilities for plant operation and maintenance), each influenced by various conflicting factors. Thinking in terms of the methodology of Figure 1.1 reduces the complexity of this problem, by categorizing the decisions according to the main elements of the organization, *viz.* its resource structure, its administrative structure, its systems, and then considering each one in the order indicated – the procedure is iterative.

Resource structure

The resource structure is the geographic location of workforce, spares, tools and information, their function, composition, size and logistics. For example, Figure 1.9 shows the Monday-to-Friday structure that had evolved at the FPP, to best suit the characteristics of a 24-hour first-line emergency workload. The emphasis is on rapid response, plant knowledge via specialization, shift working, and team working with production. In theory, the shift-groups had been sized to match the reactive workload with the lower-priority jobs being used to smooth the workload. The weekday centralized group carried out second-line work to include weekend preparation, reconditioning and also acted as a first-line work overspill for the shift-groups.

Figure 1.10 shows the structure that matched the second-line weekend workload. The shift roster was arranged to ensure that two of the four shift-groups are available for 12 hours on Saturdays and Sundays (to include some overtime). Contract labor was used to top-up, as necessary the internal labor force. A similar approach was used for the annual shutdown, but in that case the contracted workforce exceeded the internally available labor. The spare parts store and tool store was an integral part of the resource structure and in this case both were centralized, serving the whole site.

The resource structure, e.g. see Figure 1.9, can be regarded as a simple matrix of plant specialization against work category (first line, second line, etc.). To enable the structure to be drawn it is necessary to construct the horizontal axis as the *plant line*, i.e. the division of the plant into its main process areas, and the vertical

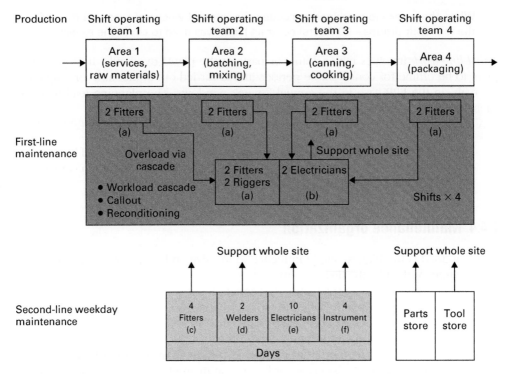

Figure 1.9 Weekday resource structure

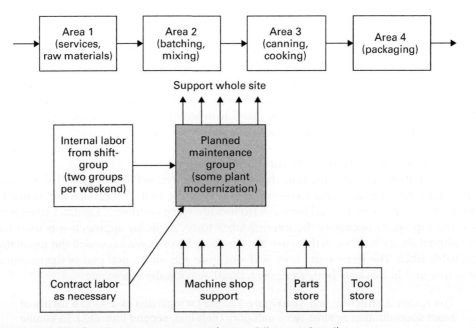

Figure 1.10 Weekend resource structure (second-line weekend)

axis as the *work-type line*, i.e. operations above the plant line and maintenance work categories below the plant line. In this case the complete structure (weekday and weekend) could have been drawn on the same diagram. It would have then been necessary to explain on the diagram how the shift teams related into the weekend teams. Resource structures provide an outline of the way in which maintenance resources are used – they need to be supplemented by a description of trade flexibility, contract usage, shift rostering and human factors, etc.

The aim of any resource structure design (or modification) is to achieve the best resource utilization for a desired speed of response and quality of work. This, in part, involves the best match of the resources to the workload. Decisions in a number of other areas (e.g. in shift rostering, the use of contract labor, inter-plant flexibility, inter-trade flexibility and production-maintenance flexibility) can influence this matching process. Flexibility is clearly the key factor here. The structure is also influenced by the availability of trade-force skills and by various human factors.

> The FPP audit revealed a number of deficiencies in the resource structure. The most important was the over-manning of the mid-week shifts (see the workload comments). The audit was carried out 13 years ago and it is not surprising that inter-trade flexibility, production-maintenance flexibility and contractor alliances were not being exploited. Human factors such as morale, motivation and a sense of equipment ownership were good.

Administrative structure

This can be considered as a hierarchy of work roles, ranked by their authority and responsibility for deciding what, when and how maintenance work should be carried out. The FPP structure is shown in Figure 1.11 (which uses the so-called organogram as the modeling vehicle). Many of the rules and guidelines of classical administrative theory can be used in the design of such structures. The model shows the maintenance administration in the context of the full administration – simplified in this case. The key decisions in the design of the maintenance administration can be divided between its upper and lower structures. Regarding the former the audit must identify how the responsibilities for plant ownership, operation and maintenance have been allocated. In the FPP case, production had responsibility for the operation of the plant, and in a sense its ownership, since they dictated how it was to be used and when it could be released for maintenance. Maintenance had responsibility for establishing and carrying out the maintenance strategy, and engineering for plant acquisition and plant condition standards. These responsibilities have to be clearly defined and overlapping areas identified.

Initially, the lower structure has to be considered separately from the upper because it is influenced – indeed, almost constrained – by the nature of the maintenance resource structure which, as explained, is in turn a function of the workload. Lower structure decisions are concerned with establishing the duties, responsibilities and work roles of the shop floor personnel and of the first level of supervision.

> The FPP was using the traditional supervisor – planner – trade-force structure. This needs to be compared with the more recent structures of self-empowered operator–maintainer shift teams and self-empowered second-line maintenance teams (see Chapter 11).

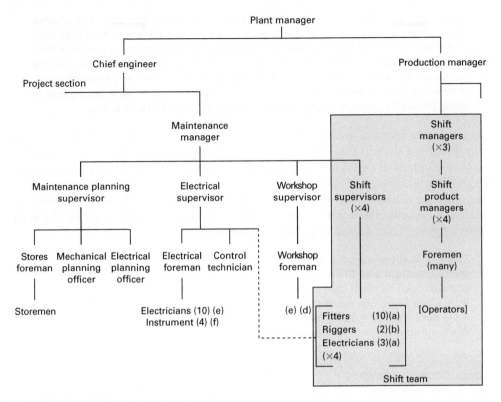

Figure 1.11 Administrative structure

1.4.5 Maintenance work planning

Figure 1.12 outlines a maintenance work planning system for the FPP resource and administrative structure previously shown. The design of this should aim to get the right balance between the cost of planning the resources and the savings in direct and indirect maintenance costs that result from use of such resources.

It can be seen that the planning system is designed around the resource structure – it has a shift planning system (first line), a weekend planning system (second line) and an annual shutdown planning system (third line, not shown in detail). The audit must identify how well each level of planning is being carried out. At each level there are key procedures to verify, e.g. at FPP's second level:

- How good is the information base in terms of standard job procedures, spare part list, history?
- Who identifies the job method for monitoring jobs?
- Are job times estimated before they are put into the forward log?
- How are multi-trade jobs handled?
- How good is the return of information in terms of quantity and quality?

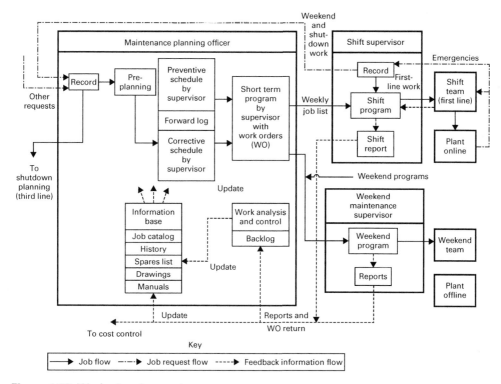

Figure 1.12 Work planning system

To understand operation of the 'weekday planning system' refer to Figures 1.9 and 1.12. Work originates from the plant areas and goes to the maintenance shift supervisor (MSS) via the operators and production supervisors. The MSS carries out priority 1 work (emergencies, etc.) and passes back lower-priority work to the planning officer (PO) for planning and scheduling. The MSS smooths the ongoing emergency workload by feeding low-priority first-line work (from the weekly planned job list) to the trade-force (see also Figure 1.8).

To understand the operation of the weekend planning system refer to Figures 1.10 and 1.12. Corrective jobs come into this system from the MSS and from other personnel, this work is priority 2 and above (plannable and schedulable). Work that can only be carried out in a major shutdown (priority 5) is passed onto the shutdown planning system. The jobs are pre-planned (spares, method, estimated time) and slotted by priority into the corrective schedule. The planning of the jobs is aided by the 'information base'. A weekly meeting (Thursday) establishes the 'weekend program' which is passed onto the weekend supervisor (one of the four MSS on a monthly rota) for detailed planning. The PO helps in co-ordinating the multi-trade jobs. Feedback to update the information base and for cost control comes back via completed work orders. In general such systems are now carried out electronically.

Figure 1.13 shows the work control system, which is complementary to the work planning system, its main function being to control the flow of work (preventive and corrective) via a job priority procedure and via the feed-forward of information about

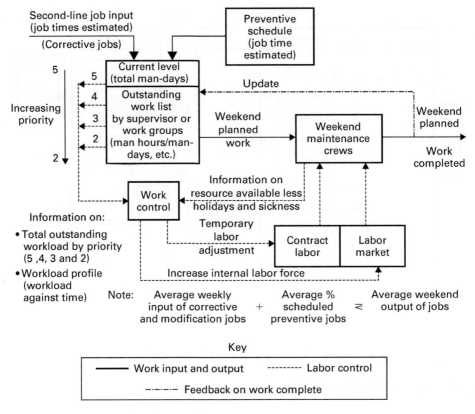

Figure 1.13 Principles of work control

future resource availability. At FPP a number of performance indices were being used to assist this process, *viz.*:

- Total man-days in the forward log.
- Man-days in the forward log by priority.
- Man-days in the backlog.
- Percent planned work completed per period.
- Percent of preventive work completed per period.

  The audit revealed that the FPP's work planning system was satisfactory for what was essentially a weekly planning system, the work is planned during the week for the weekend.

  It was my opinion that the work planning system (and the associated software) would have to be up-rated if major jobs were to be planned at short notice during the week (see Section B of this case study).

1.4.6 Maintenance control system

This is needed to ensure that the maintenance organization is achieving its objectives (see Figure 1.1) and to initiate corrective action (e.g. change the life plan, if it is not).

My own opinion is that the best practical mechanism for controlling the *overall maintenance effort* would be a properly designed maintenance costing system. This (see Figure 1.14) could be designed to provide a variety of outputs, including 'Top Tens', or Pareto plots indicating areas of low reliability, high maintenance cost, poor output performance, etc.

The FPP audit identified that the plant had a costing system similar to that outlined in Figure 1.14 but used cost centers that were accountancy oriented rather than equipment oriented. In addition, the maintenance expenditure was not linked in any way to the output parameters.

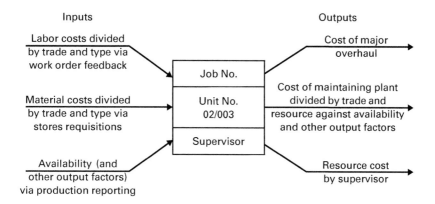

Job No.	Plant code		Trade and supervisor		Work type
	Plant	Unit	Electrician	Night shift	Preventive
521	02	003	2	NS	2

Figure 1.14 Outline of maintenance costing system

Even if properly designed, a maintenance costing system has to be a high-level, longer-term system, providing a means of controlling the overall maintenance effort. This needs to be complemented by control systems operating at a lower level and on a shorter time scale.

1.4.7 Maintenance documentation

Figure 1.1 indicated that some forms of formal documentation system – for the collection, storage, interrogation, analysis and reporting of information (schedules, manuals, drawings or computer files) – are needed to facilitate the operation of all the elements of maintenance management. Figure 1.15, a general functional model of such a system

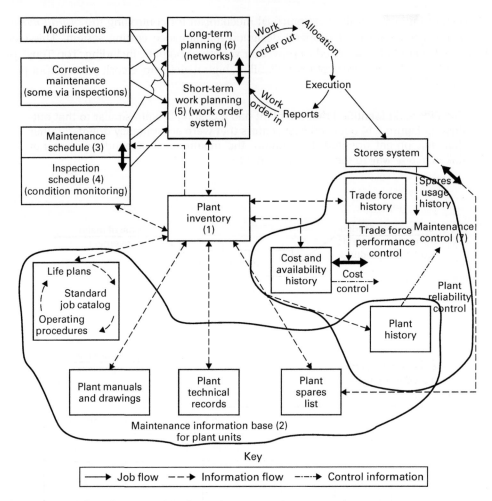

Figure 1.15 A functional model of a maintenance documentation system

(whether manual or computerized), indicates that it can be seen as comprising seven principal inter-related modules (performing different documentation functions). Considerable clerical and engineering effort is needed to establish and maintain certain of these functions (e.g. the plant maintenance information base). The control module, in particular, relies on an effective data collection system. Almost all of the companies that I now audit have computerized maintenance documentation systems.

The best way of understanding the generic functional documentation model of Figure 1.15 is to start with the plant inventory (Module 1). This is a coded list of the equipment that has to be maintained, e.g. a mixer (see Figure 1.4). The essential maintenance information needed to maintain the mixer (and the other units listed in the inventory) is held in the information base (Module 2), e.g. life plans, history, spares lists, etc. The preventive work listed in the life plans of the various equipment is carried out via the preventive and inspection schedules (Modules 3 and 4). This work and the corrective and modification work are fed into the 'short-term work planning system' (Module 5) and there are major shutdowns into the 'long-term work planning system' (Module 6). The feedback of information from the work planning system provides maintenance control (Module 7) and also updates the information base.

The bold double arrows in Figure 1.15 indicate that the possible linkages between the maintenance documentation system and other company information systems, *viz.*:

- Maintenance costing to financial management.
- Spare parts list to stores management.
- Work planning to shutdown scheduling (e.g. Primavera).
- Work planning to condition monitoring.

The majority of the systems I have audited have these functions connected, i.e. electronically – in fact, the most recent audit involved an integrated package – all the functions are on the same database. An audit needs to investigate each of the main modules of Figure 1.15, and also the sub-functions within each module, e.g. the spare parts list. In addition it needs to identify the level and degree of integration with the other company functions.

> The maintenance package at the FPP was a stand-alone computerized system. The audit revealed that this was satisfactory for the weekend planning system that was then being used (i.e. 13 years ago). For its time the plant information base was good and was being kept up to date (history excepted).

(Maintenance documentation and the other systems outlined in this case study are covered in depth in the third book of this series – *Maintenance Systems and Documentation*, ISBN 07506 69942.)

1.4.8 Audit summary

A business-centered methodology, in conjunction with models and procedures that describes in more detail each of its elements, has been used as a framework to audit the maintenance department.

The audit revealed a number of problems, in particular shift over-manning caused by lack of clear definition and measurement of the shift emergency maintenance work. In addition, the organization needed modification – improved inter-trade flexibility, the creation of operator–maintainer self-empowered teams, closer production-maintenance integration – to bring it up to international benchmark levels.

Review Questions

R1.1   You have been asked by your Managing Director to explain in a concise way what exactly is BCM. Write down an explanation keep it as short as possible.

R1.2   Define maintenance strategy.

R1.3   Consider how the 'market demand for the product/service' and/or the 'supply of raw materials' can affect the maintenance strategy for the following physical asset systems:

(a) A sugar refinery.

(b) A petroleum refinery.

(c) A local passenger bus fleet.

1.5 Part B: An alternative maintenance strategy for continuous operation (see Table 1.4)

The existing maintenance strategy at the FPP was based on carrying out offline maintenance during the weekend windows of opportunity and during the once-per-year holiday window.

Little attempt had been made to exploit the excess capacity of the plant, or spare plant to schedule offline work while the plant was operating. The new, continuous, operating pattern (continuous for up to 4 weeks) meant that offline maintenance would have to be carried out in this way. Indeed, the life plans and schedule would have to move in the direction indicated in Table 1.4. This, in turn, would change the workload pattern (also indicated in Table 1.4).

Table 1.4 Changes in maintenance strategy to accommodate continuous operation

- The first-line work would extend to 21 shifts per week. However, investigation of the mechanical emergency workload had revealed considerable over-manning. When the first-line work was defined as '*the work that must be carried out during the shift of its occurrence*' and subsequently activity sampled, it was shown that it could be carried out by five fitters.
- The second-line work (line shutdowns, unit shutdown, preparation for shutdown, services, inspection) was more difficult to forecast in terms of pattern and size. The main peaks would come during line shutdowns at a frequency of about once per week for two shifts. The size of the workload was unlikely to decrease (even with better preventive maintenance) because the plant was going to be more heavily utilized.
- The third-line major work could still be carried out during the holiday window.
- A movement toward shutdowns of complete sections of plant based on the longest running time of critical units (e.g. the hydros – about 4 weeks). The frequency of these shutdowns will, as far as possible be based on running hours or cumulative output. However, for critical items, inspection and condition monitoring routines may be used to indicate the need for shutdowns, which will provide more flexibility about shutdown dates.
- All plant designated as non-critical, e.g. as a result of spare capacity, will continue to be scheduled at unit level (e.g. the smaller mixers).
- A much greater dependence on formalized inspections and condition monitoring routines, for reasons given in (a) and also to detect faults while they are still minor and before they become critical.
- A concerted effort either to design-out critical items (short life or poor reliability) or to extend their effective running time.

Exercises

E1.1   From the above comments it will be realized that immediate organizational changes are needed to match the new mode of operation.
        Outline a revised resource structure to match the new plant-operating pattern and workload (the existing resource structure is shown in Figures 1.9 and 1.10). Modify the administrative structure to cope with any changes made to the resource structure (at this stage limit the changes to only those necessary to cope with the changed operating pattern).

E1.2   How would the new mode of operation affect the work planning system? Advise management on any changes required.

1.6 Part C: A longer-term view of organizational change

(This section uses the guideline solutions to Exercise E1.1, therefore it is advisable to answer Exercise E1.1 before reading this section.)

The organization outlined in the guideline solution to Exercise E1.1 (see Figures 1.17 and 1.18) – or in your own solutions – incorporated the immediate changes necessary for continuous operation. Their purpose was to allow the company to increase the plant availability (and output) while holding the resource costs steady. It may well be that with the experience of operation the size of the day-group of artisans will be reduced. However, in the medium and long term, when this organization is benchmarked against the best of international standards within the food processing industry, further improvements can also be identified (see Exercise E1.3).

Exercise

E1.3   Provide the management of the FPP with a model of a maintenance organization (a resource structure and administrative structure) that will bring them up to international benchmark levels.
        In order to answer this question you may need to carry out a literature search of FPP maintenance organizations (or use your own experience).

1.7 The strategic thought process

The case study has shown that the maintenance department requires managerial strategic analysis in the same way as any other department. The thought process that was involved is indicated in Figure 1.16. It starts with the sales–production reaction to market demand, the resulting change in the plant-operating pattern and the increased plant operation time. This, in turn, requires amended maintenance life plans and a modified

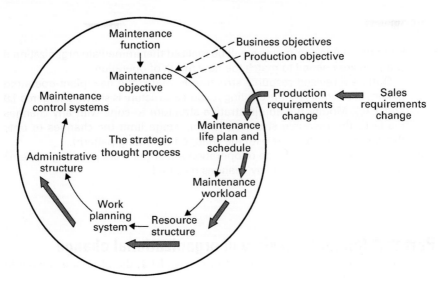

Figure 1.16 The influence of the market demand on maintenance strategy

maintenance schedule. Thus, the maintenance workload changes, which brings in the training the need to modify the maintenance organization and systems.

Understanding and applying this type of strategic through process is the cornerstone of effective and fruitful maintenance-management analysis [1,2].

Review Questions

R1.4   The sales department of the FPP wanted to increase output and the production department agreed to this. Can you explain the effect this had on the following:

- unit life plans,
- preventive maintenance schedule,
- maintenance workload,
- maintenance organization.

R1.5   From your answer to R1.4 and using Figure 1.20 explain the concept of the 'strategic maintenance-management though process'.

References

1. Wilson, A., *Asset Maintenance Management*, Conference Communication, Farnham, 2000.
2. Mather, D., *The Maintenance Scorecard*, Industrial Press, New York, 2005.

Review Questions Guidelines

R1.1   Any decision involving the way maintenance is carried out should take into consideration its effect on the company's bottom line. For example, a reorganization might influence company profitability through changes in plant availability
and maintenance resource costs.

R1.2   A maintenance strategy involves the complete maintenance-management procedure which includes setting maintenance objectives, determining the preventive maintenance schedule and setting up the maintenance organization.

R1.3   (a) The supply of raw cane sugar is seasonal lasting about 6 months over the
Summer/Autumn period. Sugarcane has a short storage life and has to be
processed shortly after cutting. The maintenance strategy of a sugar refinery is based on maintaining the plant over the 6-month sugarcane growing
season to ensure high plant availability over the 6-month plant-refining
period.

(b) Petroleum refineries are mostly production limited, and involve high capital cost plant. The maintenance strategy is concerned with maintaining the
plant during agreed shutdowns to achieve the longest possible production-
operating period.

(c) A local passenger bus fleet provides a service rather than a product. Major
maintenance is carried out using the 'spare buses in the fleet'. Minor maintenance is carried out in the low bus demand periods (the maintenance
windows).

R1.4   This is explained clearly in the notes in Section 1.7.

R1.5   See Section 1.7.

Exercise Guideline Solutions

E1.1   To match the new workload pattern the maintenance organization would also
and   have to change. The most likely resource structure (see Figure 1.17) would be
E1.2   based on a first-line, 21 shift-group (the mechanical manning per shift being
reduced to five fitters) and a second-line day-group of 15 fitters operating 5 days
per week. This, in turn, would require a change the administrative structure as
shown in Figure 1.18.

Because of the changes in the way the work would be scheduled (the mid-
week work peaks would occur at relatively short notice via the condition monitoring of the lines) it was also necessary to advise management that their work
planning system would need to be improved, in order to be far more flexible
and dynamic.

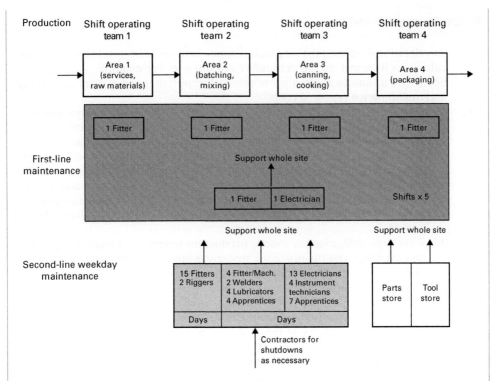

Figure 1.17 Maintenance resource structure for continuous operation

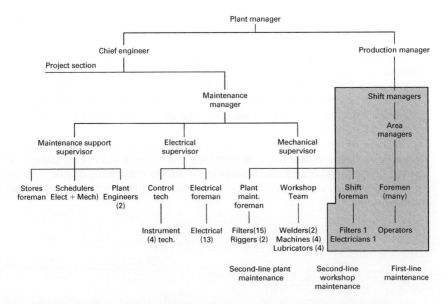

Figure 1.18 Maintenance administrative structure for continuous operation

E1.3   A proposed improved maintenance organization is shown in Figure 1.19 (resource structure) and Figure 1.20 (administrative structure). The proposals incorporate the following actions:

- The introduction of self-empowered plant-oriented operator–maintainer teams.
- The introduction of self-empowered trade teams.
- Increase in the number of engineers, plant located for maintenance support.

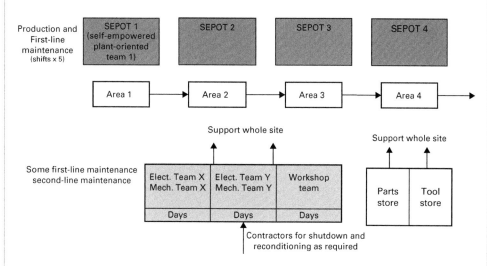

Figure 1.19 Organizational vision: resource structure

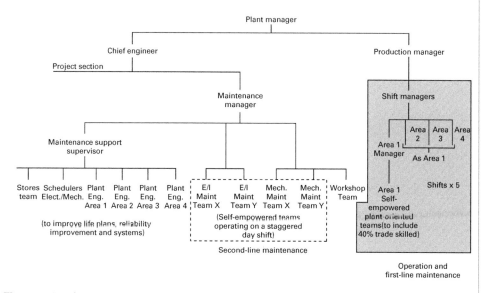

Figure 1.20 Organizational vision: administrative structure

2 Maintenance organization in outline

'A model is a picture of reality.'

With apologies to Ludwig Wittgenstein

Chapter aims and outcomes

To explain what a maintenance organization is, what it does, and how it can be modeled.

On completion of this chapter you should be able to:

- define the function of a maintenance organization;
- categorize the maintenance organization into its main elements;
- understand how to model a maintenance organization;
- understand the main internal and external factors that can affect the design of a maintenance organization.

Chapter route map

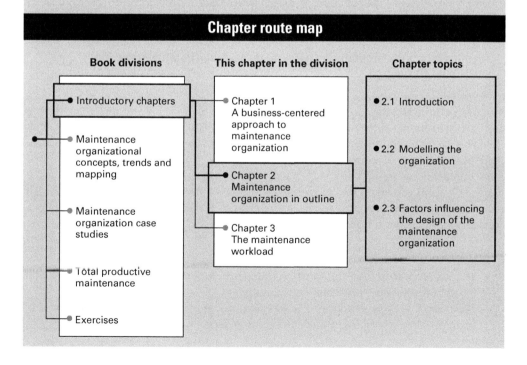

Book divisions	This chapter in the division	Chapter topics
• Introductory chapters	• Chapter 1 A business-centered approach to maintenance organization	• 2.1 Introduction
• Maintenance organizational concepts, trends and mapping	• Chapter 2 Maintenance organization in outline	• 2.2 Modelling the organization
• Maintenance organization case studies	• Chapter 3 The maintenance workload	• 2.3 Factors influencing the design of the maintenance organization
• Total productive maintenance		
• Exercises		

Key words
• Organization
• Administrative structure
• Synergy
• Organization change
• Human resource management

2.1 Introduction

The primary task of the maintenance organization is to match maintenance resources (men, spares, tools and information) to the maintenance workload, so that the following maintenance organizational objective can be attained:

Sustaining, at minimum total cost, plant which is capable of producing the desired level and quality of output.

In order to achieve this, the organization needs to be designed so that the performance of the trade-force (a function of its utilization and motivation), of the availability of spares, tools and information, and of the efficiency of work planning is maximized.

In other words the organization needs to be designed to achieve maximum organizational efficiency.

Designing (or modifying) a maintenance organization involves many interrelated decisions (Should the work be carried out through an alliance? Where to locate the manpower? How to extend inter-trade flexibility? Where do we allocate responsibility to for maintenance information or for spare parts?), each such decision being influenced by many conflicting factors.

The approach reviewed in Chapter 1 and outlined in simplified form in Figure 2.1 reduces the complexity of maintenance organizational design by categorizing the decisions according to the following main elements of the organization:

- *Structure*:
  - The *resource structure*: the location, mix, size, function and logistics of the maintenance resources – primarily the manpower.
  - The *administrative structure* (the so-called organizational chart): the allocation of managerial responsibilities and interrelationships.
- *Systems*:
  - The *short- and long-term work planning system*.

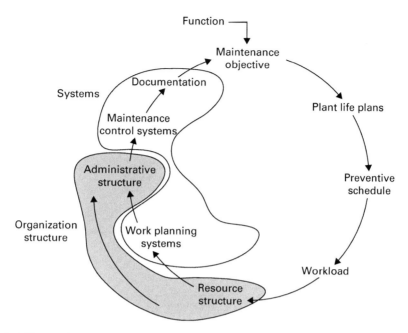

Figure 2.1 The main elements of maintenance organizations

2.2 Modeling the organization

In Chapter 1 it was shown, by considering the maintenance of a food processing plant (FPP), how the elements of a maintenance organization may be modeled.

Resource structure (Figures 1.9 and 1.10)
Administrative structure (Figure 1.11)
Work planning and control (Figures 1.12 and 1.13)
Costing (Figure 1.14)

While there are clear benefits from undertaking such an analysis it is also important to understand how these elements interrelate to allow the organization to function. *The organizational whole is greater than the sum of its elemental parts – it has synergy.*

One way of visualizing a maintenance organization is as a three-dimensional structure, as a *pyramid of personnel*. The maintenance staff and the plant operators are at the base of the pyramid – *the resource structure* – and the management make up its remainder – *the administrative structure*. All the positions in the structure have work roles, i.e. duties, responsibilities, interrelationships, etc. (see Figures 2.2 and 2.3).

The *work planning system* can be represented as an information and decision-making system running across the structure (see Figure 2.4). Other systems can be represented in a similar fashion.

For practical reasons a maintenance organization is best mapped as a series of linked, two-dimensional models, *viz.* resource structure, administrative structure, work planning systems, etc. However, once the mapping is complete it is always useful to visualize the organization operating as a whole, in three dimensions.

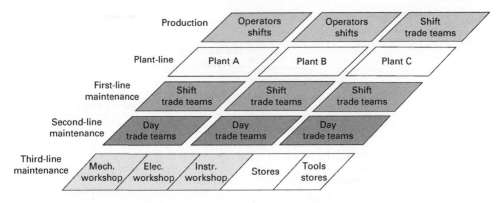

Figure 2.2 Two-dimensional model of the resource structure

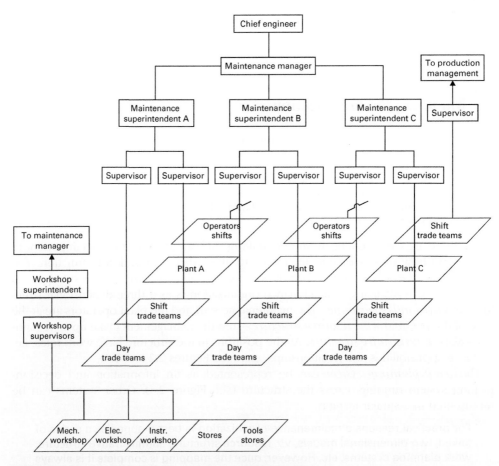

Figure 2.3 Three-dimensional model of an organization

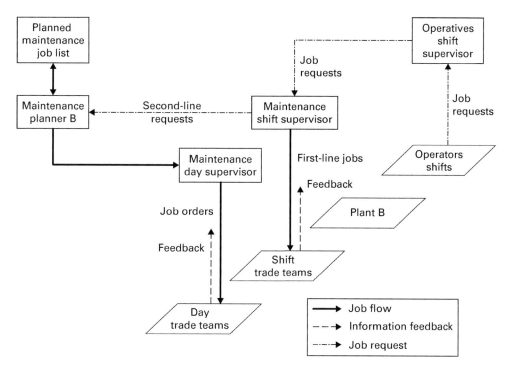

Figure 2.4 Work planning as a horizontal information system

2.3 Factors influencing the design of the maintenance organization

When designing or modifying a maintenance organization the approach outlined in Figure 2.1 needs to be followed. The maintenance schedule is influenced by many factors to include the plant-operating pattern (which is a function of the product demand), statutory safety requirements, etc. The maintenance schedule defines the maintenance workload which in turn has the largest single influence on organizational design.

The following examples illustrate this relationship:

- A base-load power station using three 500 MW turbo generators. Traditionally each generator has a life plan based on 3-yearly major overhauls, each lasting for about 8 weeks. This generates a workload of the type shown in Figure 2.5(a). The station management would be forced to consider contract labor to handle the work peaks. In addition they may have to consider shift working to handle the high-priority work occurring on a 24-hour basis.
- The FPP (see Chapter 1) – operated 15 shifts per week, 50 weeks per year to satisfy product demand. The maintenance schedule was built around the weekend windows and the annual shutdown, generating a workload of the type shown in Figure 2.5(b). The FPP management had to use mid-week shift maintenance teams (to cover the high-priority work) and a weekend-planned maintenance group. Contract labor was needed

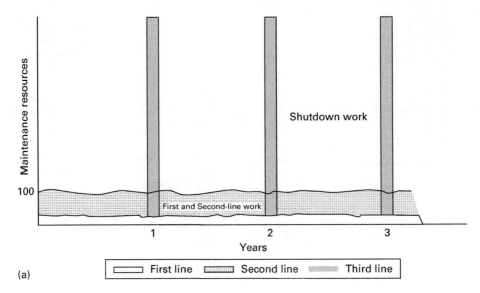

Figure 2.5(a) Power station workload

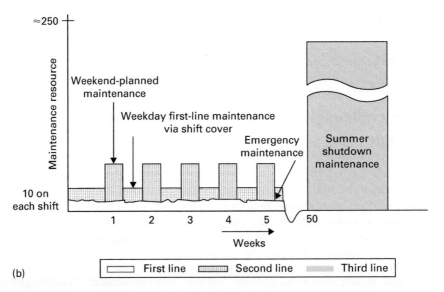

Figure 2.5(b) FPP workload

during the annual shutdowns. This example also illustrated how a change in production policy can have a major effect in the maintenance workload and organization.

- A sugar refinery operates continuously for 6 months to match the sugarcane harvesting period and is then offline for the next 6 months. The major preventive and corrective maintenance is scheduled for the offline period in order to provide high availability during the online period. The sugar refinery management has to provide shift maintenance cover during the online period and a planned maintenance group during the offline period – in this case contract labor is not required (see Figure 2.5(c)).

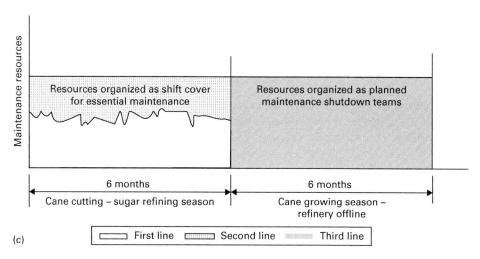

Figure 2.5(c) Sugar refinery workload

> It must also be emphasized in each of the above examples that if the scheduled preventive maintenance work was not carried out (for whatever reason) the nature of the maintenance workload would change – the high-priority corrective work would increase – and this in turn would lead to a 'fire-fighting organization'.

These examples serve to illustrate the *internal factors* that influence maintenance organizational design. These internal influences are often accompanied by *external factors*, e.g. human resource management policy (concerning such matters as production-maintenance integration, adoption of self-empowered teams, etc.), pressure to set up company–contractor alliances, etc. Figure 2.6 summarizes these internal and external influences on organizational design.

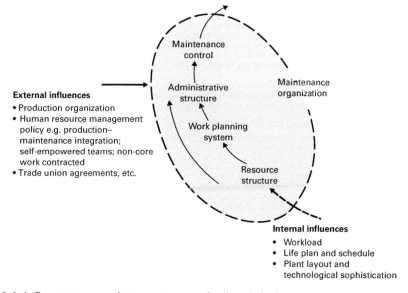

Figure 2.6 Influences on maintenance organizational design

Review Questions

R2.1   List the main internal factors that can affect organizational design.
R2.2   List the main external factors that can affect organizational design.

The final introductory point is that *an organization must be **dynamic**, it needs to be responsive to changes in its environment* (both internal and external). Such changes can be revolutionary or, as is more often the case, evolutionary.

- In the late 1980s I had the opportunity to audit the maintenance department of a large Harbor Authority. The harbor had changed over a number of years from a mainly commercial port to a tourist port and the maintenance work-load had decreased significantly. Because of out-of-date work practices, the size of the maintenance workforce had remained the same (work had expanded to fit the time available). A major reorganization was unavoidable.
- The workforce of a large UK petrochemical plant had resisted change over many years and by the early 1990s the plant had become uncompetitive. In order to survive, new work practices were accepted (in particular decentralization into manufacturing units, downsizing of the administrative structure and adoption of operator–maintenance teams) that reduced the personnel by 50% – a revolutionary change.

Exercise

E2.1   For your own company identify the main 'internal factors' that influences the size and shape of the maintenance organization.

Review Questions

R2.3   Describe the operating pattern and maintenance workload of the ammonia plant outlined in Case study 6 (Chapter 12). How does the workload (that this operating pattern helps to generate) influence the design of the main-tenance organization?
        Identify any external factors that might have had an influence on the organization.
R2.4   What was the main external influencing factor during the 1990s that changed the maintenance organization of both UK and Australian power stations?

Review Question Guidelines

R2.1   Factors that can affect the shape, size and constitution of the workload. These include:
        (a) The plant-operating pattern (a function of product demand, catalyst changes, plant structure, etc.).
        (b) Neglect of the preventive routines (can cause an increase in the emergency corrective work).

R2.2   Resistance to organizational change (industrial relations problems). Management's decision to use company–contractor alliances. Human resource management policy (pressure for greater maintenance–production integration and/or self-empowerment, etc.).

R2.3   The ammonia plant is a continuously operating production limited process. The maintenance–production policy is to operate the plant for as long as possible (≈50 months) before coming offline for major maintenance (≈4 weeks). The workload follows this pattern of operation requiring a small maintenance team during the operating periods but an influx of up to 250 contractors during the shutdown period. (It should be noted that the ammonia plant also causes the urea plant to follow the same operating pattern and shutdown resources are also required for this plant as well.)

   The main external factor that could change the organization was the possibility of a major extension of the company–contractor alliance.

R2.4   Both the UK and Australian power generation industries were privatized during the 1990s and this resulted in major changes to the way maintenance was carried out, e.g. changes in objectives, strategy and organization. In the case of the UK the workforce in power stations was considerably reduced. The privatization was accompanied by changes in industrial law that weakened the bargaining power of the trade unions.

3 The maintenance workload

'A picture is worth a thousand words.'

Napoleon Bonaparte

Chapter aims and outcomes

To show how to categorize, measure and map the maintenance workload.

On completion of this chapter you should be able to:

- categorize a maintenance workload by its strategic and organizational characteristics;
- understand how the organizational characteristics of the maintenance workload affect organizational design;
- map a maintenance workload by the variation in resource usage with time;
- understand how to use the workload categories in order to assist the forecasting of workloads.

Chapter route map

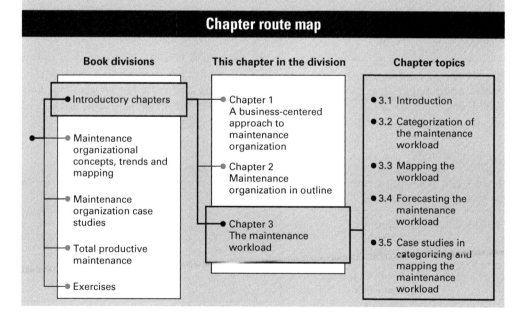

Book divisions	This chapter in the division	Chapter topics
Introductory chapters	Chapter 1 A business-centered approach to maintenance organization	3.1 Introduction
Maintenance organizational concepts, trends and mapping	Chapter 2 Maintenance organization in outline	3.2 Categorization of the maintenance workload
Maintenance organization case studies	Chapter 3 The maintenance workload	3.3 Mapping the workload
Total productive maintenance		3.4 Forecasting the maintenance workload
Exercises		3.5 Case studies in categorizing and mapping the maintenance workload

Key words

- Maintenance workload categorization
- Emergency maintenance
- Forecasting maintenance work
- Maintenance work measurement
- Activity (work) sampling

3.1 Introduction

The previous chapter used the business-centered methodology to show how the workload has the largest single influence on organizational design (see Figures 2.1 and 2.6 which defines this relationship). Therefore, before considering the problems of organizational design it is essential to be able to categorize, map and forecast the maintenance workload.

3.2 Categorization of the maintenance workload

It has long been the custom to categorize maintenance work as being either preventive, corrective or modification. The last, although strictly not maintenance, is usually included because the maintenance department is often involved in carrying it out (especially if it is part of a design-out exercise). Table 3.1(a) describes the characteristics of the workload using this categorization. Such a categorization is of most use when evaluating the effectiveness of life plans, i.e. assessing how effective the preventive work is in controlling the level of corrective work.

However, at this stage of the course we are concerned with the categorization of the workload as an aid to organizational design, so it is more sensible to do it as shown in Table 3.1(b) rather than as in 3.1(a), i.e. categorizing the work by its planning and scheduling characteristics, which is shown in more detail in Table 3.2. Table 3.3 shows an actual categorization for a few remotely located small power stations.

Table 3.1(a) Categorization of work by strategy characteristics

Corrective	Emergency Deferred Workshop
Preventive	Routines (online) Services Major (shutdown)
Modification	Revenue (minor) Capital (major)

Table 3.1(b) Categorization of work by its planning and scheduling characteristics

First line	Corrective emergency Corrective deferred (minor) Preventive routines (online)
Second line	Corrective deferred (major) Corrective workshop Preventive services Modification (minor)
Third line	Corrective deferred (major) Preventive major (shutdown) Modification (major)

Table 3.2 Detailed categorization of maintenance workload by organizational characteristics

Main category	Subcategory	Category number	Comments
First line	Corrective emergency	1	Occurs with random incidence and little warning and the job times also vary greatly. A typical emergency workload is shown in Figure 3.1. This is a workload generated by operating plant, the pattern following the production-operating pattern (e.g. 5 days, three shifts per day, etc.). Requires urgent attention due to economic or safety imperatives. Planning limited to resource cover and some job instructions or decision guidelines. Can be offline or online (*in situ* corrective techniques). In some industries (e.g. power generation) failures can generate major work, these are usually infrequent but cause large work peaks.
	Corrective deferred minor	2	Occurs in the same way as emergency corrective work but does not require urgent attention, it can be deferred until time and maintenance resources are available (it can be planned and scheduled). During plant operation some small jobs can be fitted into an emergency workload such as that of Figure 1.8 (smoothing).
	Preventive routine	3	Short periodicity work, normally involving inspections and/or lubrication and/or minor replacements. Usually online and carried out by specialists or used to smooth an emergency workload such as that of Figure 3.1.
Second line	Corrective deferred major	4	Same characteristics as (2) but of longer duration and requiring major planning and scheduling.
	Preventive services	5	Involves minor offline work carried out at short- or medium-length intervals. Scheduled with time tolerances for slotting and work smoothing purposes. Some work can be carried out online, although most is carried out online during weekend or other shutdown windows.
	Corrective reconditioning and fabrication	6	Similar to deferred work but is carried out away from the plant (second-line maintenance), usually by a separate trade-force.
Third line	Preventive major work (overhauls, etc.)	7	Involves overhauls of plant, plant sections of major units. Work is offline and carried out at medium- or long-term intervals. Such a workload varies in the long term as shown in Figure 3.1. The shutdown schedule for large multi-plant companies can be designed to smooth the company shutdown workload.
	Modifications	8	Can be planned and scheduled some time ahead. The modification workload (often 'capital work') tends to rise to a peak at the end of the company financial year. This work can also be used to smooth the shutdown workload.

Table 3.3 Categorization of station workload by organizational characteristics

Work level	Category	Description
Typical first-line work	A	Requires to be done within the shift in which it arises.
	B	Requires to be done within 24 hours of it arising.
	C	Minor corrective work that does not fall into Category A or B but does not require planning and is of relatively short duration.
	D	Minor routine preventive work, e.g. 500 hours service that does not require a high degree of skill and can be carried out on a routine basis.
Typical second-line work	E	Major corrective work that starts as Category A or B jobs.
	F	All corrective jobs that benefit from some form of planning and have a scheduling lead time less than 24 hours. Such jobs do not require a major influx of resources.
	G	Modification work that has the same planning characteristics as Category F.
	H	Preventive maintenance work that has the same planning characteristics as Category F, e.g. this would include all services other than the major outages.
Typical third-line work	I	Work that might involve considerable planning and scheduling effort in terms of job methods and major spare part resourcing. In addition, involves an influx of labor to resource peaks or has a specialist skill content.

Obviously the shape and constitution of workloads vary across different industries. Consider the following examples:

- In power generation, the emergency corrective jobs tend to be infrequent and/or can mostly wait for attention until the day shifts. Thus, shift working is not usually required. Such work is covered by some form of callout system. On the other hand the major shutdowns cause large and periodic third-line workloads that invariably require a major influx of contract labor.
- In food processing plants the emergency corrective jobs are small, frequent and high priority (see Figure 3.1). Such work requires shift cover. The major shutdowns usually occur annually and involve much shorter and smaller work peaks requiring only limited use of contract labor.

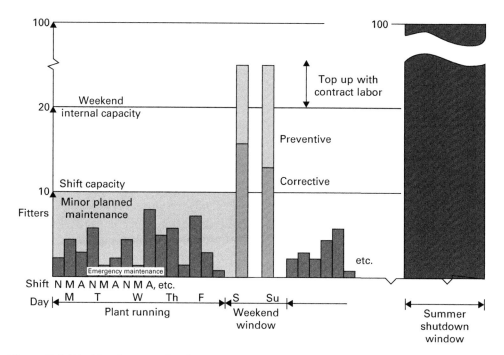

Figure 3.1 Workload pattern for fitters

Review Question

R3.1   Describe the essential characteristics of the first-line workload, the second-line workload and the third-line workload.

Exercise

E3.1   Use Table 3.2 as a guide to categorize the workload of your own maintenance department (or a department you can get access to).

3.3 Mapping the workload

One way of mapping a maintenance workload for a plant, plant area or trade group is shown in Figure 3.1, which shows the workload for the fitting group at a food processing plant of Chapter 1. We shall refer to this example throughout the following explanation of the general characteristics of the maintenance workload.

3.3.1 First-line workload

Mainly the emergency corrective work, jobs in this category have to be carried out immediately or within the shift of their occurrence – and are therefore impossible to schedule. At best, the average level of such work can be forecast. Also classifiable as first-line work are the simple deferred corrective jobs and the preventive routines (Categories 2 and 3 of Table 3.2), work which is often used to smooth the emergency workload (see Figure 3.1). *It is the emergency corrective work that determines the type and size of the first-line resource.* This is especially true of shift work where the plant operates over a full 24-hour day.

> In spite of these comments the author has observed during his extensive auditing experience that very few organizations make any attempt to define and measure their emergency corrective workload. This coupled with the often low level of shift supervision can lead to over-manning.

In our example (see Figure 3.2), the first-line mechanical resource is sized at 10 fitters working a shift system to cover 15 mid-week shifts plus 2 weekend shifts for planned maintenance.

For the reasons given above the mid-week shifts were over-manned.

It is also important to note that the first-line workload, and the operator's workload should be studied in depth before deciding on maintainer–operator flexibilities and the adoption of self-empowered maintainer–operator teams.

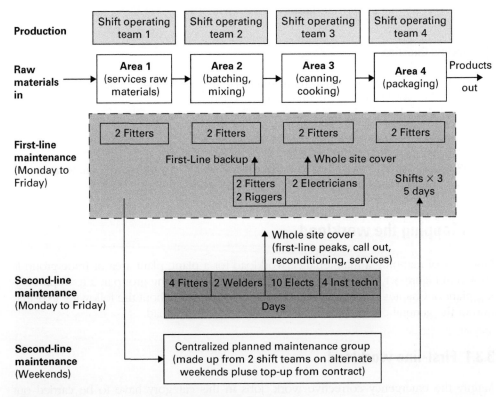

Figure 3.2 Resource structure: food processing plant

Review Questions

R3.2   You have commissioned consultants to measure and map your mechanical workload and they have provided you with the workload profile shown in Figure 3.1. The consultants have pointed out that they consider the shift trade-force is underperforming and that you should carry out a 'work sampling' exercise to establish their utilization. Carry out a brief search to enable you to explain what 'work sampling' is, and how it can be used to provide you with a realistic estimate of shift utilization.

R3.3   In general a shift maintenance crew is used to cover the emergency maintenance jobs. One way of deciding on the size of such a crew is to model the situation as a queuing model. Carry out a brief search and/or refer to Section 4.5.6 to enable you to explain the use of a 'queuing model' in such a situation. If you were asked to work out the optimum shift gang using queuing theory what information would you require and what assumptions would you make.

3.3.2 Second-line workload

Consisting mainly of:

(a) the deferred corrective work that has a scheduling lead time of more than 24 hours;
(b) the various preventive routines/services;
(c) removed-item work.

These are Categories 4, 5 and 6, respectively, of Table 3.2. These jobs are usually less than 2 days in duration and require relatively few artisans (often only one).

The preventive routines/services can be planed and scheduled in the longer term.

The deferred corrective work comes in on a continuous basis and needs to be prioritized, planned and scheduled. The second-line plant resource groups need to be sized to handle the average input of this work plus the scheduled routines and services. In our example the second-line weekend group is made up of 20 fitters (two of the four shifts on alternate weekends) plus contract top-up.

The removed-item work is in general carried out by a combination of contract reconditioning and a centralized internal workshop. The minor reconditioning work can sometimes be timed to smooth the second-line workload. In our examples there is a small workshop that provides a reconditioning and fabrication service.

The flow of work between the first-line shift groups and the workshop/weekend groups is shown in Figure 3.3.

The emergency maintenance jobs (first-line input) have an unpredictable duration, a random incidence and need to be carried out within the shift of their occurrence This results in a workload with short-duration intense peaks. If the number of shift fitters is set below the peak demand the 'peak jobs' cascade to the day resource and to the weekend group.

It can also be seen that the weekend group needs to be sized so that:

$$\begin{array}{ccc} \text{The average weekend} \\ \text{output of jobs} \end{array} \geq \begin{array}{c} \text{The average weekly input of} \\ \text{second-line jobs plus overspill} \end{array}$$

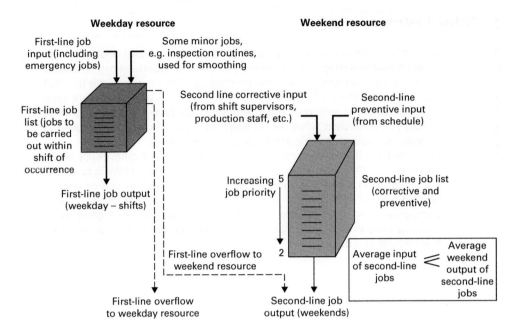

Figure 3.3 Visualization of the flow of maintenance work

The priority system and contract labor can be used to control second-line workload fluctuations.

Figure 3.3 also illustrates the importance of an efficient work planning system to control the *flow of work* and to ensure the efficient use of maintenance resources.

3.3.3 Third-line workload

Comprising the major shutdown and plant overhauls and any capital projects or modifications, its main characteristics are that it creates major peaks in resource requirement at medium- or long-term intervals (and also involves many interrelated jobs that have to be completed in a specified time – typically in a few weeks). Plants that present a true third-line workload of the type shown in Figure 3.1 are forced to bring in contract labor to supplement the internal resourcing of such peaks. Multi-plant companies (e.g. electricity utilities having several stations) can often arrange their schedule of major shutdowns so as to smooth their overall third-line workload and hence minimize their requirement for contract labor (see Figure 3.4). A large peak/trough ratio gives an indication of the need for the regular use of contract labor.

3.4 Forecasting the maintenance workload

Before modifying an existing maintenance organization, or designing a new one, the fullest possible information about the expected workload must be acquired. In order to do this it is important that the workload is categorized, e.g. see Table 3.2 and a clear definition is established for each category. This is particularly important for the emergency maintenance category.

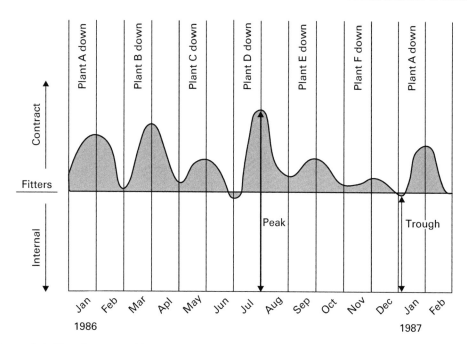

Figure 3.4 Shutdown workload, multi-plant company

As a minimum, information about the expected workload should include estimates – for each major plant or area and for each trade, and for a representative and adequate period of time – of the following.

3.4.1 First-line workload

(a) The emergency maintenance workload, i.e. the demand (and in particular, the maximum demand) in men per shift.

> The size of the first-line workload is best represented as a queuing model (see Section 4.5.6). Thus, the workload information required to establish the optimum shift size would be the average incidence of emergency jobs per hour and the average duration of emergency jobs.

(b) The preventive routines and other major first line work, i.e. the average demand, in man-hours per day.

3.4.2 Second-line workload

(c) The deferred corrective workload, i.e. the average demand in man-hours per week. This should be further categorized by priority and by the plant status required for its execution (i.e. shutdown, alongside other work, etc.).

(d) The minor preventive (e.g. services) workload, i.e. the average demand in man-hours per week. This should be further categorized by priority and by required plant status.

(e) The removed-item and fabrication workload, i.e. the average demand in man-hours per week (this would normally be amalgamated into a company-wide demand per week). There should also be an indication of whether the work should be contracted out and whether this should be to a center of maintenance excellence.

3.4.3 Third-line workload

(f) The expected major workload, i.e. the start-time, duration and size (in man-hours per day) of each major overhaul (over a period of 5 years, say, for a power station). The workload diagram for each trade could be shown against the same time scale, enabling trade linkages to be indicated.

In multi-plant companies evaluation of the long-term workload on a company-wide basis would facilitate workload smoothing. For example, see Figure 3.4, which shows the third-line workload for a chemical manufacturing company having several plants in the same complex.

The various plant shutdowns were staggered throughout the year to smooth the workload. A resulting peak/trough ratio, for the third-line workload, of approximately 0.7 minimized the demand for contract resource.

Notes on workload forecasting:

(i) Forecasts of workloads (b), (d) and (f) above can be derived from the actual historic workloads (deduced from work order cards and/or management experience) and the future maintenance schedule.

(ii) Forecasts of workloads (a), (c) and (e) can also be based on the actual historic workloads but account must also be taken of the likely impact on the maintenance strategy – remembering that there is always a time lag before the corrective load responds to the preventive input.

Forecasting for new plant is very much more difficult and must rely on management experience, manufacturers' information and experience of similar plant.

(iii) Unless some form of maintenance work measurement system is being used, e.g. comparative estimating, the estimated times in (a)–(e) will be based on what has gone before, i.e. will take no account of the organizational inefficiencies that may formerly have been present, and it will sometimes be necessary to make an allowance for this.

> The point that is being made is that the 'historic workloads' take no account of the 'labor performance', work practices or planning efficiency. It is possible to use the technique of activity sampling to provide an estimate of workforce utilization and performance.

Review Question

R3.4   By using the three main categories of maintenance work explain the essential workload characteristics of the following industrial processes:
(a) An alumina refinery.
(b) A petroleum refinery.
(c) A brewery.

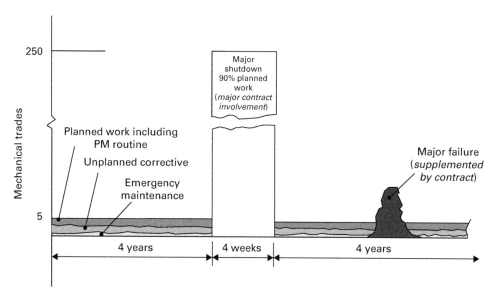

Figure 3.5 Estimate of mechanical workload profile for an aluminum plant

Exercise

E3.2   Use Figure 3.1 and/or Figure 3.5 to sketch the workload profile of the mechanical trades of your own maintenance department.

3.5 Case studies in categorizing and mapping the maintenance workload

3.5.1 Ammonia plant

Because of the lack of historic work order data only a simple estimate of the workload could be made (see Figure 3.5). The study indicated that the main preventive effort involved 400 man-weeks of fitting work during the main shutdown – this was well carried out. This should be compared with the 1000 man-weeks of fitting work between the shutdowns when the plant is online – about 50% of this on-going workload proved to be ineffective, poorly documented, out-of-date preventive routines (see Case study 6 of Chapter 12).

3.5.2 Chemical plant

This plant will be discussed in detail in Case study 1 of Chapter 8. The point to be made here is that the categorization of the workload (see Table 3.2) was of considerable help in identifying the company's core and non-core maintenance work, *viz.* first-line work has a center of gravity toward the company's core effort while the third-line work might lie well toward non-core. The difficulty is often deciding if all, or some, of the second-line work is core or non-core – this is where the categorization helps. The ability to estimate the future workload (size and pattern) is also of help in setting up the company–contractor contract.

3.5.3 Agricultural chemicals

This shows how a large multinational company manufacturing agricultural chemicals on a multi-plant site – categorized its workload and used this information to aid its organizational design.

The company identified each job that made up the workload according to the criteria listed in the main column of Table 3.4. They then categorized each job in the right-hand

Table 3.4 Criteria applied to work activities

	First line		Second line	Third line
Proposed criteria	*Shifts*	*Days*		
Small jobs less than 1 hour, small leaks, spanner jobs				
Planning not required (straightforward job)				
Maybe a little organization required, less than 4 hours work				
Tools, materials, technical information, joints				
Need to be organized before being worked on				
Requires day support to shift core				
Preventive maintenance work-patrol/check list				
Leaks, oil levels				
Complex/multi-skill requiring planning				
High frequency (per shift/day), greasing, oil checks, may be complicated				
Low frequency (per week/month)				
Demands immediate response				
Demands urgent response				
Can wait for greater than 1 week				
Requires specialist skills				
Requires local skills				
Requires some plant skills				
Requires specialist equipment/machinery				
Requires doing in center of excellence				
Requires contractor				
Workload shedding may be a problem				
Variety of work may be significantly affected				
Have we split up what is an engineering transformation, i.e. splitting whole tasks: multiple responsibility?				
Activities may be clustered				
Any other criteria you feel may be necessary				

columns into first, second or third line. In addition they knew the total man-hours spent on each activity. This resulted in the following distribution of labor by category:

- First line: 20%
- Second line: 60%
- Third line: 20%

They argued that the responsibilities for first-line work, and for the necessary resources, were best carried locally, within each plant. In addition, the resource group for second-line work should be shared between a number of plants and that for third-line centralized or put out to contract.

Because the total man-hours spent on each category were known, the maximum size for each group could be estimated. They further proposed that the nature of the fluctuations of the workloads in each category was such that the sizes of the first-, second- and third-line groups should each be set to a minimum and that the work peaks should be allowed to cascade from first to second to third line and then to contract.

3.5.4 Alumina refining

Illustrates how a workload profile can be mapped using information that is unavoidably limited and of low quality. The profile was established to:

- obtain a feel for the performance and utilization of the trade groups;
- assist an organizational redesign.

The plant concerned was a large, complex, continuously operating alumina refinery. As a whole it never came off-line maintenance was undertaken at plant unit level (e.g. bauxite mill), because of the extensive redundancy, which existed at this level. The off-line work was therefore scheduled at fixed operational intervals in order to spread the workload throughout the year.

Because the plant was large many trade groups carried out the maintenance. The management felt, however, that specialized, centralized groups needed to be set up to deal with the more sophisticated work. One such group was the mechanical drives group (MDG) who were responsible for the maintenance of the gearboxes, couplings and so forth of the kilns, mills, etc. of the whole plant. This group worked only on the day shift and undertook the first-line work, and also the second-line plant work and reconditioning. The first-line shift crew (a separate team) were only permitted to maintain this equipment in the event of an emergency. The author could see the advantages of the MDG specialization but felt it had gone too far. His view was that the MDG was under-utilized.

As a first step to reviewing the situation the work profile of the MDG was estimated. It was constructed (see Figure 3.6) after:

- Reviewing the off-line preventive schedule and the histories of shutdowns.
- Discussing the off-line failure histories with the trade-force and supervisors and examining the work order history.
- Asking the supervisors to estimate the average number of MDG fitters on first-line work.

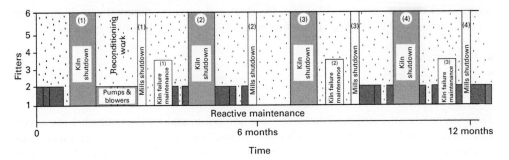

Figure 3.6 Estimated workload pattern for MDG

The review showed that the workload was divided as follows:

- First-line maintenance: 20%
- Second-line plant maintenance: 40%
- Reconditioning: 40%

To a large extent the reconditioning work was being used to smooth the second-line load, the overflow being contracted out.

The author was concerned about the following aspects of the arrangement:

- The first-line work on mechanical drives should be carried out by the specialist shift team. If necessary their skills should be improved to enable them to perform this work satisfactorily.
- Much of the second-line plant work could be carried out by the area plant mechanical teams, with specialist assistance as necessary from the MDG.
- The MDG should concentrate on carrying out quality workshop-based reconditioning. Even in this area, careful consideration should be given to contracting out work which would be better carried out at centers of excellence.

Review Question Guidelines

R3.1
- The key constituent of first-line work is emergency maintenance. Jobs in this category have to be carried out within 8 hours (a shift) of their occurrence. In general such jobs are less than a shift duration:
- Typically second-line jobs are less than a shift in duration, require few artisans and have a scheduling horizon from 24 hours to a few weeks. Such work benefits from planning and scheduling and can use a priority system to allow for work smoothing.
- Third-line jobs are those that normally can only be carried out during a major shutdown. In the large process industries this usually results in a large peak of work stretching over several weeks. Many of the jobs are large, multi-resource and interconnected. Such workloads have to be planned many weeks/months in advance of the shutdown.

R3.2   Work sampling can be used as a means of obtaining information about the proportion of time the shift trade-force spends on different activities. Snap observations of the men are made at random times throughout the working period.
Thus, if *n* random observations are made of a maintenance fitter and he is
found to be inactive on *x* of these occasions then the percentage inactivity is
simply $(x/n) \times 100$. The number of observations *n* that needs to be carried out
to provide the desired precision can be obtained from

$$n = \frac{4p(100 - p)}{l^2}$$

where *l* is the desired percentage precision and *p* is the estimated percentage
of time spent on the activity.

R3.3   A multi-channel queuing model is shown in Figure 3.7.

A queue forms when the incidence of jobs arriving and the repair rate are
probabilistic and for short periods, the arrival rate exceeds the repair rate.

In order to decide on the number of shift fitters (the number of channels) it is
necessary to balance the costs of the fitters against the cost of keeping the jobs
in the queue (unavailability cost), i.e. the more fitters the less the queue length.
In order to use queuing theory the following information is needed:
(a) mean arrival rate of first-line jobs;
(b) mean repair rate of first-line jobs;
(c) the queue priority

The main assumptions are that the arrival rates and the repair rates can be
described by a Poisson distribution; the average repair rate is less than the
average arrival rate; one fitter can tackle any first-line mechanical job.

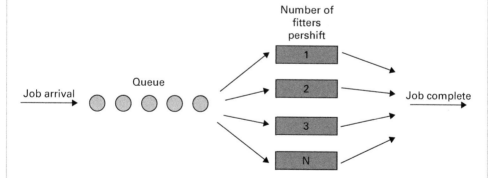

Figure 3.7 A multi-channel first-line maintenance queue.

R3.4   (a) *Alumina refinery*: The plant is described in outline in Section 4.2. In terms
of the workload the main distinguishing characteristic is that the refinery
never goes off-line. There is sufficient redundancy at plant stream/unit/item
level to allow the maintenance to be carried out while the refinery contin-
ues operating (in some cases at reduced level). Therefore, if the major plant
stream/unit outages are spread evenly throughout the year this enables the
third-line workload to be smoothed.

(b) *Petroleum refinery*: A continuously operating plant with a major shutdown every 2 years for about 4 weeks. Thus, the third-line workload is made up of major peaks of work every 2 years. There is some first-line work but it can be dealt with by call out.

(c) *Brewery*: The main problem here is the first-line work in the bottling/packaging plant. This is similar to the food processing plant workload shown in Figure 3.1. The first-line workload (small, numerous high-priority jobs) requires shift maintenance cover. (Note the difference between this first-line work and that of the petroleum refinery.)

PART 2

Maintenance organizational concepts, trends and mapping

4 Maintenance resource structure

'We trained hard . . . But it seemed that every time we were beginning to form up into teams we would be reorganized. I was to learn later in life that we tend to meet any new situation by reorganizing; and a wonderful method it can be for creating the illusion of progress while producing confusion, inefficiency and demoralization.'

Petronius Arbiter (210 BC)

Chapter aims and outcomes

To show how a resource structure can be mapped, modeled and if necessary modified – and to show how to identify the key decisions that affect its shape and size.

On completion of this chapter you should be able to:

- map an existing resource structure;
- define the function of a resource structure;
- understand the characteristics of the maintenance resources (artisans, spareparts, tools and information);
- understand the key decisions that influence the shape, size and operation of the resource structure;
- use a systematic procedure for designing a resource structure for a new plant or for modifying an existing resource structure.

Chapter route map

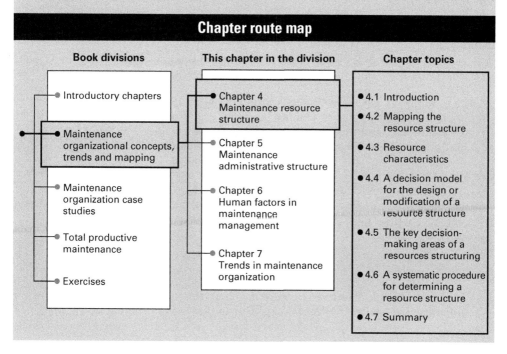

Key words

- Resource structure
- Plant layout
- Departmentalization
- Logistics
- Decision model
- Resource smoothing
- Non-core work and core work
- Company–contractor alliances
- Trade-force flexibility
- Trade consolidation
- Inter-plant flexibility
- Shift working flexibility

4.1 Introduction

The maintenance resource structure, an example of which was outlined in Figure 2.2, is concerned with *matching the maintenance resources (men, spares, tools) to the maintenance workload*. Setting up (or modifying) a resource structure involves deciding on the geographic location of personnel, tools, spares and information; their function, shift roster, composition and size; and their logistics.

4.2 Mapping the resource structure

This will be described via an example taken from a maintenance-management audit of an alumina refinery (see Figure 4.1).

Its various sub-processes were located as shown in the plant layout diagram (Figure 4.2), which also identifies the locations of the trade groups.

> The group code, e.g. Raw Materials group (a), is used to identify the group on the plant layout and also to identify the same group on the resource structure (see Figure 4.3), and the administrative structure (see Figures 5.1 and 5.2), i.e. the code provides a linkage across these three main models.

This ties up with Table 4.1 which shows the functions, compositions, size and shift rosters of the trade groups.

The resource structure (see Figure 4.3) maps the trade groups by work function down the vertical axis (first line, second line, etc.) and by plant specialization or location along the horizontal axis. The operator groups are shown above the plant equipment line.

For example, group (a) is made up of 13 fitters on days carrying out second-line work in the grinding area.

> When drawing the resource structure it is best to start by drawing the 'plant equipment line' as the horizontal axis. This is drawn with the aid of the plant

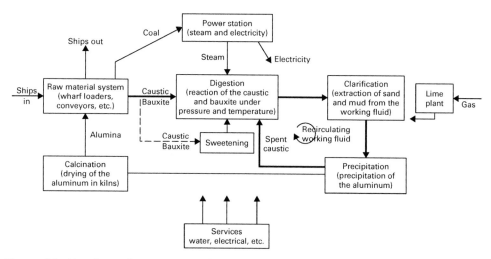

Figure 4.1 Alumina refinery process flow

layout (to identify plant areas) and the administrative structure (to identify departmentalization). In this case it starts with 'raw materials' and ends with 'primary distribution'. The vertical axis can then be added (operation above the plant line and the three maintenance categories below the plant line. Table 4.1 can then be used to locate each of the maintenance and operator groups onto the mapping.

Additional labor information – shift roster, use of inter-plant flexibility can also be indicated on the mapping (see Figure 4.3). However, other important labor information (human factors, inter-trade flexibility, operator–maintainers) is best described with reference to the resource mapping. A complete labor inventory is shown in Table 4.2 (simple indices can also be used to identify some important characteristics, such as trades/non-trades ratios.

Information on spares and tools (location, centralized–decentralized, logistics) can also be shown on the structure or on a linked diagram (see Figure 4.4).

Exercises

E4.1   Draw a resource structure for the maintenance department of your own organization (or one you can get access to). In order to do this it would be useful to firstly draw a plant layout (use Figure 4.2 as a guide) and then to construct a table of the kind outlined in Table 4.1 (remember you must first draw the plant line with the operators above this line and the three categories of maintenance below this line).

E4.2   Draw up a 'labor inventory' for the maintenance department of your own organization and check that it ties up in terms of trade numbers with the trade numbers on your resource structure.

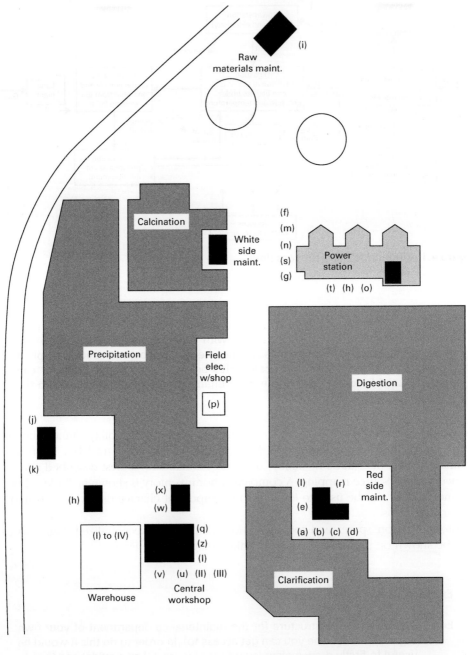

Figure 4.2 Plant layout

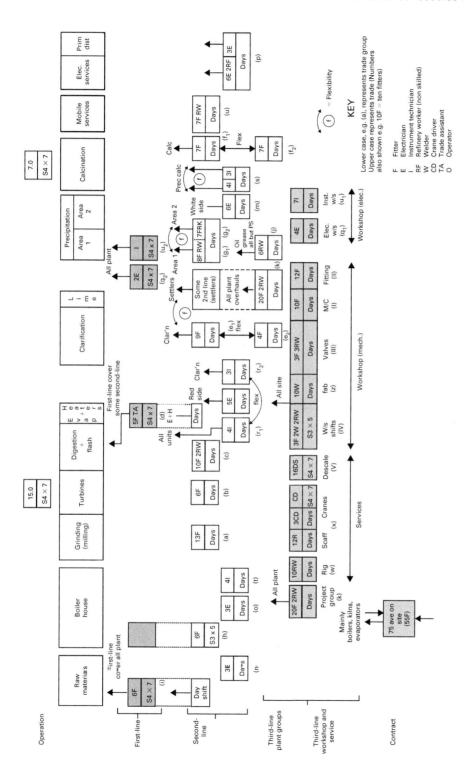

Figure 4.3 Alumina refinery, resource structure

Table 4.1 Extract from listing of trade group functions

Trade group name	Location	Composition	Shift roster	Work function
Raw materials mechanical	Wharf area workshop	24F	6F on a 4 × 7 roster	On Monday-to-Friday shift, material-handling equipment, second-line work. On all other shifts plant-wide first-line work, other than where there is local cover.
Raw materials electrical	Wharf area workshop	3E	Days	Material-handling equipment, first- and second-line work.
Boiler house mechanical	Boiler house mechanical workshop	18F	6F on a 3 × 5 roster	First- and second-line cover for boiler house Monday to Friday.

Table 4.2 Inventory of personnel

Staff		Waged inventory	
Engineering managers	12	Trades	
Engineers (including allowance for plant engineering support)	17	Fitters	194
		Welders	16
Supervisors		Electricians	35
Direct	43	Instrumental Technology	29
Planning	9	Total	274
Training	4		
Total	56	Non-trades (RW)	
Clerical	4	Trades assistants	22
		Lubrication	6
		Crane drivers	7
		Scaffolding	12
		Descale and others	74
		Total	121
Total staff	89	Total waged	395

4.3 Resource characteristics

Before discussing the problem of how best to match the resources to the workload it will be instructive to review the characteristics of the maintenance resources – manpower, spares, tools and information (the characteristics of the workload were reviewed in Chapter 3).

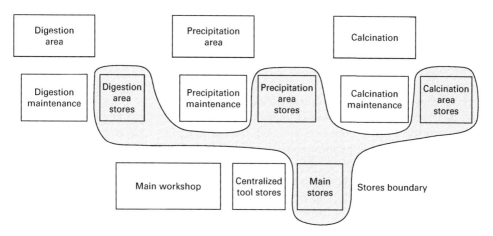

Figure 4.4 Aluminum refinery stores structure

4.3.1 Manpower

This may be classified according to the technical area in which it is employed (mechanical, electrical, instrumentation, building, etc.), further divided according to craft (fitter, welder, electrician, etc.) and, if necessary, subdivided into specialization (boiler, fitter, turbine fitter, etc.).

The quality of labor available will depend mainly on the environment within which the company operates, on the technical and craft training system, on the availability of retraining and specialist training, on the availability of contract labor and on the influence and attitudes of trade unions.

The factors that influence the *morale* and *motivation* of the maintenance workforce are similar to those influencing other shop floor workers. However, the maintenance tradesman is one of the few shop floor workers who still has considerable autonomy over his day-to-day actions and decisions. In addition, maintenance work has many of the attributes that promote worker satisfaction – craftsman status, pride in the quality of the work, varied and interesting job content. An important human factor at shop floor level is the sense of *equipment ownership* – which can apply to both the operators and the maintainers. Of increasing importance is *team working*, especially between operators and maintainers. Perhaps the most important human factor is *goodwill towards the company* – a characteristic which is not easy to promote via activities operating at shop floor level only (Human factors is discussed in Chapter 6).

The nature of these various factors differs enormously from one country, or one company, to another and the local situation regarding them must be fully understood before any organizational redesign is attempted.

4.3.2 Spare parts

The objective of spares organization is to achieve the optimal balance between the cost of ordering and holding (depreciation, interest charges, rental, etc.) and the cost of stockout (loss of sales due to unavailability, temporary hire charges, etc.). The main difficulty in this simply stated task arises from the variety and complexity of the many thousands of different items (of widely varying cost, lead times and usage rates) required to sustain a typical operation. Each spare part requires its own inventory policy and, in a sense, presents an individual problem of control.

To facilitate the setting of control policies spare parts can be classified as either *fast moving* (demand per year greater than three) or *slow moving* (three or less). The fast movers can be further classified as *adequate-warning* or *inadequate-warning* items. The slow-moving inadequate-warning category often accounts for a large proportion of the stockholding costs. To further facilitate their management, spares should also be classified, of course, according to their function (abrasives, bearings, etc.).

Companies in the developing world (or remote from suppliers) often experience long and variable lead times that cause considerable difficulty for the setting and controlling of spares inventories – which can then cause problems in the execution of maintenance strategy. Options for local reconditioning of parts should then be a major consideration.

With regard to spares, the main resource structure decision concerns the function, location and number of stores. For example, in Figure 4.2 there was a single centralized stores, the main computer-controlled warehouse. In addition, each main workshop (highlighted in the figure) had a minor parts store (see Figure 4.4). An associated secondary problem is the logistics, i.e. the management of the movement of spares – including that of component parts and 'rotables' (see Figure 4.5).

4.3.3 Tools

Although the objective of the organization of tools is similar to that of spares, the control problem is different because tools are not, in the same sense, consumable. Tools, like spares, can be categorized, the simplest division being as follows:

● Small (sometimes supplied to individual artisans).
● Large (held, for issue, in a tool stores).
● Lifting gear and scaffolding (held separately and usually subject to periodic testing).
● Electronic (held separately and often in a controlled environment).

The main task with returnable tools is the development of a system for monitoring their loan and maintaining them (or replacing them if necessary) when returned. A simple tool control system is shown in Figure 4.6.

4.3.4 Information

Included under this heading are all documents, catalogs, manuals or drawings that might facilitate maintenance work. They fall into several categories, *viz.*:

● *Training*: used primarily for initial training of the trade-force on new equipment (e.g. logical fault-finding manuals).

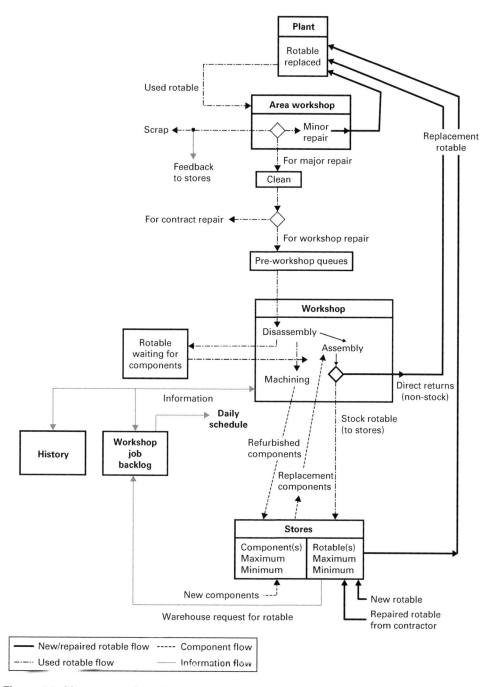

Figure 4.5 Movement of rotables

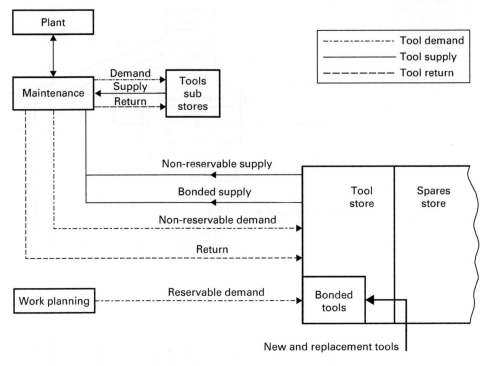

Figure 4.6 Outline of a tool storage and control system

- *Reference*: *might* be consulted before carrying out a job (e.g. manuals, item histories, spares catalogs).
- *Instruction*: *must* be consulted before carrying out a job (e.g. work orders, compulsory job instructions, safety instructions).
- *Scheduling*: used to record and schedule the way in which work is carried out (e.g. preventive routines).
- *Control*: used to store and analyze plant history, costs, etc.

Each of the above categories has different characteristics. Some of the questions that need to be asked are:

- How is the information to be held (on paper, on computer or on some combination of these)?
- Where is it to be held (centrally, locally or in some combination of these)?
- Who is to use such information (the trade-force or the management)?

This kind of inquiry is particularly important when building up a user-requirement statement when procuring a computerized maintenance information system. The questions cannot be answered effectively without reference to models of the kind shown in Figure 4.3.

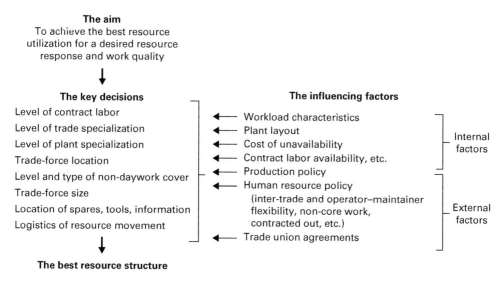

Figure 4.7 A model of the resource structure decision problem

4.4 A decision model for the design or modification of a resource structure

A decision model for the design or modification of a resource structure is shown in Figure 4.7.

> *The aim is to achieve the best balance between the cost of the resources and the quality of service it provides.*

In practice, this aim will need to be defined for each situation and will most likely be:

> *to achieve the lowest resource cost for a desired response and work quality.*

Although such an objective may be difficult to quantify it can be used to judge the relative merits of possible modifications to the structure, or of alternative designs. What the basic problem boils down to is:

> *deciding on the best way to match the maintenance resources to the workload, to achieve the desired aim.*

It can be seen that this 'matching' can be achieved through a number of key decisions, e.g. 'determining the level of contract labor', deciding on the type of non-daywork cover, etc. These decisions are influenced by many factors, e.g. contract labor availability, the unavailability cost associated with first-line emergency jobs, etc.

4.5 The key decision-making areas of resource structuring

It will be instructive at this point to consider each of the key decisions in more detail before moving on to outline a systematic procedure for the design/modification of a resource structure.

4.5.1 Contract labor

Deciding on the extent to which outside labor is used. Traditionally, contract labor has been used for the following reasons:

(i) *Resourcing peaks in labor demand (mainly for third-line work)*
Improves the planning function's ability to match resources to a fluctuating work-load which, in turn, improves overall labor utilization. The disadvantages include: a slower response than that of internal labor (the larger the peak, the greater the lead time for resourcing it); lack of plant knowledge; lack of identification with the company; and increased hourly labor cost. These can be only partially compensated by detailed job contracts and internal supervision of work quality.

(ii) *Specialized work*
The advantage of employing external labor increases as maintenance work becomes more sophisticated and specialized (e.g. gas-turbine maintenance) and, as is often the case with such work, more peaky in its workload pattern.

(iii) *Reconditioning units or assemblies*
This has considerable advantages where sophisticated equipment is needed for reconditioning or quality checking and where such equipment would not be fully utilized internally. The disadvantages can be long reconditioning lead time and high cost.

The pros and cons of using contractors for maintenance work are summarized in Table 4.3.

> In the resource structure of Figure 4.3 contract labor is used for reconditioning the more complex or sophisticated rotables, e.g. large gearboxes, where special equipment or expertise is required. In addition, there is a pool of contract labor continually on-site, which varies in size depending on the demand. In this case the contractors smooth out the second-line work peaks (there is no real third-line work) and are allocated the 'dirty' jobs. Generally speaking, the pool is used as a sink for jobs that are not wanted by the internal labor force. Most medium- or large-size companies have customarily used contract labor to supplement their own (often large) internal labor forces.

Recently, criteria have been developed for categorizing the maintenance workload into core work (that work essential to the companies main function) and non-core work (that work which is not central to the companies main function). For example, Table 4.4 lists the criteria laid down by Riddell during his reorganization of the maintenance department of a large chemical company (see Chapter 8).

Table 4.3 Employing contractors: the benefits and problems

Benefits
- Facilitates resourcing of peak demands
- Facilitates reduction of overhaul duration
- Stabilizes the size of the internal workforce (at minimum levels for the maintenance problems)
- Enables internal trade-force size to be controlled in the early stages of new plant operation
- Allows internal trade-force to be allocated to quality jobs
- Contract organization may have specialist skills and resources
- Helps to keep internal overtime under control
- Helps to suppress costs of internal maintenance equipment

Problems
- Contractors do not always have resources readily available
- Contractors have no feeling of 'ownership' of the plant
- Contractors need validating for skills and safety knowledge
- Job definition needs to be more detailed and precise than for internal workers
- Difficult to check productivity of a contractor
- Problems can arise regarding the relationship between contract artisans and internal artisans.
- Union problems can arise (e.g. use of non-unionized contract labor)
- Contractor objectives are different from those of the company, they are not concerned with the long-term aims of the plant

Table 4.4 Criteria used to identify a core maintenance service

- Critical to one or more of the business units on the site
- Provides a rapid skilled response to cover emergency maintenance
- Provides a specialized resource or skill which is not readily available from outside contractors
- Involves many short-duration jobs scattered throughout a wide area
- Local plant or site knowledge is needed
- Close interaction with operations or with the users of the service is essential

He argued that a contractor can better supply the resources for all non-core work, relieving the company of the associated man-management and industrial-relations problems, so that it can concentrate on its core business. Such a policy has been used for many years in the maintenance of large building complexes. For the estimated workload shown in Figure 4.8, e.g. the proposed organization was as outlined in Figure 4.9. Although there was a need for a resident maintenance group for first-line work it was considered that such work was non-core and it was made the contractual responsibility of an outside company.

As explained, the above contracting-out was not done for specifically financial reasons, but to enable the management to concentrate on main function. The contracting company, however, still had to make many of the resource structure decisions for the

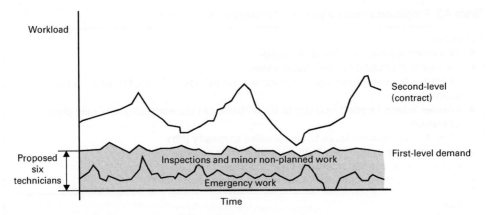

Figure 4.8 Estimated workload for a new building complex

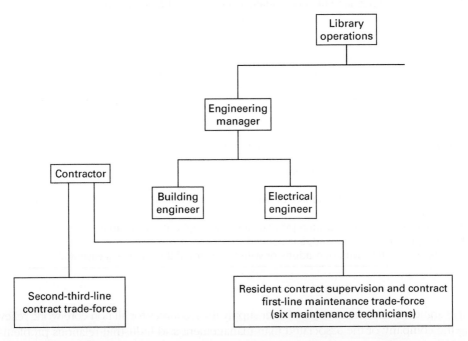

Figure 4.9 Proposed maintenance organization for a new building complex

non-core work – regarding such matters as composition and location of the trade groups, flexibility, shift working, etc. The adoption of this policy means that the decision to contract out becomes the most important one in the design or modification of the resource structure. It follows that the categorization of the workload shown in Table 3.2 could be extended to the identification of core and non-core work. This might be accomplished using a format of the kind shown in Table 4.5.

Table 4.5 Proposed tabular guidelines for establishing maintenance workload

Main category	Subcategory	Catalog number	Job description	Trades		Core work	Non-core
				Main	Sub		
First line	Emergency	1					
Second line	Deferred corrective, etc.	4					
Third line	Major overhaul	7 etc.					

Review Question

R4.1   List the traditional uses of contract labor for carrying out maintenance work in large industrial complexes.

4.5.2 Trade-force composition

Identifying the various trades, operator grades and unskilled grades to be used; this includes defining work roles, skills and the degree of flexibility between trades, between artisans and operators, and between artisans and unskilled workers. In general, the greater the division of work (boiler fitter, turbine fitter, electronic technician, etc.) the greater the skill of the individual trades.

In the UK and many other countries it has been customary to divide the maintenance workforce into various trades and sub-trades and also into several categories of unskilled worker. Each individual trade has been union protected and its skills highly demarcated. This lack of flexibility causes inefficiency in the planning of multi-trade jobs.

In terms of maintenance resource design the question of trade specialization and flexibility can be explained via reference to Figure 4.10.

Where the work requires skill and where the workload can be made relatively smooth there are considerable advantages in trade specialization (e.g. high-pressure welding). This is the situation that often exists in the second-line reconditioning workshop. On the other hand, the second-line plant maintenance groups more often than not carry out jobs that require a range of skills, although one skill is usually predominant. In these situations inter-trade flexibility is of paramount importance, i.e. retention of the basic core skill – fitting, say – with 'add-on' skills in other areas to facilitate inter-trade flexibility (see Figures 4.11(a) and 4.11(b)). These are, however, only very general observations; the author has encountered situations in oil refineries where the engineering manager was adamant that he still needed specialization for second-line plant groups. In the electrical and electronic area, e.g. he felt that the following technicians were needed.

Specialist	Generalist	Specialist
HT electrical	electrical/instrument	electronic/instrument

In some industries there are considerable advantages in amalgamating the roles of operator and first-line maintainer, creating an operator who undertakes a range of first-line

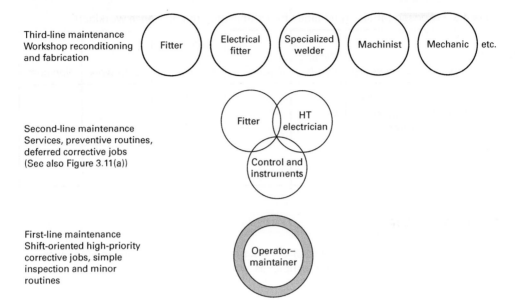

Third-line maintenance
Workshop reconditioning
and fabrication

Fitter   Electrical fitter   Specialized welder   Machinist   Mechanic   etc.

Second-line maintenance
Services, preventive routines,
deferred corrective jobs
(See also Figure 3.11(a))

Fitter   HT electrician   Control and instruments

First-line maintenance
Shift-oriented high-priority
corrective jobs, simple
inspection and minor
routines

Operator–maintainer

Figure 4.10 Relationship between maintenance work categories and trade flexibility

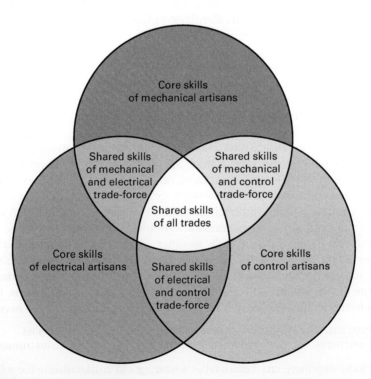

Core skills
of mechanical artisans

Shared skills
of mechanical
and electrical
trade-force

Shared skills
of mechanical
and control
trade-force

Shared skills
of all trades

Core skills
of electrical artisans

Shared skills
of electrical
and control
trade-force

Core skills
of control artisans

Figure 4.11(a) Inter-trade flexibility

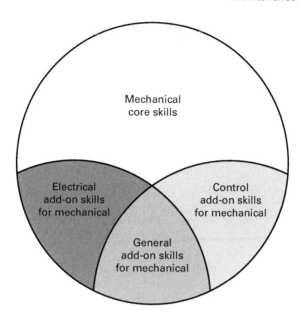

Figure 4.11(b) Skills needed by mechanical tradesman to facilitate flexible operations

work (electrical, mechanical or electronic) for a *small area of plant or process stream*. When applied to shift workers this can lead to considerable labor productivity gains. One common way of achieving this is to recruit artisans as operators.

> In the example of Figure 4.3 considerable training had improved the range of skills of the individual artisans. However, because of industrial relations problems the inter-trade flexibility was restricted to the consolidation of the fitting skills into a single mechanical tradesman ('F' for fitter in the figure). In addition there was very limited flexibility across the interfaces, *viz.* operator/mechanical, electrician/instrument technician and fitter/electrician.

Labor flexibility, particularly with regard to simpler work, can be improved in the longer term in two principal ways. Firstly, through productivity agreements and other management – workforce bargains, thus reducing demarcations (see Figure 4.10), e.g. the mechanical tradesman could engage in general fitting, welding, cutting, metal forming, etc. Secondly, through formal training program, both internal and external, to extend the tradesman's skills. The benefits of improved flexibility include easier work planning and higher utilization. This, however, has to be weighed against the costs of the productivity deal, of training and of the installation of the scheme.

In the *short term* the resource structure has to be designed, or redesigned, within the constraints of the existing flexibility agreements between management and trade unions.

Review Question

R4.2   With reference to Figure 4.3 discuss the advantages of introducing inter-trade flexibility across the second-line trade-force.

4.5.3 Plant specialization

Deciding the extent to which the trade-force is dedicated to the maintenance of a single plant, area or unit type. In a large company the extremes can range from a *plant-flexible* tradesman (usually centrally located) who is expected to work on all plant to a *plant-specialized* one (usually decentralized) who only works in a single area or on a particular equipment type (e.g. only on compressors).

The advantage gained through plant specialization is improved work quality through greater plant knowledge and sense of ownership. This is especially the case where artisans are delegated the authority to control their own work. To a certain extent there is also a better response to job requests. Plant specialization also lends itself to the setting up of self-empowered plant-oriented teams (SEPOTs), i.e. of maintainers and operators jointly responsible for an area or section of plant (on days or shifts). This in turn may lead to the creation of the operator – first-line maintainer described in the previous section.

The main disadvantage with plant specialization occurs where there is a peaky workload. In such situations it is difficult to achieve high labor utilization. This is most evident when there are numerous plant-specialized groups each made up of highly demarcated single trades. This is especially true if a proportion of the groups are shift working.

> By and large, this is the situation of the example in Figure 4.3. The structure is traditional and has evolved over many years into numerous single tradegroups. There are three first-line, plant-flexible, single tradegroups and 22 second-line plant-located single trade groups. In addition, there are 11 single trade workshop groups. It is inevitable here that the trade-force utilization will be low and work planning particularly difficult. In such situations the labor utilization can be improved through inter-plant flexibility, e.g. in Figure 4.3 there is inter-plant flexibility across the digestion and clarification instrument technicians (groups t_1 and t_2) – thus peaky workloads can be balanced.

If the advantages of plant specialization are required (and they are becoming increasingly important because of the trend towards plant ownership and team working, and because of the increased focus on assuring product quality) then it must be combined with flexible working practices and, where possible, self-empowerment.

4.5.4 Trade-force location

Deciding, e.g. whether workshops should be centralized or dispersed (a decision which tends to be connected with plant-specialization decisions). Plant-flexible trade groups are normally located centrally. The plant-specialized area groups can be located centrally (or in a central workshop area) or close to their designated area (which is usually the case). The location of a trade group specialized in the maintenance of an equipment type will clearly depend on the distribution of such equipment.

In addition to the above possibilities groups can also be designated as 'roving'. This is especially suitable where a particular unit type is in use at widely scattered locations (e.g. compressors in a large oil field).

The main benefits of decentralizing the plant-specialized groups are increased speed of response and a stronger sense of team working with the operators in the locations concerned. This is especially the case if production and maintenance both report to the same authority. If plant-oriented teams are to be developed the plant-specialized maintainers must be located near to their plant and to the plant's operators.

The main disadvantage of decentralized plant-specialized groups is the difficulty of achieving flexible labor movement between trade groups (this is even more difficult if plant-oriented teams have been adopted). In theory, inter-plant flexibility can be used to move labor from groups with a low workload to those with a high one. In practice, this is particularly difficult because of human factor reasons. People do not like moving out of their groups and do not like accommodating strangers within their group.

In the case of Figure 4.3 the company felt there were advantages in making the first-line shift-groups centralized and plant flexible, i.e. each group covered first-line work for their own trade across the complete plant. Amalgamating the first-line workload in this way made for better first-line trade utilization, especially if the peaks could be cascaded to the day-groups. Obviously these first-line groups (especially mechanical) had to receive plant-specific training in first-line maintenance across a wide variety of equipment.

In the case of the second-line maintenance the company felt that advantages of plant-specific knowledge and response (it was a big plant) outweighed the advantages of centralization. The opposite of this was true for the services and workshop groups.

Review Question

R4.3 With reference to Figure 4.3 discuss the advantages and disadvantages of centralizing the second-line trade-force in a single workshop and improving their inter-plant knowledge of equipment maintenance.

4.5.5 Non-daywork maintenance cover

Involves deciding the way in which maintenance activity outside the normal daywork is resourced (i.e. outside, say, 08.00–17.00 hours Monday to Friday). Possibilities include shift working, staggered day-shifts, overtime, callout, or combinations of these.

The need for non-daywork maintenance arises mainly for the following reasons:

- There may be a demand for emergency maintenance cover for plant operating outside normal daytime hours.
- Planned offline maintenance may be scheduled to be undertaken outside normal production times or during a major overhaul.

In the case of non-daywork emergency cover, the advantages of shift working are rapid response and the fostering of team spirit between production and maintenance shift workers, if their shifts coincide. The disadvantages are the usual ones associated with decentralization, but magnified by the increase in the number of small shift-groups – a situation in which supervision and planning is inherently difficult. Utilization can often be improved by centralizing shift cover or using a callout system. The greatest gains in utilization in this area, however, have come about by increasing flexibility across the interface between the first-line maintainer and the operator (in some cases shift operators have been trained to carry out essential first-line maintenance).

With the resource structure of Figure 4.3 all first-line maintenance is carried out by shift-groups, because the plant is in continuous operation; in addition there is a callout system for key personnel. In this case, it would appear that there would be benefits from combining the groups into a single centralized first-line shift-group located in a well-equipped workshop.

For non-daywork scheduled activities the advantage of shift working lies in the quicker completion of major overhauls, which is particularly important where downtime is costly (e.g. in power generation). The disadvantage is in the difficulty of co-ordinating the work between several different groups of workers. A further problem is caused by the peaky nature of overhauls. Shift working flexibility is therefore needed if high labor utilization is to be achieved – i.e. when the shift workload drops, the center of gravity of the shift roster should move towards day working.

The more usual way of resourcing a peaky workload such as the above is through an overtime arrangement. In most cases this has proved to be the most flexible and economic solution. In many situations, however, the use of overtime has been abused. It has become a means of supplementing low basic wages and the trade-force has come to expect overtime as of right. Jobs in normal daywork are deliberately slowed to extend into the overtime period; those, such as major shutdown work, that are to be carried out on overtime are deliberately prolonged. This human factor problem has been overcome in many companies by the introduction of *annualized-hours agreements*. An agreed annual level of overtime payment is awarded in 52 weekly installments, regardless of the actual hours worked. The burden of the implementation of the scheme rests firmly with the trade-force, the agreement often being bought-in as part of a self-empowerment program. The trade-force in turn agrees to get the work done as quickly as possible. Actual overtime is reduced and plant availability improved.

The main point that needs to be stressed is that resourcing non-daywork cover has to be considered in relation to workload pattern, work roster agreements, cost of unavailability, required speed of response, etc.

> The experience of the food processing plant (discussed in Chapter 1) illustrates this very well. The company felt that the most economic way of covering the Monday-to-Saturday workload was to use shift working from Monday to Friday and then to use the shift workers on overtime to carry out the second-line weekend work. An alternative would have been some form of shift roster to ensure that at least half of the trade-force were in on Saturdays and Sundays. Other possibilities would have been to use only contract labor at the weekends or a separate trade group employed only to carry out 2 × 12 hours weekend shifts.

Exercise

E4.3   Carry out a literature search to identify companies who have introduced 'annualized-hours agreements' with their 'maintenance trade-force'. Use the case studies to understand the advantages and disadvantages of such agreements.

4.5.6 Sizing the trade-force

This involves deciding on the number of maintenance artisans allocated to each work-shop or plant area. This number is a function of the workload, of the motivation of the men and of the efficiency of work planning.

The most complex and difficult sizing problem concerns the first-line trade groups responsible for the high-priority (mostly emergency) jobs. This is, particularly, the case where the trade groups are working on shift rosters (see e.g. the first-line shift-groups of Figure 4.3). The duration of such jobs may be quite unpredictable and their inci-dence quite random but they will need to be undertaken within the shift in which they occur. This results in a workload with short-duration intense peaks as in Figure 4.12.

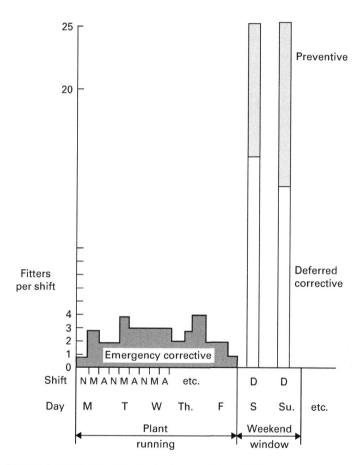

Figure 4.12 Biscuit factory, Monday-to-Friday workload (fitters)

A simple queuing theory model of the above situation is illustrated in Figure 4.13. The objective is to identify the trade group size which minimizes the total cost of unavailability and labor. If the size is set at a level well below that needed to meet peak demand, then the cost of labor will be low but the unavailability will be high. Conversely, if it is set at a level above that needed to meet peak demand then waiting cost will be zero but labor cost will be high. Clearly, the main factor is the cost of unavailability. In many modern industrial plants the cost of unavailability is of a much higher order than the cost of labor, so any peaks in repair demand caused by emergencies must be covered. This will inevitably lead to low labor utilization unless compensatory measures are taken.

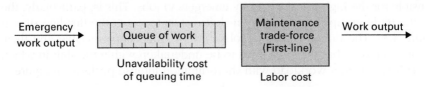

Figure 4.13 Simple queuing model for emergency maintenance

The principal alternatives are:

(i)   workload smoothing by the inclusion of work of a lower-order priority (see Figure 3.1);
(ii) using inter-plant labor flexibility to resource the peaks (there will, of course, be an inevitable penalty in the shape of the unavailability costs caused by travel time);
(iii) allowing the peaks to cascade to the second-line groups (supplemented by callout in the case of shift work);
(iv) centralizing emergency cover, which will improve utilization, because the workload will be smoother, but has the disadvantage of slower response.

These alternatives can be used singly or in combination. In our example (see Figure 4.3), a combination of (i), (iii) and (iv) are used.

If the workload can be planned and scheduled (e.g. as it was for the second- and third-line trade groups of Figure 4.3) then for a given level of trade-force performance it is not difficult to decide on the best size of trade group. If such a workload fluctuates in the longer-term, inter-plant flexibility can be exploited to smooth the peaks. Alternatively, the peaks can be allowed to cascade to a third-line trade group (as existed in the example, Figure 4.3) or to contract labor.

4.5.7 Location of spares, tools and information

Identifying an optimal or, at least, an effective positioning of these resources is a task which is secondary, but closely related, to that of locating the trade-force.

Decentralization of the trade-force creates the need for decentralized sub-stores for tools and parts, in order to facilitate rapid response (see Figure 4.4). This has to be considered against the accompanying disadvantages of increasing the costs of holding and of stores administration (especially if shift work is involved). If attention is not given to the administration of the sub-stores, slack control will lead to duplication of parts-holding on the one hand and to more frequent incidence of stockouts on the other.

The need for decentralized information holding will also arise. Although information can indeed be copied and held in different areas it is essential to have a master information base (the transfer of information from which has been made much easier by the advent of computers).

4.5.8 Logistics

Deciding how the resources are to be moved around the site, e.g. planning the movement of repairable parts between plant, workshop, external contractor and stores (see Figure 4.5). These decisions are secondary, but closely related, to those of resource location.

Review Questions

R4.4 'The design of the maintenance resource structure is about matching the resources to the workload'. List the following:
(a) The main maintenance resources (do not include time or money).
(b) The main decisions that have to be taken to achieve the 'matching'.
(c) Some of the 'factors' that influence the decisions.

R4.5 The author has come across the following saying:
'small enough to care but large enough to cope'
Discuss this saying in relation to the resource structure of the agricultural chemical plant (see Figure 12.9).

R4.6 'Flexibility is the most important characteristic of the trade-force if *dynamic matching* between the workload and the trade-force is to be achieved'.
Discuss this statement and list the 'trade-force flexibilities'.

4.6 A systematic procedure for determining a resource structure

It will be appreciated from the preceding discussion that the design of a new resource structure or the modification of one for an existing plant is a complex task. With new plant there will be considerable uncertainty regarding the influencing factors, in particular regarding the size and pattern of the workload, which at best can only be estimated (with some allowance made for its increase as the plant ages). Where a resource structure has been in existence for a number of years there should be a recorded and detailed history of both workload and resource, and if there is a problem it is usually some mismatch between them. Poor management or artificial constraints on decision-making may have led to a considerable excess of resource above the level needed to deal with the true workload. Clearly, modifying an existing resource structure and formulating one for a new plant are tasks which call for very different approaches, proposals for which are now outlined.

4.6.1 For a new plant

(i) Understand the resource characteristics, giving particular attention to those that are particular to the situation under study.

(ii) Draw a plant layout and estimate the composition, size and pattern of the workload arising for each plant and trade. This should be categorized into first, second and third line, and wherever necessary the core and non-core work be identified (see Tables 3.2 and 4.5).

(iii) Determine the level of response which production will find acceptable for emergency maintenance in each plant and area.

(iv) Formulate the maintenance trade-force structure, as follows:

(a) *For each trade, outline an initial first-line structure which will meet the response requirement for the anticipated emergency work.* This will involve the determination of numbers, locations and shift rosters. Consider possible associations of trades, and of maintenance and production labor, to form plant-based or product-based teams. Estimate the probable level of scheduled minor work, such as lubrication routines, that can be carried out by the first-line trade-force during normal hours (and which can be used for work smoothing). *Keep the first-line trade group as small as possible commensurate with the workload* – using 'cascade to second line' and 'callout' arrangements as necessary.

(b) *For each trade, formulate an initial second-line structure which will meet the anticipated ongoing scheduled workload but not major shutdowns or overhauls.* Such a structure might consist of an independent centralized pool or, as in the example of Figure 3.3, several small decentralized trade groups. In the food processing plant it involved setting up a weekend trade group on overtime, drawn from the Monday-to-Friday first-line groups. *Again, the trade-force size should be kept to the minimum commensurate with the estimated workload, any peaks being resourced by cascade to third line or contract, whichever is available.*

(c) *For each trade, formulate an initial second-line structure which will meet the expected reconditioning and fabrication workload*, taking into consideration possible contributions from the other work groups or opportunities for contract reconditioning.

(d) *For each trade, outline an initial third-line structure which will meet the planned major workload and, in some cases, the anticipated unplanned major outages.* The most usual situation is that there is a need to resource major – work peaks arising during complete plant shutdowns which only occur at long intervals. This will necessitate restructuring the internal labor force into a project-type structure, allocating artisans according to their knowledge of particular plant. Where necessary, the level of contract labor required to supplement the internal labor force should be estimated and a contract procedure established which will ensure the supply of such labor when needed (e.g. preferred contractors or possibly contract alliances).

In large multi-plant companies the need might be to resource a continuing, but fluctuating, major workload (see Figure 3.4), in which case a permanent major-work trade group could be established. The existence of such a group might have a considerable effect on the rest of the structure. The group should be sized to meet the trough of the workload, the peaks being resourced via contract or overtime.

(e) Using the information obtained during steps (a)–(d) formulate a proposed *complete* trade-force structure. This formulation should rationalize the initial structures by exploiting, wherever possible, opportunities for flexibility – inter-trade, inter-plant, shift-related or overtime-related. The structure should be arranged so that:

  – work cascades, in the ongoing structure, from first line to second line to contract;
  – labor cascades from the ongoing work to weekend shutdowns to major plant shutdowns.

  Because of the uncertainty in the size and pattern of the workload for new plant it is prudent to restrict the size of the permanently employed trade-force until experience has been gained.

(v) Formulate the spare parts and tools structure, taking account of the trade-force structure established in Step (iv).

(vi) Formulate the resource logistics for the combined structure established in Steps (iv) and (v).

Note: The way non-core work is handled will depend on the criteria used for its definition. At the one extreme it might mean work not directly concerned with production, i.e. maintenance of building services (painting, plumbing and so on). This might involve a small resident contract team with appropriate supervision. The company specifies the work (via its maintenance department) but the contractor is responsible for the labor and resource structure decisions.

At the other extreme, non-core work might be defined as all maintenance other than first line. In such a situation the company would have to set up a contract administration to specify the work and monitor its quality. Once again, however, the contractor is responsible for the labor and the resource structure decisions (e.g. see Figure 4.8). Alternatively the company could decide to set up a company – contractor alliance (see Chapter 8) to carry out all of the non-core work.

4.6.2 For an existing resource structure

The previous procedure has to be modified. Steps (i)–(iii) are changed, because the existing workload and resource structure have to be mapped.

> The result of such an exercise – carried out as part of a maintenance-management audit of an alumina refinery – was shown in Figure 4.3. Other information from the audit is shown in Figures 4.1 and 4.2, and in Tables 4.1 and 4.2.

The mapping would include not only the information outlined in Steps (i)–(iii), but much more. For example, higher management may have decided that non-core work should be identified and contracted out, and also that shop floor 'ownership' should be fostered by amalgamating the maintainer and operator roles into some form of self-empowered teams. The mapping may also reveal that the company is over resourced – perhaps because its operations have been cut back but its maintenance resources have not. The information obtained as a result of the mapping can be used in conjunction with the procedure of Step (iv) to modify the existing structure in order to improve its effectiveness.

The structure shown in Figure 4.14 was a proposal which resulted from conducting such an analysis on the structure shown in Figure 4.3. It was accompanied by the following observations:

- The first-line work should be clearly defined and an estimate made of its pattern and size throughout the refinery. Using this information, it might be possible to determine the size of a centralized and workshop-located shift-crew (mechanical, electrical and instrumentation – using inter-trade flexibility where possible) to replace the several existing sources of shift cover. Such a first-line crew should also carry out first-line work during the day-shift allowing, as far as possible, the second-line area crews to carry out the scheduled second-line work. With suitable training, more of the first-line work might well be carried out by the operators.
- The second-line work should be clearly defined. It would appear, e.g. that a distinction can be made between the ongoing schedulable work and the major work (unit overhauls). The point being made is that it is necessary to distinguish the work (mechanical, electrical or instrumentation) i.e. best carried out by an area resource (for reasons of specialized knowledge, response, teamwork) from work such as overhauls that are best carried out by a centralized or contract resource. To a certain extent this is already done by the overhauls group (k) of Figure 4.3. Using this reasoning, the area second-line groups should be sized and the excess manpower (if any) moved back to form a centralized third-line plant resource to supplement the existing project group. This third-line group should be set at the minimum size and peaks in its workload should be cascaded to contract.
- Coupled with better production scheduling, adopting the above approach would mean that, initially, improvements in productivity would be gained by reducing the usage of contract labor and not by reducing the company labor force.
- The central workshop workload was not analyzed either as regards its size or as regards the basis adopted for deciding whether reconditioning and fabrication should be undertaken internally or externally. It was recommended that such an analysis should be carried out and as much work as possible should be contracted out. The impression, a purely subjective one, had been gained that much of the work carried out within the workshops could be handled by outside contract. The main point here is that support activities of this kind should not be allowed to gain a momentum of their own (the company's business is alumina refining not engineering).

Exercise

E4.4   Use the procedure of Section 4.6.2 to review the resource structure used by your own company that you modeled via Exercise E4.1. If necessary draw a revised resource structure.

Review Question

R4.7   A number of companies have based their design of the resource structure on a 'work cascade' as shown in Figure 4.14. Discuss the advantages of such a structure using the idea of a work cascade.

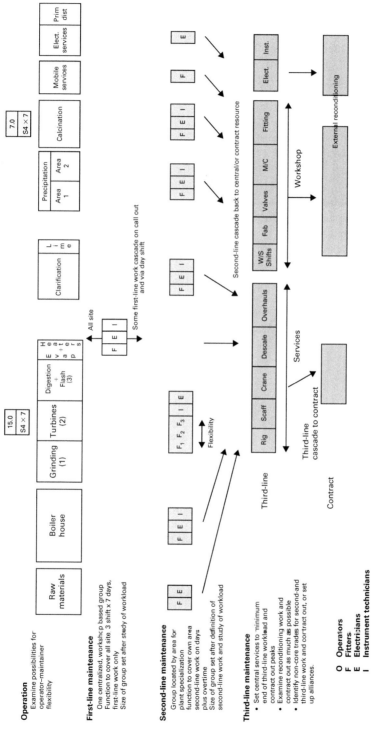

Figure 4.14 An approach to improving the resource structure

4.7 Summary

The design or modification of a resource structure is a complex problem involving a number of interrelated decisions (see Figure 4.7) some of which affect the *shape* of the structure (e.g. location, plant specialization) and some its *size* (e.g. trade specialization). What we are seeking is the *best shape and size to match the distribution and pattern of the maintenance workload.* Some of the key points to be borne in mind when carrying out this task are the following:

- Although there is no one best type of solution the cascade structure, as in Figure 4.14, tends to suit the general characteristics of the maintenance workload.
- If dynamic matching of the trade-force to the workload is to be achieved, *flexibility* is the most desirable characteristic to be fostered in the trade-force, i.e.:
  - inter-trade flexibility,
  - maintainer–operator flexibility,
  - inter-plant flexibility,
  - flexibility of location,
  - shift working flexibility,
  - flexibility to use contract and/or temporary labor.
- The design of the resource structure must always take into consideration the effect of that structure on the administrative structure and on work planning. *It is only one part of the organization (see Figure 2.1).*

Exercise

E4.5 Modification of a strip mill resource structure.
   A resource structure for a strip mill is shown in Figure 4.15.
   The mill is made up of 10 plants (Plants A–J) linked together in a batch process operating 52 weeks per year, 7 days per week and three shifts per day. The trade-force in each plant is supervised by a plant supervisor (mechanical-days). The plant supervisors plan and supervise all maintenance work in their areas and are helped on shifts by four shift supervisors (two on evenings and two on nights) responsible for shift artisans on a company-wide basis. At least one shift supervisor is electrically qualified. Electrical advice can be obtained from a centralized electrical engineer. All supervisors and the electrical engineer report to a maintenance manager.
   The *ongoing* workload (non-shutdown) in each area is made up as follows:

- 25% first-line emergency work (to be carried out within the shift of occurrence);
- 25% minor schedulable corrective work;
- 25% preventive maintenance routines;
- 25% preparation for down-shifts.

The present trade-force size can cope with the emergency work in their respective areas without keeping production waiting. Under normal circumstances one fitter can cope with the mechanical emergency jobs in each area. A recent activity sampling exercise has shown that the maximum company-wide demand per shift for electricians is five. The mechanical

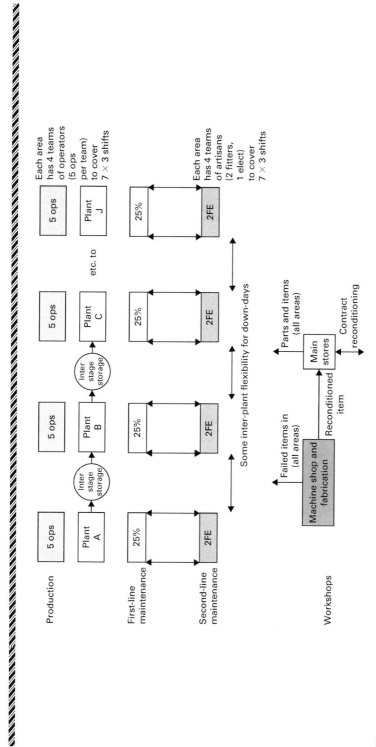

Figure 4.15 Resource structure for strip mill

equipment uses very different technology in each of the areas while the electrical equipment is similar. In exceptional situations it is possible to use inter-plant flexibility to resource peak emergency jobs.

Every 10 days each plant is shutdown for two shifts (down-shifts) for servicing and major planned work (on a schedule to avoid more than one plant being shutdown at a time). During the down-shifts the demand for labor exceeds the area supply by a factor of three. The down-shift workload in each area is carried out by resources from within that area (via overtime) and by limited inter-plant flexibility. Contract labor is not used because of trade union problems. Likewise inter-trade and operator–maintenance flexibility is not being used. The unions representing the trade-force have agreed to consider improving flexibility as a part of a productivity deal.

Management are concerned that the utilization of the trade-force is very low. They have asked you to provide them with ways of improving trade-force utilization. In particular they would like you provide an outline of a modified resource structure that would improve organizational efficiency (a better matching of the resources to the workload). If necessary they are prepared to accept a staged modification – short term and medium term. The answer should include a list of changes and the reasons why they have been made.

Review Questions Guidelines

R4.1   This is discussed in Section 4.5 under the following headings:
- Resourcing peaks in labor demand.
- Specialized work.
- Reconditioning/fabrication.

R4.2   If inter-trade flexibility is introduced it should reduce the size of the trade-force for a given workload. It improves trade utilization.

R4.3   Advantages:
- Improved utilization due to the combining of the second line 'area workloads' into a 'company second-line workload' – this will lead to work smoothing.
- Utilization and performance should also improve due to easier supervision/control, work standards, training and work planning.

Disadvantages:
- Loss of ownership, plant knowledge (especially with mechanical trades since there is a variety of equipment across the site), team working with production (increased horizontal polarization).
- Slower response.

R4.4   (a) Manpower (artisans), spares, tools and information.
(b) Use and level of contract labor:
- level of inter-plant flexibility;
- location of resources;
- level of inter-trade and operator–maintainer flexibility;
- non-daywork maintenance cover;
- size of the trade-force, etc.
(c) Unavailability cost of emergency jobs:
- trade unions;
- human resource policy;
- plant layout (see Figure 4.7).

R4.5   For example take the ammonia maintenance group of the Fertec A resource structure. They are responsible as a 'self-empowered team' for carrying out the ongoing maintenance of the ammonia plant and are accountable to the ammonia plant manager. They are small enough to feel a sense of ownership for the equipment, i.e. 'to care'. Unfortunately in the authors opinion they were not large enough 'to cope'. Often as a result of training/holiday/sickness the mechanical artisans were reduced and not able to cope with the workload (see the alternative resource structure of Figure 12.11).

R4.6   'Matching the trade-force to the workload' is a self-evident statement. Dynamic matching means that as the workload changes with time the resources are sufficiently flexible to follow the changes. The main list is as follows:
● inter-trade flexibility;
● production-maintenance flexibility;
● the flexibility to use contract and temporary labor;
● shift working flexibility;
● inter-plant flexibility.

R4.7   The advantages of a 'cascade structure' are based on the unique characteristics of the maintenance workload. The first-line workload has short frequency peaks. The trade-force size can be set below the peaks and the peaks cascaded. This makes for an improved first-line labor utilization. (Remember the first-line jobs have to be carried out, or started, in the shift of their occurrence.) Similarly it is often the case, in spite of prioritizing jobs, that the second-line workload will also have longer frequency (and larger) peaks. These peaks can either be cascaded to the third-line workforce or to contract. This helps in improving the utilization of the second-line resource and so on.

Exercise Guideline Solution

E4.5   The short-term resource structure is shown in Figure 4.16(a).

The first-line decentralized shift cover has been retained for mechanical but reduced to one fitter per shift – the peaks cascaded to the second-line group. This move has achieved a reduction in shift cover of some 40 fitters. The electrician shift cover has been centralized and reduced to four per shift giving a saving of 20 electricians – again the peaks are cascaded to second line. The second-line groups are responsible for carrying out the down-day work, all other non-emergency work and the first-line overspill. The overspill must be kept to less than 10% of the second-line workload otherwise it will disrupt the work program. The second-line group is made up of 32 fitters and 15 electricians – this provides an overall saving of some 13 artisans. This saving should be possible because of increased utilization of the trade-force resulting from the restructuring.

The medium-term structure is shown in Figure 4.16(b). In order to operate such a structure considerable union-management movement will have had to been made in inter-trade and operator–maintainer flexibility and in the use of contractors for in-plant maintenance. It is envisaged that mechanical and electrical artisans would be recruited as manufacturing technicians (operator–maintainers) to supplement the existing retrained operators. This structure could achieve up to 30% reduction in resource costs.

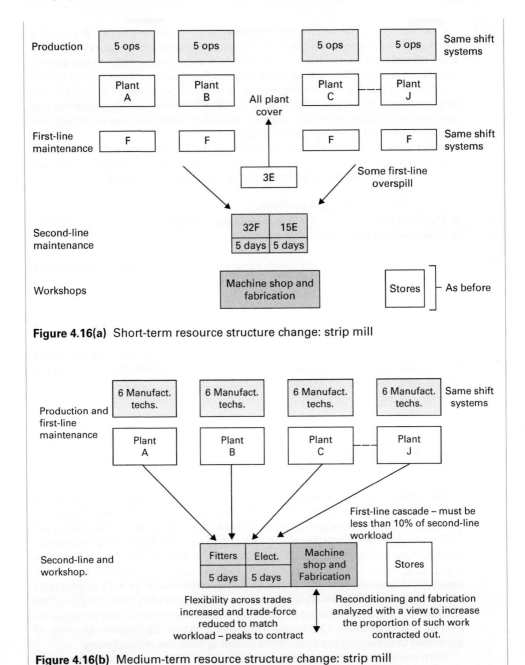

Figure 4.16(a) Short-term resource structure change: strip mill

Figure 4.16(b) Medium-term resource structure change: strip mill

5 Maintenance administrative structure

Chapter aims and outcomes

To show how a maintenance administration can be mapped, modeled and if necessary modified.

On completion of this chapter you should be able to:

- map and model existing administrative structures and link them to their corresponding resource structures;
- understand the classical views on the design and operation of administrations, e.g. span of control, chain of command;
- appreciate the characteristics that are particular to a maintenance administration;
- understand a procedure to guide the design or modification of a maintenance administration.

Chapter route map

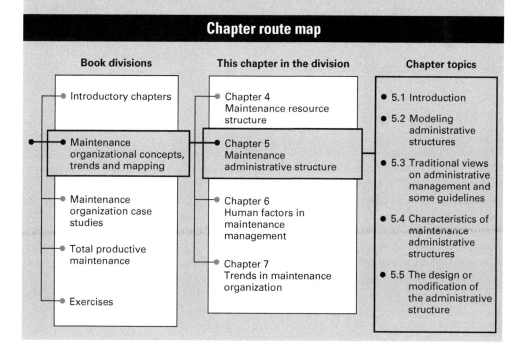

Book divisions	This chapter in the division	Chapter topics
Introductory chapters	Chapter 4 Maintenance resource structure	• 5.1 Introduction
Maintenance organizational concepts, trends and mapping	Chapter 5 Maintenance administrative structure	• 5.2 Modeling administrative structures
Maintenance organization case studies	Chapter 6 Human factors in maintenance management	• 5.3 Traditional views on administrative management and some guidelines
Total productive maintenance	Chapter 7 Trends in maintenance organization	• 5.4 Characteristics of maintenance administrative structures
Exercises		• 5.5 The design or modification of the administrative structure

Key words

- Organogram
- Job description
- Administrative theory
- Accountability
- Span of control
- Self-empowered teams
- Chain of command
- Staff and line authority
- Manufacturing units
- Business units
- Collateral relationships
- Matrix organizational structures

5.1 Introduction

The administrative structure, one of the principal elements of the maintenance organization, is a complex of managerial roles for deciding when and how an industrial plant should be maintained. It differs from a resource structure in that the latter is concerned with the composition and location of the shop floor resources, whereas it is concerned with allocating the management responsibility for carrying out the work. Its principal functions are:

- the initial formulation, and on-going modification, of the maintenance objectives, strategy, organization and control (including resource budgeting);
- the management of the maintenance resources (a necessary part of which is the transmission of the objectives, policy decisions and other information from senior management to the shop floor).

5.2 Modeling administrative structures

One way of mapping an administrative structure is to use an organization chart (or 'organogram!') in which position titles are located so as to show their various responsibilities and lines of communication. Each title can be supplemented by a full *position description*, and an *organizational manual* can clarify the relationships between the various roles. An example of such a structure, used for administrating the alumina refinery maintenance resources (see Figure 4.3), is shown in Figures 5.1 and 5.2(a) and (b).

Mapping the organization chart is an essential part of the author's audit method [1]. This information is supplemented with inventories of the personnel (see Table 4.2) and also additional administrative models (see, e.g. Figures 5.3 and 5.4).

Figure 5.3 indicates the roles of all of those who either operated or maintained the digestion sub-process of the refinery – *this model exemplifies the maintenance characteristics of the administration.*

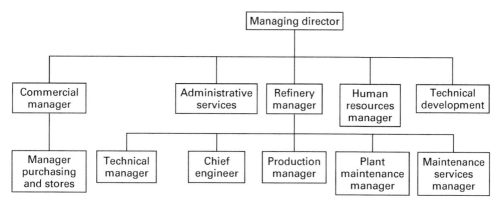

Figure 5.1 Senior administration, alumina refinery

Within the outer dotted line all of the personnel are directly involved with the digestion area plant. In spite of this there are no common digestion objectives across this group. The various trade groups, engineers and production personnel report functionally to their own functional manager. The long chains of command increase the 'friction' across the groups.

Figure 5.4 is a plant responsibility model – it shows the area of plant responsibility of each supervisor.

It should be noted that the production area supervisors area of plant responsibility (see Figure 5.3) does not match the areas of plant responsibility of the maintenance supervisors. This works against the idea of 'plant-oriented teams'.

Exercise

E5.1 (a) In Exercise E4.1 you drew a plant layout and resource structure for the maintenance department of your own company. Use Figures 5.1 and 5.2 as a guide to draw an administrative structure of your company. Remember to use a simple code to link the trade-force across the three main diagrams.
      (b) If necessary draw a simplified administrative structure that illustrates the administrative characteristics (see Figure 5.3).
      (c) Draw a plant responsibility model – at supervisor/team leader level (see Figure 5.4).

5.3 Traditional views on administrative management and some guidelines

A link between levels, like that shown in Figure 5.2(a) between the digestion mechanical superintendent and the mechanical maintenance supervisor (grinding), is the key manager–subordinate relationship. The essence of this is that the supervisor has the

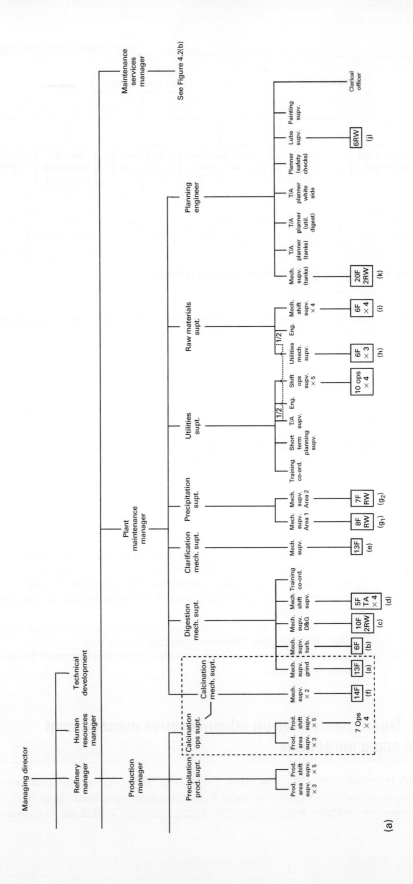

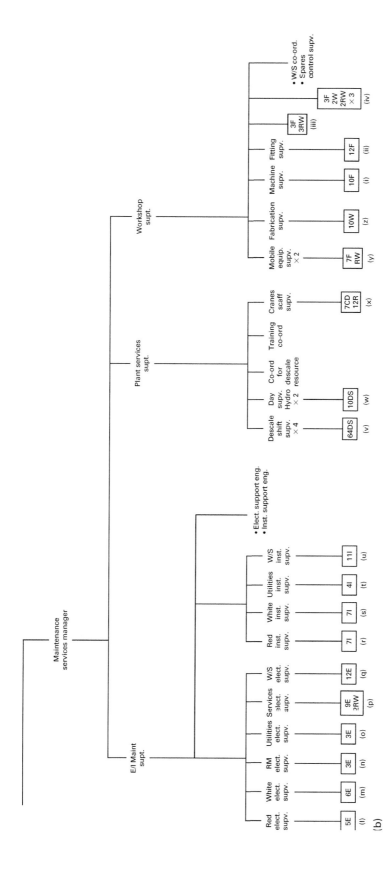

Figure 5.2 Extract from maintenance administrative structure, alumina refinery

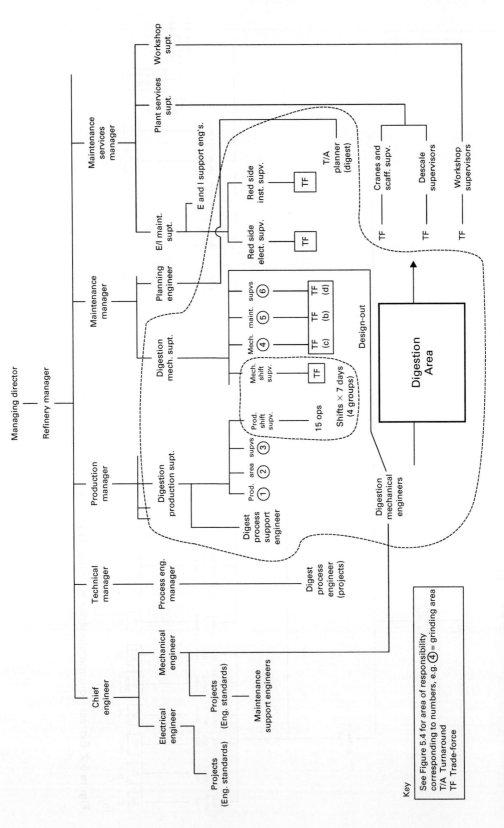

Figure 5.3 Digestion process administration

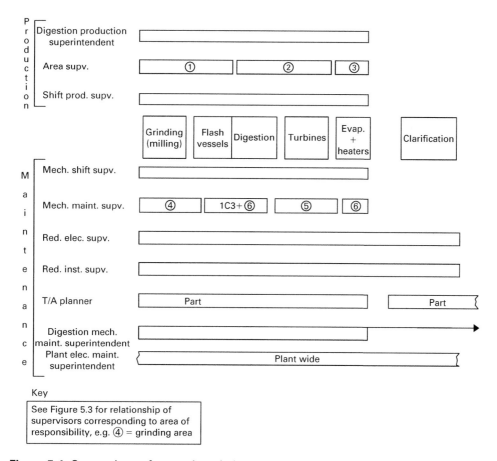

Figure 5.4 Comparison of supervisors' plant responsibilities, digestion process

responsibility for ensuring that his own and his team's work achieve the desired results. For this, the supervisor must have the *line authority* over decisions within his responsibility area. The superintendent *delegates* duties (in this case mechanical maintenance) to the supervisor and also the authority for the supervisor to use the necessary resources (in this case trade group (c), see also Figure 5.3). The supervisor is *accountable* to the superintendent for achieving the desired results. The superintendent remains accountable for this work to the maintenance manager, i.e. authority is delegated as far down the line as possible but responsibility is not shed by doing this (see Figure 5.5).

One man can only effectively manage a limited number of subordinates. It has been suggested that this number lies somewhere between 3 and 12 depending on the complexity of the decision-making (e.g. the digestion mechanical superintendent has a *span of control* of 5). Because of this constraint most organizations comprise several subordinate management levels. In the example of Figure 5.2(a) the *chain of command* passes down through five levels, from managing director to shop floor. Because there are clear advantages in having a short chain of command, some compromise must be reached between the length of this chain and the span of control. This is sometimes

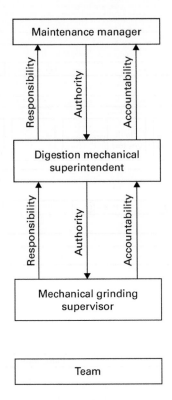

Figure 5.5 Formal relationships in the administrative structure, digestion process

achieved by breaking a large structure into smaller ones, e.g. '*manufacturing units*', see later – a form of *decentralization*.

The foregoing observations refer only to line relationships (the transmission of decision-making power down through the hierarchy and into the various work areas) but the 'horizontal' transmission of information and, in certain cases, of decision-making power is also needed. The principal relationships here are:

(i) *Collateral*: those in which the work carried out in one area impinges on that of another, independent, area (i.e. between the shift mechanical supervisor and the shift production supervisor of Figure 5.3).

(ii) *Staff*: those in which the occupant of a managerial role has staff authority in a defined area of another manager but does not have line (managerial) authority over him. In the example of Figure 5.3 the digestion mechanical superintendent (in agreement with the chief engineer) gives the digestion mechanical engineers the authority to make decisions and to give instructions to his staff in the limited area of design-out maintenance.

Classical theory dictates that each individual should be responsible directly to one person only; this principle – of *unity of command* – is the basis of the line relationship. However, a number of modern structural arrangements modify this in dividing an individual's activities so that he is responsible for different duties (or aspects of the duties) to different managers. Such a structure would occur in Figure 5.3 if a digestion area group (all personnel within the dotted line) were to be formed, with group objectives and responsibilities and a group leader. Staff within the group would then report both to the group leader (for all work carried out in the digestion area) and to their functional manager. Where there is more than one such plant-operating group (POG) in a large process plant the organization can be called a *matrix*. In order to avoid conflict in such arrangements the two managers must communicate closely about the duties of their subordinates and about the way they convey their instructions (see also Figure 12.14 – Case study 6).

Even small organizations can have many complex relationships and it is therefore advisable that there is a *job description* for the work of each individual in the hierarchy. This should set out in clear, unambiguous, terms the job's main functions and objectives, and the individual's limits of responsibility and authority, both financial and with regard to personnel. It should state to whom and for whom the individual is responsible; this should include staff and other dual reporting relationships.

Because of the interdisciplinary nature of most maintenance work it is also necessary to:

(i) establish *standing committees* for joint decision-making areas (in the situation of Figure 5.3 there is a weekly meeting for maintenance work planning, involving the maintenance and production supervisors, a stores representative and the maintenance planner);

(ii) establish *ad hoc committees* for special projects.

To conclude this survey of traditional administrative theory it is necessary to say something about *administrative control*. The basic system by means of which a manager controls his team is illustrated in Figure 5.6.

The digestion mechanical superintendent is concerned with work and with decisions which involve a time scale much longer than that of the decisions of his supervisors. The former carries out his task by communicating the necessary instructions, and the aim of the work, to his supervisors. They, in turn, instruct their work groups on how to complete their tasks. Information feedback to the supervisors enables them to control the completion of the work in the short term; information feedback to the superintendent enables him to control the performance of his supervisors, and hence the completion of the work, in the long term. *This is an example of a vertical control system.*

5.4 Characteristics of maintenance administrative structures

Having reviewed some of the key points of classical administrative theory we are now in a better position to identify and discuss some of the principal difficulties of administrating the maintenance resources.

5.4.1 The maintenance–engineering interface

It is usual (see Figure 5.3) to separate the engineering responsibilities for the procurement of *new* plant from those for the maintenance of *existing* plant. Although this has advantages it also presents difficulties, *mainly caused by lack of clarity in the overlapping areas of engineering responsibility for the plant.*

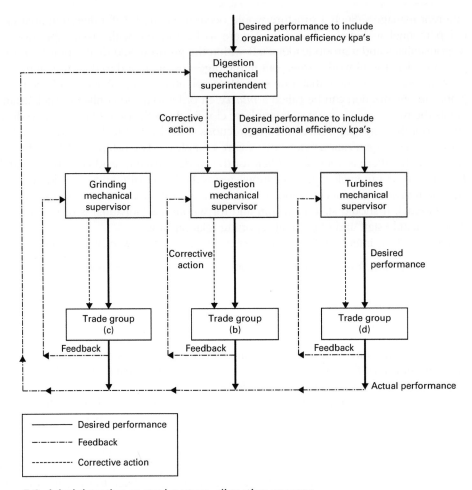

Figure 5.6 Administrative control system, digestion process

Situations in the mining industry have been observed where the engineering department was responsible for mobile equipment when it was off-site (e.g. out for contract overhaul) and the maintenance department was responsible for the maintenance of the equipment when it was on-site. There was confusion over who 'owned' the equipment, who 'owned' the maintenance budget and who should specify the overhaul work (see the Coalcom example in Chapter 10).

The engineering department often 'owns' the professional engineers responsible for maintenance improvement (i.e. for design-out maintenance). The digestion mechanical engineer of the Figure 5.3 example was located in the digestion plant area but reported to the engineering manager. Conflict existed regarding his job priorities – should he have been concentrating on project work in the digestion plant or on design-out maintenance? Design-out ended up being neglected in spite of the low reliability exhibited by the plant.

Major difficulties are also experienced in the feedback of maintenance information (from the maintenance departments information system to the engineering department) to aid the specification of new plant.

The major problem here is usually lack of adherence to the basic rules of administration. For example, the overlapping areas of responsibility (arising from collateral relationships) must be clearly defined and understood by all.

Review Question

R5.1   Some of the main problems of a maintenance organization occur across the following departmental boundaries:

- engineering–maintenance
- production–maintenance
- stores–maintenance

Can you identify any 'common thread' that links these problems?

5.4.2 The maintenance–production interface

Conflict, can, and often does, occur across the maintenance–production interfaces. This again is mostly caused by lack of definition of overlapping responsibility areas. This can lead to the entrenched view that 'they (the operators) bust the plant; we (the maintainers) fix it'. This causes 'horizontal polarization' – a conflict of attitudes and communications between the various groups of an organization (see Figure 5.7).

This is most evident in large organizations of the type shown in Figure 5.3, highly functionalized at the top with long chains of command down to the operators and maintainers – it is then very difficult to get the many disparate groups shown within the dotted line of Figure 5.3 to work together to drive the plant.

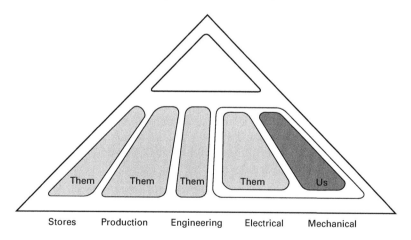

Figure 5.7 Horizontal polarization in an administrative structure

The example of Figure 5.3 illustrates that large functionalized organizations with centralized authority for maintenance and engineering decision-making have many advantages, including, inter alia:

- uniformity of engineering standards,
- high level of technical knowledge,

- high level of craft knowledge and skills,
- easy introduction of new technologies on site.

These are particularly important when an extremely large and integrated process, such as a petroleum refinery, is being run. Centralized administrations, however, have difficulty in establishing 'ownership', a vital ingredient in the successful operation and maintenance of plant. In the example of Figure 5.3 this characteristic could be introduced via the following actions:

- identifying process areas which have a clear production function and which can support a POG (see, e.g. the digestion group of Figure 5.3, shown within the dotted line);
- identifying the production and maintenance objectives for such groups;
- identifying the scope for interdisciplinary teams (of up to 10 personnel) within the group (team objectives will need to be identified and made compatible with group objectives). The team may also focus on a plant or process area, i.e. be *plant oriented*. One way of identifying the teams is via 'equipment responsibility diagrams' of the kind shown in Figure 5.4. Such teams can become self-empowered;
- carrying out a major educational and training program aimed at production–maintenance–engineering group and team building.

These changes may result in a modified administrative structure, as in Figure 5.8 proposal where a digestion-operating group is suggested. In many respects, and especially if a group leader were to be appointed, this would be a matrix structure, i.e. the functional reporting structure would have been retained but the group members would also focus, as a group, to 'drive the plant'.

An alternative (see Figure 5.9) might be to create plant manufacturing units (PMUs) – sometimes called mutual recognition units (MRUs) [2]. This would differ from the matrix structure in that it would involve a structural change, the functional reporting set-up being divided into smaller units. The digestion area would become one of a number of manufacturing units within the company. It would have considerable autonomy, having its own budget and management. Such an arrangement is more suitable where a company is made up of a number of clearly identifiable plants. Such units have not proved particularly successful for integrated plants.

It will be noticed in both Figures 5.8 and 5.9 that as far as possible an effort has been made to align the 'plant area responsibilities' (A–C) of production and maintenance. In the longer term this may help in the establishment of self-empowered plant-oriented teams (SEPOTs). (SEPOTs are discussed in detail in Section 7.7, Chapters 9 and 11.)

Review Question

R5.2   The administrative structure of the ammonia plant is based on manufacturing units (see Figure 12.14 of Case study 6):

(a) Explain what is meant by a manufacturing unit.
(b) List the main advantages of using manufacturing units.
(c) List the main problems that Fertec A and B were experiencing with their manufacturing units.

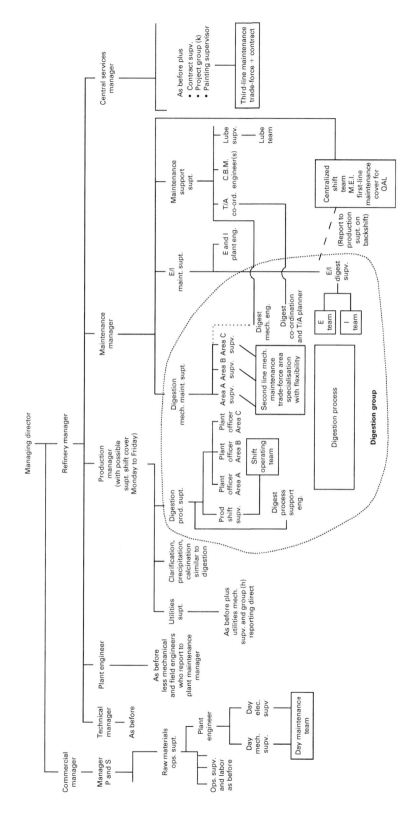

Figure 5.8 Proposed administrative structure based on POG

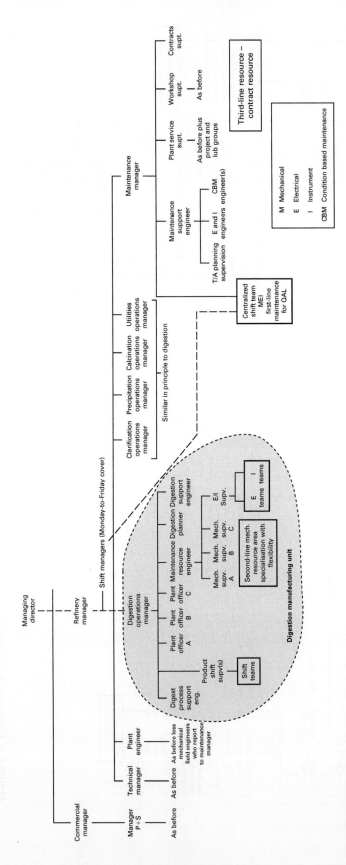

Figure 5.9 Proposed administrative structure based on manufacturing units

5.4.3 Responsibility for spare parts management

The rational objective for spares holding is to minimize the total of procurement, holding and stockout costs. Traditionally (see Figure 5.2), the responsibility for spares management has lain outside the maintenance domain. Thus, maintenance specifies the spare parts, sets the *initial* order level and uses the parts, while the commercial department is responsible for the cost of the stores and the spares inventory policy. The natural tendency is for maintenance to over-specify and overstock and for the commercial department to do the opposite. The responsibilities of the holder of spares and the user of spares must be clearly identified and systems of communication established for which the rules of operation (checks and balances) are clearly described and understood.

5.4.4 Vertical polarization

Considerable antipathy can build up between the various levels of an organization – especially if they are numerous and the organization is large (this has been particularly the case in the UK). The greatest degree of antipathy is often between the shop floor and the higher levels of management (*vertical polarization*) – a conflict in attitudes, objectives and communication (see Figure 5.10). This can cause problems throughout the organization (not just in the maintenance area). For example, at shop floor level the characteristic that is of particular importance, and is diminished by such polarization, is *goodwill towards the company*. This is perhaps the most important of the human factors, probably the dominant one. The impact of other human factors, such as motivation and the sense of equipment ownership, stems from this.

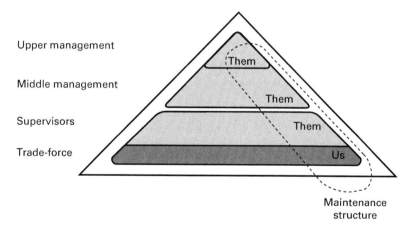

Figure 5.10 Vertical polarization in an administrative structure

Introducing 'manufacturing units' or POG can have a positive effect in reducing vertical polarization. At shop floor level the introduction of plant-oriented teams and self-empowerment can help to break down antipathy towards management. The largest negative factor in this area, however, is lack of shop floor job security. This can have a negative effect on all the human factors.

5.4.5 The relationship between the professional engineer and the maintenance supervisor

Supervisors mostly come from the trades, do not have professional engineering qualifications and only rarely move into the upper reaches of management. They are, however, unique in that they constitute the only level of management that looks downwards to non-management personnel. In addition, they tend to be less mobile within the organization than professional engineers and are the main source of trade and plant-oriented knowledge. More recently, their direct man-management role has been threatened by the implementation of self-empowered teams. This has been a principal cause of friction between the supervisors and those above them.

A vehicle for achieving a better understanding of the above problem has been developed by Riddell [3] who considers that the traditional work roles of the maintenance supervisor can be represented by a grid of duties (see Figure 5.11) comprising four domains, *viz.*:

1. upward-facing technical (UT)
2. downward-facing technical (DT)
3. upward-facing personnel (UP)
4. downward-facing personnel (DP)

He points out that irrespective of the organizational changes that will take place these duties will always have to be carried out by someone. The trend toward the self-empowered team means that many of the UP and DP duties will be taken on board by the team and its leader. The UT and DT duties are tending to be carried out by technician-advisers and planners, who in general act in advisory positions to the teams. Clearly, these roles are key technical links between the professional engineers and the teams or the shop floor.

As Riddell affirms, *the supervisor has not become extinct, he has undergone a metamorphosis*. It is important that senior management recognize this and provide the necessary counseling and training.

Review Question

R5.3   (a) Identify the four domains that describes the work role of the traditional maintenance supervisor.

       (b) For each domain list at least one duty/activity.

       (c) Explain how these duties are carried out when an administration uses self-empowered plant-oriented maintenance teams.

5.4.6 Major overhaul administration

A problem that is particular to maintenance management is the need, in many industries, to change the on-going organization to cope with the demands of a major overhaul.

		Work diversity	
		Technical role	**Personnel role**
Janus-like traits	**Upward facing** (Part of management team)	**Upward technical (UT)** • Influencing the maintenance goals • Involvement in setting his own and his team's goals • Influencing the maintenance strategy • Involvement in setting preventive maintenance program • Involvement in work order and other maintenance information systems • Using condition monitoring systems and equipment • Collecting reliability and maintainability data and passing to engineers • Advising on design-out maintenance • Co-operating with other staff on technical/work matters in maintenance, production, stores, safety, engineering functions.	**Upward personnel (UP)** • Communicating men's concerns and ideas – acting as their advocate • Influencing personnel policies and decisions on – tradesmen and apprentice recruiting, selection, training, promotion, control and disciplinary procedures, pay differentials, bonus payments, overtime, amenities, dismissals, redundancies • Influencing policies and decisions on – foremen selection, training, development • Training new foremen and young engineers • Giving advice on industrial relation problems and disputes, negotiations with unions • Co-operating with other staff on personnel matters in personnel, safety, maintenance functions
	Downward facing (Leader of own team)	**Downward technical (DT)** • Producing PM schedules in accordance with PM program • Making decisions on corrective maintenance – what is to be done, when, how and by whom • Setting job methods and work standards • Deciding on materials, tools, and information needed for each job • Implementing maintenance systems and ensuring their continued proper use • Monitoring work output and performance, deciding corrective action to achieve team goals and implementing that action • Investigating plant/equipment problems, seeking immediate solutions – if available implementing • Developing and improving job methods, tools and work standards	**Downward personnel (DP)** • Communicating the firm's department goals and policies • Communicating team targets and plans • Allocating jobs to men and maintaining team activity • Motivating each member of team to achieve job targets • Involving team in identifying new targets • Guiding, training each man in: (a) job knowledge and skills, (b) use of maintenance systems • Setting behavior and relationship standards, monitoring these in team and improving • Controlling and disciplining men in accordance with agreed policies • Resolving individual's personal problems • Settling disputes and negotiating on minor industrial relations issues with shop stewards within agreed procedures • Deciding on working conditions, hours, payments and amenities within agreed policies

Figure 5.11 A grid of maintenance supervisor's roles (*Source*: H.S. Riddell)

Figure 5.2 showed the administrative structure for the alumina refinery when it is in normal operation. When, however, major parts of the refinery (e.g. the kilns in the calcination area) are shut down for overhaul the resource and administrative structures in those areas have to change – to forms that are more appropriate for a *project* type of activity. The idea is illustrated in Figure 5.12, where it is indicated that the main link between the overhaul and the on-going administrations is the turnaround manager, who also acts as project manager.

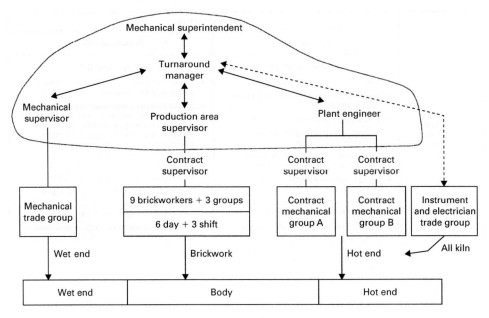

Figure 5.12 Administration for turnaround work

Review Question

R5.4   Case study 6 of Chapter 12 (see Figure 12.15), shows that a matrix structure was being used at senior management level of the company. Discuss the relationship between the reliability engineers (see also Figure 12.14) and the ammonia plant mechanical engineer in terms of the way maintenance and design improvements are carried out.

5.4.7 Summary

The problems discussed above can be divided into those that are general, i.e. vertical polarization and the rest, which are particular to the maintenance administration. The basic difficulties highlighted in items Sections 5.4.1 and 5.4.2 stem from the size of the operation. Large integrated plants make for large organizations and there is a pressure to specialize by function at a high level of the administration – to create a specialist engineering section which will set standards for equipment and also specify and procure it, to create a maintenance section which itself might be departmentalized by function into mechanical and electrical, etc. Thus, the duties and responsibilities for areas of the plant or of the process are usually set within each function, or trade, without thought for POG. For example, see Figure 5.4 which shows a mismatch of the responsibility of supervisors across the plant process. Thus, in order to 'drive the plant' in such situations a major effort of co-ordination is needed *and careful thought should be given to achieving the right balance between functionalization and the creation of POG and plant-oriented teams* [4].

5.5 The design or modification of the administrative structure

The design of a maintenance administrative structure is concerned with:

- Determining the responsibility, authority and work role (the decision-making bounds) of each individual concerned directly with the management of maintenance resources.
- Establishing the relationships, both vertical and horizontal, between each individual concerned directly or indirectly with the management of maintenance resources.
- Ensuring that the maintenance objective has been interpreted for, and understood by, each individual concerned directly with the management of maintenance resources.
- Establishing effective systems for co-ordination of – and for communication between – each individual concerned directly and indirectly with the management of maintenance resources.

Many of the rules and guidelines of classical administrative management – concerning such matters as chain and unity of command, span of control and so on – can be used to assist the design of a maintenance administrative structure. A procedure for such design, the aim of which should be to facilitate administration at least administrative cost, is shown in Figure 5.13.

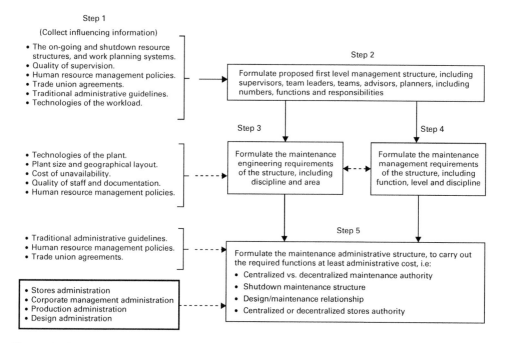

Figure 5.13 Decision procedure for formulating a maintenance administrative structure

Step (2) is concerned with the bottom-up influence on the *lower* structure – with the composition, duties and administration of the trade groups and first-line tradesmen or tradesmen-operator teams. Steps (3) and (4) address the *upper* structure and take account of top-down influences, the former being concerned with the engineering needs of the structure (e.g. Is there a need for a separate engineering group or can this be combined with the maintenance needs?) and the latter with identifying the maintenance management requirements (e.g. Should the managers be single discipline or multi-discipline? How many levels of management are required? Is a separate planning section needed? and so on). All of this has finally to be considered, Step (5), in the light of the rest of the structure.

During many years of consultancy the author has only once been involved in setting up an administrative structure for a *new* plant, the task has nearly always involved improving the structure for an *existing* plant and has been carried out as a part of an audit, after the life plans, workload and resource structure have also been reviewed. In such situations it is important to map and review the existing administration (of production and engineering) in order to identify the problems, which may be the result of having too many levels of management or of poor managerial performance. *If such problems can be identified the objective of the review is to redesign the structure to enable it to better carry out its function and at reduced cost.*

The mapping of the plant layout, and of the resource and administrative structures, of the alumina refinery (see Figures 4.1–4.3 and 5.1–5.4) were part of a maintenance audit. It can be seen from Figure 4.14 that a considerable immediate reduction in the level of the trade-force numbers and cost was achievable – *mostly by reducing the dependency on contract labor.*

In the longer term, the development of improved inter-trade flexibility should lead to increased organizational efficiency and further reduced numbers. Clearly, this modified resource structure would have a considerable bottom-up influence on the existing administrative structure shown in Figures 5.1–5.3. For example, because the trade-force would be reduced, and self-empowerment schemes implemented, fewer supervisors would be needed. In addition, there would be top-down pressure to reduce the levels and concentration of management while encouraging production–maintenance integration. In addition, there would be moves to set up company–contractor alliances.

One way to accomplish this structural slimming would be to adopt the manufacturing unit approach of Figure 5.9.

Exercise

E5.2 In Exercise E5.1 you mapped the maintenance administrative structure currently in use in your company. Using this information carry out the following tasks:
  (a) Make a list of what you consider to be the main problems with the administration.
  (b) Draw a modified administration to overcome the problems listed in (a).

Review Question

R5.5 With reference to Figures 5.1, 5.8 and 5.9 describe the main characteristics of the following organizational structures:
  (a) An administration based on 'plant groups'.
  (b) An administration based on 'manufacturing units'.
  (c) A traditional functional administration.

Choose one of these three administrative arrangements for each of the following plants and explain your choice:

(d) An aluminum smelter
(e) An old petroleum refinery
(f) A large, complex and relatively new alumina refinery.

References

1. Kelly, A., *Maintenance Management Auditing*, Industrial Press, New York, 2005.
2. Jacques, E. and Clement, S., *Executive leadership.*
3. Riddell, H.S., A supervisory grid to understand the role of the foreman in the process industries, *Proceeding Institution of Mechanical Engineers: Part E, The Journal of Process Engineering* 203, 1989.
4. Moore, R., *Making Common Sense Common Practice*, Gulf, 1999.

Review Questions Guidelines

R5.1   The 'common thread' is best explained via the stores-maintenance boundary. The stores objective from a company point of view can be explained as:

Minimize the sum of holding costs + stockout costs.

The maintenance department is normally responsible for 'what to hold' and the initial order quantity. The stores department is responsible for 'holding the stock' and are expected to control the inventory and the holding cost – they try to keep the spares inventory down. The maintenance department want to avoid stockout and try to keep the spares inventory up. Thus there is often conflict. In other words, the responsibility for a company function has been split across two departments. Unless the overlaps and objectives are clarified horizontal polarization results. (Think about the other two interfaces in the same way.)

R5.2   (a) The ammonia plant administration is based on manufacturing units. In each unit the plant manager has the responsibility for both operations and maintenance and has a budget and the authority to enable this work to be carried out. The manufacturing unit is partly autonomous and is regarded as a 'profit center'. The unit can take decisions to use additional contract resources and can also expect help and advice from the reliability group.

(b) The unit is relatively small so that 'everybody knows everybody' – this can engender *'esprit de corps'*. There is a sense of 'belonging to a group' and an ownership for the plant. It is easier to set ammonia plant objectives than with a functional administration. Vertical and horizontal communication is easier and this works against polarization.

(c) Fertec were experiencing numerous problems resulting in the main from poor leadership and lack of definition of the process teams and maintenance teams *'modus operandi'*.
   - The process teams were trained and paid to carry out first-line maintenance but were refusing to do this work. Senior management had allowed this to happen. This was disrupting the second-line planned work and causing polarization between maintenance and production.
   - The role and responsibility of the maintenance team (and the process team) had not been clearly specified resulting in communication problems

between the teams and the other members of the unit, e.g. Could the mechanical engineer tell the maintenance team to carry out a job or should he refer back to the plant manager? This area needed clarifying.

R5.3   (a) Upward and downward technical.
Upward and downward personnel.

(b) Upward technical – collecting reliability data and discussing it with the engineers.
Downward technical – making decisions on corrective maintenance – trouble shooting.
Upward personnel – communicating tradesmans concerns to senior management.
Downward personnel – maintaining team discipline.

(c) Most of the activities are shared out among the team leader and team members (see, e.g. Figure 5.11). Some of the technical duties are carried out by a planner and/or technical officers (advisors).

R5.4   It will be seen in Figure 12.14 that the technician engineers, e.g. machine engineering officers, are transferring from the reliability group to report to the ammonia plant engineer. Under this arrangement the ammonia plant engineer is regarded as the asset custodian – he is responsible for life plans, design-out-maintenance, etc. The reliability group engineers (professional engineers) act in an advisory capacity especially in their designated areas of specialization. Figure 12.16 shows the author's proposals for the administration – note that he has the maintenance teams reporting to the ammonia plant engineer.

R5.5   (a) Figure 5.8 illustrates an administration based on plant groups. The structure remains a 'functional structure', e.g. the operators report to a company production manager. There is no one manager solely responsible for digestion. However, one of the existing managers, e.g. digestion production superintendent may also have a role as the digestion co-ordinator. He and other personnel meet as a digestion group and set digestion area production and maintenance objectives. This is a form of matrix structure and the various responsibilities/meetings/communication lines will need to be set up clearly.

(b) Figure 5.8 illustrates an administration based on a manufacturing unit. The characteristics have been outlined in the answer to 5.1(a).

(c) Figures 5.1(a) and (b) illustrate a functional organization. The administration is departmentalized by function, e.g. production, maintenance. In large organizations this results in long chains of command which can generate both vertical and horizontal polarization.

(d) An aluminum smelter is made up of a number of separate plants using different processes with a degree of inter-plant storage. This structure lends itself to PMUs. Most of the smelters across the world use manufacturing units.

(e) An old petroleum refinery could conceivably use any of the three structures. However, it is a large integrated process plant and a functional structure is the most likely structure to be used. The author has seen a petroleum structure based on 'groups' which was adopted to overcome polarization – it worked well.

(f) Again an alumina refinery is a large integrated plant which does not lend itself naturally to manufacturing units. In addition, the plant is new and likely to experience 'commissioning' problems. For these reasons the most likely structure is functional.

6 Human factors in maintenance management

'Heaven has no rage, like love to hatred turned, nor Hell a fury like an 'artisan scorned.'
with apologies to William Congreve 1701

Chapter aims and outcomes

To show how individual and group behavioral characteristics can influence the way in which maintenance work is carried out.

On completion of this chapter you should be able to:

- define 'human factors' in an industrial management context;
- identify and explain the effect of individual and group behavioral characteristics on maintenance work;
- construct questionnaires for auditing maintenance human factors.

Chapter route map

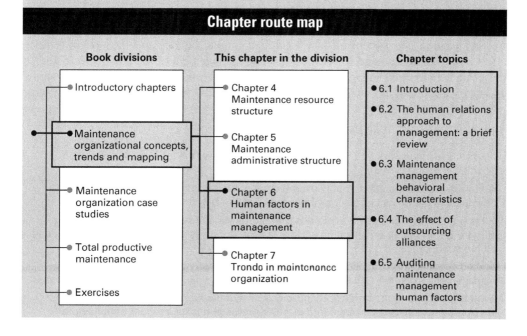

Book divisions	This chapter in the division	Chapter topics
Introductory chapters	Chapter 4 Maintenance resource structure	6.1 Introduction
Maintenance organizational concepts, trends and mapping	Chapter 5 Maintenance administrative structure	6.2 The human relations approach to management: a brief review
Maintenance organization case studies	Chapter 6 Human factors in maintenance management	6.3 Maintenance management behavioral characteristics
Total productive maintenance	Chapter 7 Trends in maintenance organization	6.4 The effect of outsourcing alliances
Exercises		6.5 Auditing maintenance management human factors

Key words

- Human relations management
- Participative management
- Autonomous work groups
- Individual behavioral characteristics
- Human factor profiling
- Behavioral theories
- Human factor problems
- Group behavioral characteristics
- 'Esprit de corps'

6.1 Introduction

In Chapters 4 and 5 I have drawn on an example of an alumina refinery to discuss maintenance organizational structure. The models on which that analysis was based were derived from the work of the administrative and systems theorists (see Table 6.1), rather than from the school of managerial theory which is centered on studies of *human relations*. We will now look at how human factors can influence the way in which maintenance work is carried out.

6.1.1 What are 'human factors' in organizations?

An organization is a system of interdependent human beings, and their characteristics affect both its structure and its functioning. The management of human relations studies the characteristics and interrelationships of individuals and groups within organizations and takes account of these factors when designing and administering those organizations.

Table 6.1 Summary of management theories

Mechanistic management: monitors and controls the way the job is performed at shop floor level; includes method, timing, and direction.

Administrative management: applies universal management functions and structural principles to the design of an organization and to its operation.

Human relations management: studies characteristics and relationships of individuals and groups within an organization and takes account of these factors when designing and administrating it.

Decision management: applies procedural and quantitative models to the solution of management problems. A theory for communications and decision-making in organizations.

Systems management: studies organizations as dynamic systems reacting with their environment. Analyses a system into its subsystems and takes account of behavioral, mechanistic, technological and managerial aspects.

Contingency management: takes the view that the characteristics of an organization must be matched to its internal and external environment. Since, these environments can change it is important to view the organizational structure as dynamic.

6.2 The human relations approach to management: a brief review

The first major development in the human relations approach was the work of Elton Mayo at the Hawthorn Plant [1]. He established that social and psychological factors were important to worker satisfaction and productivity. Considerable advances were made during the period 1950–1970, most notably by Maslow, Herzberg and McGregor, in understanding worker motivation [2,3,4].

Maslow identified and ranked what he considered to be the needs of the individual, i.e.:

Higher needs

5. Self-fulfillment
4. Autonomy
3. Self-esteem

Basic needs

2. Sociality
1. Security

Herzberg also divided the needs of the individual into those that are basic (biological) and those that are higher (growth). He then identified and quantified the factors affecting these needs, see Figure 6.1.

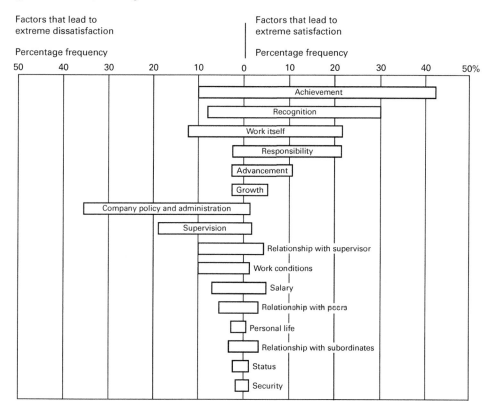

Figure 6.1 Factors affecting job attitudes

He pointed out that it is the factors bearing on the higher needs that can affect job satisfaction and that, in the industrial setting, these are to be found in the job content. Factors which influence the basic needs are those affecting job dissatisfaction and these are concerned with the job environment. He emphasized that it is the factors which bear on the job content that are the true motivators and that a motivated worker is responding to an internal stimulus – he wants to get the work done.

McGregor's work – his so-called 'Theory X' (the then traditional view that the worker needs to be controlled and directed because of his inherent dislike of work) and 'Theory Y' (the idea that the majority of workers can be self-directing if they have job satisfaction and become committed to an objective) – provided managers with an insight into the characteristics of the worker.

The behavioral scientists of this period argued that work had become over-controlled and boring. They were advocating changes of the following kind:

- Replacement of detailed instruction by clarification of objectives.
- Increase of responsibility and provision of greater chance of achievement by making the job of planning, organization, directing and controlling a joint function with employees.
- Study of the organization of jobs and trying to design them so as to give greater satisfaction of human needs.
- Replacement of control activities by those which seek to emphasize the manager as helper, supporter and tutor – in order to develop abilities.
- Setting out to build effective teams within the workforce.

During the last 20 years there have been many exercises in the application of this approach. Some of the early ones, focusing on job redesign with emphasis on autonomous small work groups, were undertaken in Scandinavia. Swedish management and unions, working together, implemented (and modified *via.* experience) many of the ideas of job enrichment and participative management [5]. In the UK, however, similar early exercises, in the 1970s, in participative management met with limited success, principally because the industrial environment was very different from that in Scandinavia and was not conducive to this style of management [6]. The UK's political and industrial environment changed in the subsequent two decades and with this came the introduction of participative management and self-empowered shop floor teams (many of the latter reflecting the Japanese concept of the autonomous operator–maintainer team). More recently, the industrial climate has changed again and brought in downsizing and contract alliances, changing yet further the style of human factors management – in a sense it has moved backwards.

6.3 Maintenance management behavioral characteristics

In Section 6.2 it has been explained that the main efforts of the human factors school have focused on identifying and understanding those elements that make an employee's work more satisfying and therefore more effective in terms of the organizational objectives. Here, we will look at human factors from a different viewpoint. We will be concerned with identifying the main ones that influence the organization's efforts towards achieving its maintenance objectives. Some (e.g. a sense of ownership of equipment, affecting reliability performance) will affect the maintenance objective *via.* output considerations, and some (e.g. motivation) *via*. the efficiency of resource usage. It is important to understand that management can take actions to change human factors; the creation of plant-oriented teams, for example might improve the sense of equipment ownership.

When identifying human factors the following points are helpful:

- It is important to differentiate between human factors and the actions that influence them (see above).
- Human factors can interact, e.g. morale affects motivation.
- Some researchers consider that some human factors, such as goodwill towards the company, can be considered as dominant.
- Some performance indicators provide a measure of certain human factors, e.g. the level of absenteeism is an indicator of morale.

I am not trying to be 'academic' about this. When auditing maintenance departments I try to get a feel for how good or bad the human factors are. There is little point in confirming that the strategy, structure and systems are good without providing corresponding information about human factors.

When seeking the key human factors in maintenance management I have found the following definition useful:

> *Characteristics which define the way in which an individual or group behaves or acts in an industrial setting can be called human factors. Those that influence the way the maintenance department operates are termed maintenance management human factors.*

The more important of these may be divided into those that can affect individual behavior, and those that can affect the behavior of industrial groupings of people – complete companies, manufacturing units and teams. As far as possible, industrial examples will be used to show how important these are to maintenance management.

Review Question

R6.1   Define 'human factors' in maintenance.

Exercise

E6.1   Carry out a brief Internet search in order to locate literature on the subject of 'human factors in maintenance management' and/or associated topics.

6.3.1 Individual behavioral characteristics

Equipment ownership
Equipment ownership is a factor which involves the degree to which a trade-force and/or operators and/or the team feel:

> *a sense of personal ownership for an equipment or an area of plant.*

This is probably the most important single factor in achieving a high level of equipment reliability. Where ownership exists the equipment tends to be operated and maintained correctly.

> This first became evident to me in the result of a major study of maintenance costs of forklift trucks in the UK. Those operated and maintained by a single operator (operator–maintenance) incurred one third of the maintenance cost of pool-operated trucks in the same industry.

One of the key organizational characteristics of total productive maintenance (the Japanese-developed strategic approach to maintenance management) is the move towards small, *self-empowered, plant-oriented operator–maintenance teams* – of up to seven operator–maintainers with the responsibility for operating a definable sub-process or area of plant and carrying out simple maintenance tasks on it, such as lubrication, adjustment and minor servicing. The teams comprise operators (trained in superficial maintenance) and artisans (given operator training). The teams are also given considerable training in the way the plant operates and the relationship between the way it is maintained and operated and its failure or its inability to produce at its design level of quality. They are encouraged, with the help of engineers, to carry out modifications to improve operation and reliability (the so-called continuous improvement or *Kaizen*). All of these actions engender a considerable level of plant ownership in the individuals and in the team – they care about the equipment in the same way as if it were literally their personal property.

> Some of the necessary ingredients for fostering ownership were present in the food processing plant (FPP) organization of Chapter 1 (see Figures 1.14 and 1.15). The operators and fitters were plant oriented. However, the separation of operators and maintainers and the shift system worked against ownership. To compensate for this, individual artisans were made responsible for carrying out the preventive work on designated equipment – both on shifts and when they were in the weekend group.

Goodwill
The state of wishing well to a person, a cause or an enterprise.

Source: a dictionary definition

This involves the artisans or operators feeling a sense of belonging with the company and wanting it to prosper. It is closely allied to 'loyalty' but is something more than this. The author considers it to be in many ways a key factor. When goodwill is evident at the shop floor level other problems seem to be more amenable to solution. It takes a long time to build up – perhaps many years of good relationships and trust in the management and the company. It is a function of the company treating the workforce fairly and with respect.

> I recently audited an Australian underground coal mine. On a scale of 1 (= no goodwill) to 10 (= excellent relationship and trust) I would have rated goodwill as of Level 1!

Motivation

Motivation is much researched and much written about, because of its importance to all industrial personnel. I consider the *behaviorist* theories (see Table 6.1) to be too general and insufficiently dynamic to describe the motivational characteristics of the shop floor. To quote from one of my earlier books:

> *'In general the industrial worker sees his job as a means of obtaining money, a lower order need, in order to satisfy elsewhere his other, higher order, needs. This view is based on the observation that people are only truly motivated when they are doing something (work, hobby, sport, home repairs) that they really want to do. Most often the worker does not experience this at work. The nature of the work is such that it is normally difficult to institute changes sufficiently to arouse true motivation' [7].*

Applying these ideas to the maintenance artisans is not without difficulty. To a certain extent, maintenance work has many of the ingredients needed to provide Herzberg's idea of worker satisfaction and motivation. It has autonomy, craftsman status, pride in the quality of the work, varied and interesting job content, etc. – all of this reinforced with the movement in many companies to self-empowerment. These work ingredients also emphasize how important trade-force motivation is to maintenance management. Maintenance workers are among the few on the shop floor who still have considerable autonomy as regards their day-to-day actions. Thus, it is difficult to check how well a preventive maintenance inspection routine has been carried out. It is also difficult to judge how well a repair has been carried out and, in some cases, whether the spares used have been the best from the company's point of view. Maintenance workers know that if they carry out inferior work the consequences of their actions take time to surface and often will be difficult to attribute to them.

In the case of the maintenance artisans, the most realistic indicators of his level of motivation are (a) the extent to which he knows what is wanted from him and (b) the level of his effort to provide it with a minimum of external control.

When trying to influence, understand or audit motivation within a maintenance department the following aspects must be taken into consideration:

- The shop floor's industrial relations history, its present position and its deficiencies.
- The factors that influence job content and job environment.
- The external social and political environment and its influence (because this governs the extent to which internal change is possible).
- The trade-force's identification with the maintenance objectives (the most important factor in their motivation).

Morale

Morale is defined as:

> the mental state of an individual with regard to confidence and discipline.
>
> Source: Oxford Dictionary

Finding a definition in a management text proved difficult; the best was:

> an individual's satisfaction and confidence with membership of an organisation [8].

The same work pointed out that productivity is not a function of morale and therefore morale is not a very meaningful concept in management thought! My own auditing experience, however, has convinced me that poor morale, whether of individuals or trade groups, most certainly affects both the quantity and the quality of maintenance work. Morale within the maintenance department may be defined as:

> *an individual's perception, which may be positive or negative, of his future work prospects, and which may be induced by the success or failure of the company employing him and the ability (leadership, organisational and engineering performance) of its management.*

As this implies, the negative factors affecting morale may be those that appear to threaten the individual's or group's future work security, e.g.:

- a company's poor economic performance;
- poor company organization and systems, inducing problems with product quality, for example;
- recent workforce redundancies and the threat of more to come.

Resentment

Resentment is defined in the dictionary as:

> *'a strong feeling of ill will against the perpetrator of a wrong or affront'.*

The following example, drawn from one of my own auditing exercises, explains this in the context of the maintenance artisans:

> *'Hell hath no fury like a fitter scorned'.* A small power station, supplying a chemical plant, consisted of a number of large diesel generators. It was maintained by five fitters, one of them a leading hand. One of the younger (very bright) fitters had been promised promotion to supervisor level but this had not materialized – and did not look like doing so. He had become resentful and obstructive (the bad apple) and this feeling had spread to two of the other, younger, fitters. They were using every IR trick in the book (bad backs, bad arms, etc.) to avoid work and undermine the rest of the trade group. Weak management had allowed this situation to fester for about a year. The condition of the diesel units was deteriorating and this was likely to have a considerable effect on the overall operation of the plant.

Protectionism

Protectionism can be defined in the maintenance context as:

> *resistance to sharing knowledge and information.*

It can be affected by other human factors such as insecurity and low morale.

> A typical example is provided by the technician who has built up considerable knowledge over many years about specific equipment but is reluctant to document his knowledge or convey it to other employees.

Parochialism

Parochialism is defined as:

> *local narrowness of view and attitude.*
>
> Source: a dictionary definition

I have encountered this in many organizations. It can occur, e.g. within the manufacturing units of a decentralized organization.

> A power station, which I was auditing, provided electricity to an alumina refinery. It was set up as semi-autonomous manufacturing unit. There was considerable narrowness of view exhibited by its manager. He was an ex-marine engineer and ran the station as if it were a ship. On each visit I felt that the gangway had to be lowered before I could go onboard. The attitude of the staff was that they were set apart and different. The refinery senior management seemed to know little about the way the power station was being operated and maintained. I established that two out of the three generating units were needed at all times for full refinery operation. However, they were all in poor condition and in need of major overhaul. It was difficult to take a unit out because of the unreliability of the two left in service. Before leaving the site I insisted that the refinery general manager discuss this problem with the power station manager.

Organizational design creates the boundaries between departments and it is management's job to minimize parochialism and its effects. It generates other human factor problems, e.g. polarization (see later).

Other human factors

I do not audit directly but are covered indirectly during the one-to-one interviews which make up the bulk of the audit program. Some of these are as follows:

Jealousy: of those on shifts exhibited by those on days, or vice versa.
Attitude: a positive trade-force attitude towards data collection.
Envy: of those promoted.
Resistance to change: to the introduction of new working methods, team working, or computer systems.
Pride: in an individual's trade and in the quality of work carried out.
Prejudice: a pre-conceived, biased, opinion or position on a subject, e.g. the maintenance view of production – 'They break it, we mend it'; the production view of maintenance – 'They do not understand our objectives – we give them a line for 4 h they keep it for twelve'.

Exercise

E6.2   Of the 13 'individual behavioral characteristics' discussed in Section 6.3.1, identify for your own company, these characteristics that have the most influence on maintenance work and plant performance.

6.3.2 Group behavioral characteristics

Culture
Culture has been defined as [9]:

> *the collective mental programming of people in an environment.*

It is not a characteristic of individuals, it encompasses a number of people who are conditioned by the same education and life experience. Thus, when auditing it is important to recognize and understand the culture of the country. For example, that of Saudi Arabia is very different from that of the USA and this can influence the organization – most of the artisans in Saudi Arabia are expatriates.

A company can have its own culture:

> A FPP which I audited was part of a USA multinational that had been operating in Australia and the UK for many years. It had developed a company culture that I had observed in both of these countries, one that put a very high premium on success, hard work, fairness, tight scheduling and efficiency of thought – it could almost be 'felt'.

Further down the organization a culture can also develop within departments:

> A petrochemical complex used a functional organizational structure in which the maintenance department was large and carried out all the maintenance, even the major shutdowns. Over many years the culture within this department had developed a mix of norms, standards and behavior weighted much more towards maintaining equipment for engineering excellence rather than achieving organizational efficiency. The department was considerably over-manned.

Esprit de corps
Esprit de corps is defined as:

> *a spirit of regard for the company or group honor and interest, and for those of each member belonging to it.*

Clearly a concept of military origin and one which I observed in the major Japanese companies during visits to that country in the late 1970s. During my auditing of some fifty companies worldwide I have not come across any other companies, departments or manufacturing units which have had an *esprit* of the kind defined above. It has been suggested that one of the reasons for breaking down large functional organizations into semi-autonomous manufacturing units is to generate *esprit de corps* in each of those units (although I have not, as yet, observed this actually occurring to any extent).

Horizontal polarization
Horizontal polarization has been defined as:

> *having opposite views and attitudes across departmental boundaries.*

This can best be explained *via.* the simple model of a functional organization shown in Figure 6.2.

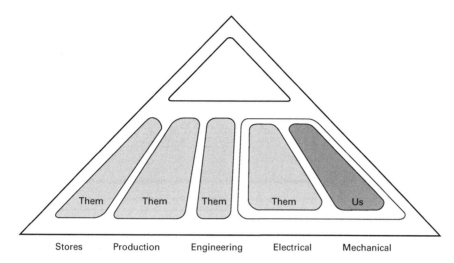

Figure 6.2 Horizontal polarization in an administrative structure

Conflict builds up across the boundaries of the main departments – *viz.* production, maintenance, engineering, stores – and to a lesser extent across the sub-departments, e.g. electrical maintenance and mechanical maintenance.

The production–maintenance conflict has been well documented. The maintenance view is that 'production built it and we mend it'. In other words 'they mal-operate and never let us have the equipment for proper maintenance'. The production view is that 'we make the money and maintenance do not understand our objectives – we give them the plant for a shift and they keep it for a day'.

> I was consulting on the maintenance of a papermaking machine. A production supervisor pointed out that a machine came down every 3–4 weeks for the replacement of a wire belt (a task of 8hours duration which the production operators carried out). When asked if this provided a window for maintenance work the supervisor replied *'We do not tell them when the machine is coming down otherwise we lose it for more than 8 hours – we keep this information to ourselves'.*

I often observe polarization across the maintenance–stores interface when these functions are the responsibility of different departments. From the company point of view the spares holding objective would be to minimize the sum of the holding and stockout costs. Maintenance try to keep the inventory high, stores management try to keep it low – hence conflict and polarization.

Figure 6.2 shows that the organization can develop the 'us and them' syndrome across the horizontal boundaries. 'We' are mechanical maintenance and everybody else (including electrical maintenance) is a 'them' – the larger the number of 'thems' the greater the polarization. Once severe polarization develops, information might flow but communication and understanding is lost.

Vertical polarization

Considerable antipathy can build up between the various *levels* of an organization, especially if these are many and the organization is large, see Figure 6.3.

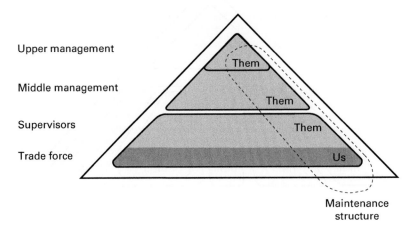

Figure 6.3 Vertical polarization in an administrative structure

The greatest degree of antipathy is often between the shop floor and the higher levels of management – a conflict in objectives and attitudes. Not only does such conflict affect communication but it also negatively affects some of the more important individual behavioral characteristics, e.g. goodwill and motivation.

The other important vertical maintenance interface is that which lies between the maintenance supervisors and their professional engineering managers. Supervisors mostly come from the trades, do not have professional engineering qualifications and only rarely move into the upper reaches of management. They are, however, unique in that they constitute the only level of management that looks downwards to non-management personnel. In addition, they tend to be less mobile within the organization than professional engineers and are the main source of trade and plant-oriented knowledge. More recently, their direct man-management role has been threatened by the introduction of self-empowered teams. In many industries their role has changed to that of technical advisor, planner and team leader. They have become uncertain and defensive. This has led to conflict and polarization.

The 'us and them' syndrome (of both the vertical and horizontal varieties) is most evident in large organizations which are highly functionalized at the top, with long chains of command down to operators and maintainers. Severe polarization in such organizations can cause complete lack of communication, organizational contraction and eventual failure.

Review Questions

R6.2   List the main 'individual' and 'group' human factors that can affect the performance of maintenance work and the reliability of equipment.

R6.3   To answer this review question you will need to refer to Figures 5.1, 5.2 and 5.9 of Chapter 5. It was proposed that the company should move from a functional organization (Figures 5.1 and 5.2) to one based on manufacturing units (Figure 5.4). If the company adopts this proposal identify the possible negative and positive human factor changes that might occur.

6.4 The effect of outsourcing alliances

So far, the discussion has been confined to a review of human factors within *traditional* organizations, those in which all the maintenance work is carried out by company-employed personnel (other than during periods of peak loading). The most recent trend in maintenance organization, however, has been towards company–contractor *alliances* where, e.g. the second- and third-line work (and perhaps the operation of the stores) are transferred to the alliance, whose workforce combines personnel transferred from the company with new personnel brought in by the contractor. My own experience indicates that this introduces some largely negative human factors, *viz.*:

- The transferred personnel suffer low morale – resenting and resisting the change, they find their position less secure. They feel that they have little in common with the contract trade-force.
- The incoming personnel lack both process and equipment knowledge and any form of goodwill towards the company
- The alliance workforce has little sense of plant or equipment ownership.

A leading contract company, when challenged with this view, argued the following case:

- The contract between the company and the alliance to deliver a 'level of service' is tightly specified by key performance indices. The alliance trade-force is aware of this and know that if the service levels are not achieved their job security will be jeopardized. So they are well-motivated.
- The contractor brings expertise in engineering and in job planning, the resulting efficiency enhancing the perception of job security and hence morale
- A sense of equipment ownership is more important within the production-oriented first-line teams than within the alliance workforce.

My experience of auditing human factors within alliance arrangements of this kind is, however, somewhat limited, so I present these views only for discussion.

Review Question

R6.4   Explain how the trend towards outsourcing maintenance work and the setting up of company–contractor alliances to carry out maintenance work has affected human factors within organizations.

6.5 Auditing maintenance management human factors

Human behavior can have a profound effect on the performance of organizations. In this chapter we have been concerned with identifying and discussing those human factors that can have an influence on maintenance performance. But although they can be identified it is much more difficult to audit them objectively. Table 6.2 shows an extract from one of the several questionnaires which are used in my own maintenance audit program, this one during one-to-one interviews with members of the maintenance trade-force.

Table 6.2 Extract from a human factor profiling questionnaire

---

MAINTENANCE AUDIT – COMPANY_____
HUMAN FACTOR PROFILING QUESTIONNAIRE
(MAINTENANCE ARTISANS)

Answer the following questions in terms of the scale below

0	1	2	3	4	5	6	7
Do not know	Not at all	Very little	A small amount	A fair amount	Quite a lot	A great deal	Completely

To what extent do you feel/believe:

1. You have a 'sense of ownership' for the equipment you maintain
2. The operators have a 'sense of ownership' for the equipment they operate
3. You have a 'feeling of goodwill' towards the company and its senior management
4. You have a high morale
5. You are motivated to work hard in the interests of the company
6. Your relationship with the production operators and supervisors is good
7. You have a good relationship with first-line management
8. You have an effective service from the stores

Continued...

It is only one relatively small part of the interviewing process. For artisans, questions on equipment ownership, motivation, morale and goodwill would be included in the interview plan, different sets of human factor questions being posed to the operators, supervisors and managers. The auditor explains the question, explaining what he means by 'ownership' and the scale adopted for its measurement. During such interviews he also records some of the individual comments about human factors, e.g.:

- 'We are a centralized group – we do not have a sense of equipment ownership'.
- 'Rotation works against ownership and plant specific knowledge'.
- 'There is no sense of ownership in the process teams, they don't even clean'.

A representative selection of such comments may be included in the audit report.

Auditing group behavioral characteristics requires a different approach, which is also illustrated in Table 6.2 in the case of horizontal polarization. Question 6 is directed at determining the maintenance view of the attitudes, co-operation and communication between production and maintenance. Other questions (not shown) attempt to determine production's view of the service they get from Maintenance.

When auditing large organizations I carry out surveys of opinion which include questions on human factors. Questionnaires in such cases are sent out ahead of the audit and returned during the audit period. The main aim of the human factors audit is to identify those factors which are affecting maintenance performance, either positively or negatively. When positive, advice is given on how they can be reinforced and maintained; when negative, how they might be eliminated or their influence mitigated. For example, if, in a traditionally functioning organization, the sense of equipment ownership is found to be poor at trade-force and operator level it may be improved by the creation of *self-empowered plant-oriented operator–maintainer teams* [10]. If such a structural modification is not possible or desirable then alternative courses of action must be sought within the traditional structure, e.g. individual artisans made responsible for specific equipment for preventive routines. While such a structural change may improve ownership it may well affect other factors in a negative way, e.g. plant-oriented teams may well increase parochialism. The point here is that organizational change requires a complex mix of structural, strategic, systems and human factors decisions. Before such decisions are taken it is essential to have as clear a picture as possible of the existing situation.

Exercises

E6.3   Construct 'human factors' questionnaires to help you to audit the maintenance artisans and operators of your own company.

E6.4   use the questionnaires of Exercise E6.3 to carry out human factors audit. Interview a selection of artisans and operators. Identify the main problem areas and propose changes to overcome these problems.

References

1. Mayo, E., *The Social Problems of an Industrial Civilisation*, HGS & A, Boston, 1945.
2. Maslow, A.A., *Motivation and Personality*, Harper and Brothers, New York, 1954.
3. Herzberg, F., *One more time: how do you motivate employees?* Harvard Business Review, January/February, 1968.
4. McGregor, D., *The Human Side of Enterprise*, McGraw Hill, New York, 1960.
5. Swedish Employers' Confederation (Technological Department), *Job reform in Sweden*, 1975.
6. Johnson, A.V., Motivation of labour, staff and management, Organisation of Maintenance, *Proceedings of Conference ISI*, 1968.
7. Kelly, A., *Maintenance Planning and Control*, Butterworth-Heinemann, Oxford, 1984.
8. Hicks, H.G. and Gullett, C.R., *Management*, McGraw Hill, Singapore, 1985.
9. Kast, F.E. and Rosenzweig, J.E., *Organisation and Management*, McGraw Hill, Singapore, 1985.
10. Yuki, G., *Leadership in Organizations*, Prentice Hall, 1994.

Review Questions Guidelines

R6.1   Characteristics which define the way in which an individual or group behaves or acts in an industrial setting can be called human factors. Those that influence the way the maintenance department operates are termed maintenance management human factors.

R6.2   Individual characteristics: ownership; goodwill; motivation. Group characteristics: culture; *esprit de corps*; polarization, etc.

R6.3   Possible positive human factor changes:
● Improved equipment ownership *via*. the first-line maintainers, the operators, the teams and the manufacturing unit.
● Improved '*esprit de corps*' within the manufacturing unit.
● Reduced production–maintenance polarization within the manufacturing units.

Possible negative human factor changes:
● Increased parochialism within the manufacturing unit.
● Increased polarization between manufacturing units and between the units and the centralized groups.

R6.4   Discussed in Section 6.4 entitled 'The effect of outsourcing on alliances'. The most important influence of these trends has been to decrease the artisans' sense of equipment ownership. It can also create polarization between the company operators/trades and the alliance trades.

7 Trends in maintenance organization

'If we want things to stay as they are, things will have to change.'
Giuseppi di Lampedusa (1950)

Chapter aims and outcomes

To review the changes that have taken place over the last 30 years to the management function in general, and to the maintenance-management function in particular. The overriding aim is to identify and discuss those changes which improve the efficiency of the maintenance organization.

On completion of this chapter you should be able to:

- appreciate the maintenance organizational trends that have emerged over the period 1970 to date;
- understand why the changes have occurred and the influence the changes have had on organizational efficiency;
- understand the principles and concepts associated with each of the organizational changes.

Chapter route map

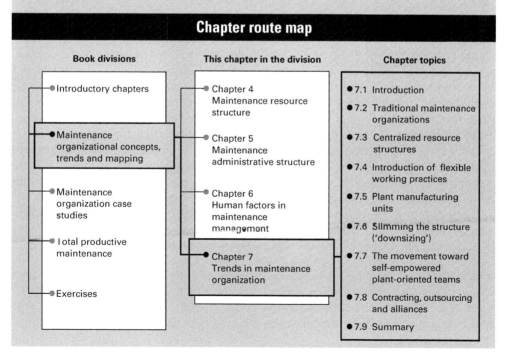

Book divisions	This chapter in the division	Chapter topics
Introductory chapters	Chapter 4 Maintenance resource structure	7.1 Introduction
Maintenance organizational concepts, trends and mapping	Chapter 5 Maintenance administrative structure	7.2 Traditional maintenance organizations
Maintenance organization case studies	Chapter 6 Human factors in maintenance management	7.3 Centralized resource structures
Total productive maintenance	Chapter 7 Trends in maintenance organization	7.4 Introduction of flexible working practices
Exercises		7.5 Plant manufacturing units
		7.6 Slimming the structure ('downsizing')
		7.7 The movement toward self-empowered plant-oriented teams
		7.8 Contracting, outsourcing and alliances
		7.9 Summary

Key words

- Functional organization
- Plant custodian
- Resistance to change
- Operator maintenance
- Business unit
- Down sizing
- Plant manufacturing unit
- Maintenance organizational trends

7.1 Introduction

During the course of the last 20 or 30 years considerable changes have been brought about in the way in which the maintenance-management function is organized. This section will review these trends and explain the principles, concepts and structure of each of the organizational initiatives, e.g. teams. The remaining sections of this module will use case studies and exercises to explain each of the initiatives in more detail.

The models of resource structure and administrative structure that have been introduced in Chapters 4 and 5 will serve as useful vehicles for mapping the various developments.

7.2 Traditional maintenance organizations

Taken together, Figures 7.1(a) and 7.1(b) model what may be regarded as the customary maintenance organization of a medium- or large-size company in the 1960s and 1970s. Figure 7.1(a) shows that the first- and second-line maintenance groups would be plant located and backed up by centralized specialist trades and workshops. The work cascades from the shift-groups to the day-groups to the central groups and where necessary to contract. Figure 7.1(b), on the other hand, shows that although most of the resources would be plant-located the authority for decision-making would be centralized. Indeed, the upper structure would be highly functionalized. Production would be responsible for operating the plant, maintenance for maintaining it. Engineering would be responsible for the design and procurement of new plant.

This is essentially the organizational structure used by the alumina refinery of Chapters 4 and 5. Although there would be advantages in such an arrangement there would also be serious disadvantages (especially where the structure had become very large), *viz.*:

- low utilization, because of the many small single-trade or single-shift maintenance and production groups – often manned up to the peak of a variable work load;
- vertical and horizontal polarization within the structure;
- high management cost due to an excess of hierarchical layers and functional positions.

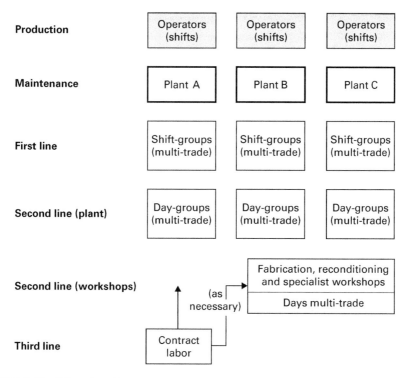

Figure 7.1(a) Traditional maintenance resource structure

In combination, these can result in poor organizational efficiency, as was the case with the alumina refinery.

> It should be emphasized that 'functional organizations' are still widely used and have advantages in some situations, e.g. for use with large, complex and integrated plants (see Section 5.4.2 and Review Question R5.3). The main problem with the so-called traditional structure was the use of a decentralized shift-oriented resource structure coupled with 'poor labor working practices', e.g. strict trade demarcation, resistance to the use of contract labor, etc.

7.3 Centralized resource structures

The main trends in the 1970s were aimed at improving shop floor utilization, this being achieved by increasingly centralizing the maintenance resource (see Figure 7.2(a)).

> The advantages of centralizing the trade group were discussed in Section 4.5.3. Combining the workload of several area maintenance teams has a natural 'workload smoothing effect', this should improve utilization. It also makes supervision and control of the trade-force easier.

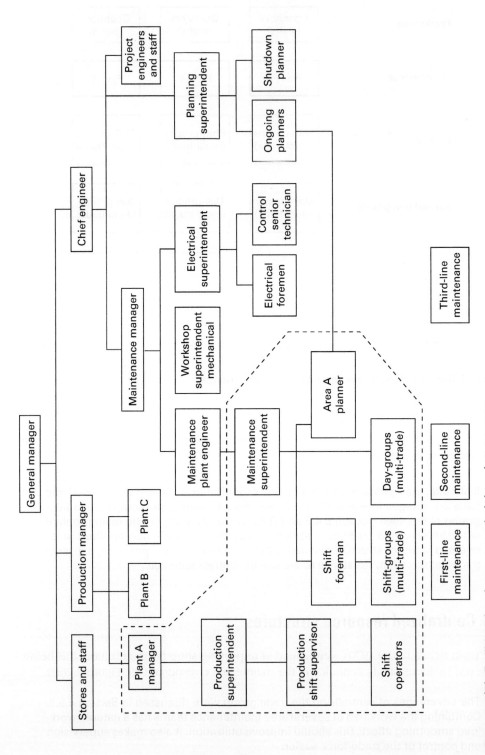

Figure 7.1(b) Traditional maintenance administrative structure

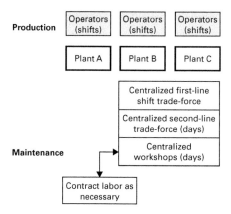

Figure 7.2(a) Centralization of trade-force with a view to improving its productivity

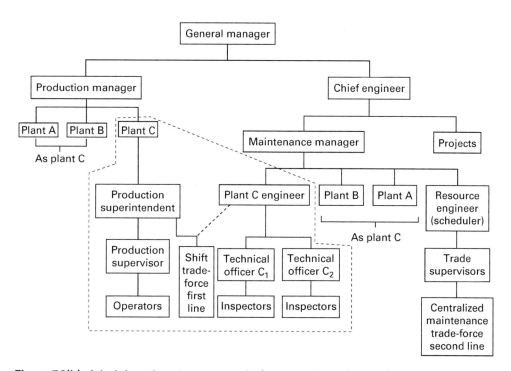

Figure 7.2(b) Administrative structure: trade-force owning jobs, engineers owning plant

This was accompanied by improved work planning and stores control. In addition, extensive use was made of maintenance work measurement systems, such as *comparative estimating*, as a basis for trade-force incentive schemes. These moves did improve trade-force productivity. In the UK, however, the extent of such gains was limited by trade demarcation. There were many differentiated trades and many categories of non-trade workers; inter-trade flexibility was very limited and informal. In addition, central-ization of the trade-force and their supervisors had a negative effect in that it eliminated their feeling of plant ownership – at best they only 'owned' a job. There was a loss of plant specific knowledge. It also exacerbated horizontal polarization.

Attempts were made to solve these problems administratively – by making the engi-neering staff responsible for the plant and locating them, as far as possible, next to the corresponding production staff (see Figure 7.2(b)).

Technical officers reporting to the engineering staff were made responsible for sub-areas of the plant. The inspector-planners reporting to the technical officers were in turn respon-sible for still smaller sections of plant. *The engineering staff were the plant custodians.*

Both the shift trade-force and the second-line resource were centralized, the former reporting to the shift production superintendent – reacting to plant-wide emergencies on a strict priority system – and the latter to a resource engineer via trade supervisors. Thus, second-line jobs originating from plant areas would be planned and prioritized by inspector-planners and sent to the resource engineer for scheduling on the second-line work program. These moves clarified administrative responsibilities but did little to break down polarization or promote team working and true shop floor ownership.

The above approach was adopted at various plants of the Central Electricity Generating Board of England and Wales (a public monopoly, now broken up and privatized) and has also been used by several steel manufacturers, including BHP in Australia and Nissan Steel in Japan. Some petroleum refiners, such as Conoco, also went down this road but with local contractors being the maintenance trade-force – even the resident second-line groups (see Figure 7.3).

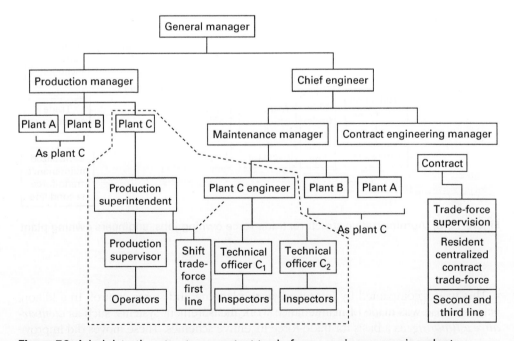

Figure 7.3 Administrative structure: contact trade-force, engineers owning plant

The Conoco arrangement of Figure 7.3 was in a sense the first move toward company – contractor alliances.

The BHP structure did not work well. The inspectors became 'paper pushers' and spent little time on the plant, they lost equipment ownership. The maintenance trade-force owned a job not an equipment. There was a vacuum of equipment ownership and the condition of equipment fell away.

7.4 Introduction of flexible working practices

Broadly speaking, the productivity of trade-forces, whether centralized or not, steadily improved throughout the 1980s as a result of a sea change in industrial relations, the general evolution being as outlined in Figure 7.4 – although it progressed more rapidly in some sectors than in others (indeed, some industries are still at Stage 1 of Figure 7.4).

In the late-1970s several companies, e.g. British Steel, negotiated productivity deals which reduced the level of unskilled maintenance labor while consolidating the numerous skilled trades into just three, *viz.* mechanical, electrical and control (*consolidation*). In the early 1980s a number of companies (also including British Steel) introduced *cross-boundary skilling*, a mechanical artisan, e.g. might be trained to work occasionally in an associated skill area, usually on specified equipment.

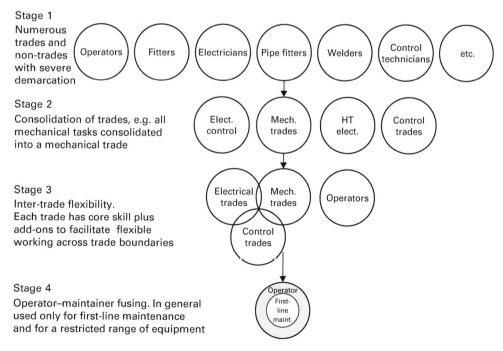

Figure 7.4 Trends in trade-force flexibility

Although excellent examples of true *multi-skilling* can be found, its development is not as widespread as might be expected. The main reason for this is the high cost, in an environment of relatively high labor turnover, of the required training. In Australia a high-profile joint initiative of government and trade unions, financed in part by an industrial training levy, has promoted skill extension. This, however, appears to have been of more benefit to the artisans than their companies. The former have extended their skills, and in many cases their payment (as part of the agreement) and job mobility while the latter have not always achieved the skills profile that they needed – and in some cases have yet to decide how best to use the skills improvements that have been generated. Some Australian companies consider that skills improvement should grow out of company needs rather than from government and trade union initiatives.

Undoubtedly the most significant trend of the late-1980s and early 1990s has been the emergence of the *operator–maintainer*. Shell Chemicals, Carrington, were one of the first companies to promote this concept (this will be discussed in Section 7.6) the most successful application of which has been to first-line shift work where – for a limited range of plant – artisan and operators have been trained both to operate that plant and to carry out first-line maintenance across all the traditional trades. Where companies (including Shell Carrington) have tried to promote a similar approach to second-line work it has not been so successful; the experience with this has been that the artisan will always revert to his main (core) skill. To sustain the quality of his work he needs to practice his wider armory of skills on a regular basis.

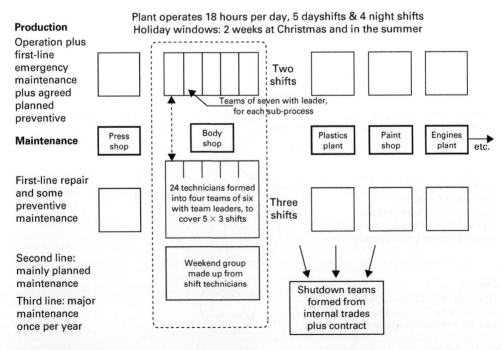

Figure 7.5(a) Resource structure, Nissan, UK

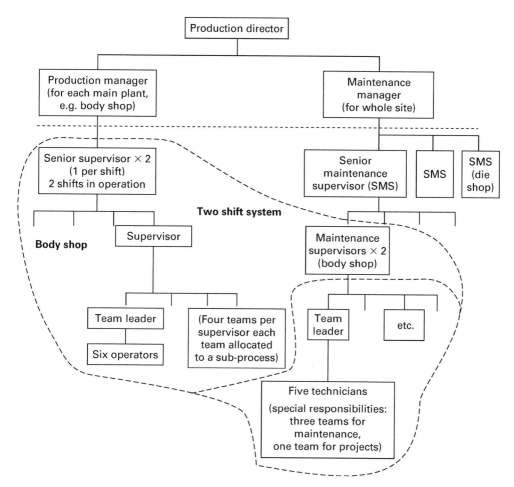

Figure 7.5(b) Administrative structure, Nissan, UK

In the late-1980s a number of Japanese companies built manufacturing plants on greenfield sites in the UK and negotiated Japanese type agreements with the trade unions – one factory union, no-strike undertakings, etc. – Nissan, in Sunderland, being a typical example. A noteworthy aspect of the latter development is that while retaining a functional administration Nissan promoted the adoption of plant-oriented operator–maintainers (see Figures 7.5(a) and 7.5(b)).

They encouraged the sense of plant ownership by training their operators to carry out first-line maintenance tasks and to be involved in a philosophy of continuous improvement, i.e. they fostered *autonomous maintenance teams*. What must be emphasized is the considerable level of training required to establish these, up to 2 years of effort is required.

In many respects, the Nissan structure of Figure 7.5 implements the idea of plant-oriented teams that was put forward in Figure 5.9. This is one part of the Japanese technique of total productive maintenance (TPM).

7.5 Plant manufacturing units

An alternative solution to the problems of very large structures is to divide them into smaller semi-autonomous units, the so-called 'ship' structure. This is a form of departmentation, e.g. the structure of Figure 7.1 is modified to that shown in Figure 7.6. In this case each 'manufacturing unit' is formed around a process (see also Figure 5.9).

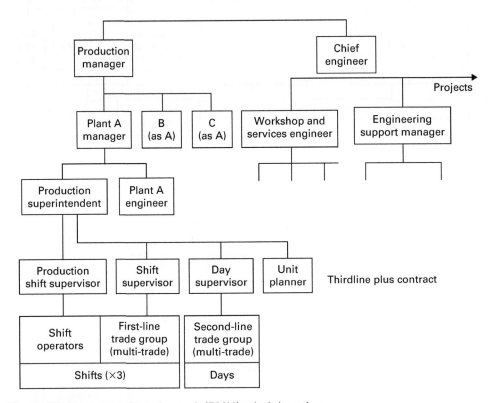

Figure 7.6 Plant manufacturing unit (PMU) administration

> The difference between a *plant manufacturing unit (PMU)* and a *business unit* is one of scale. The latter would be large enough to operate as a self-contained business (sales, production, maintenance, finance), but under the umbrella of a large organization. The former would be a part of a major plant but would have an identifiable product and would be semi-autonomous (production, maintenance, budget).

The author first encountered this approach, and the human issues involved, in selecting and training PMU staff in British Steel in the late-1970s. In the 1980s and 1990s it seems to have developed into something of a fashionable trend, many companies having moved in this direction, including (in the UK) Shell Chemicals of Carrington and Courtaulds Chemicals of Derby, and (in Australia) Alcan and Queensland Alumina. Others, such as

Glaxo in the UK, have used a similar approach but formed the unit around a product line. It must be emphasized that such reorganizations usually come about for non-maintenance reasons and provide the following *general* advantages:

- Responsibility for costs and profits can be better identified.
- At PMU level, co-ordination and planning of work is improved.
- Setting of objectives and their translation into terms accepted by the staff and work-force are facilitated.
- The ideas and techniques of total quality management (TQM) (see Figure 7.7), are more easily introduced.
- *Esprit des corps* is improved.

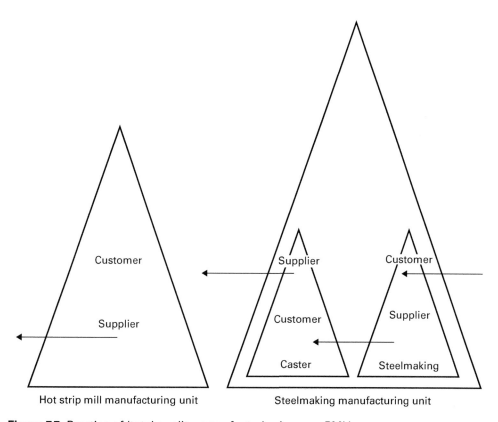

Figure 7.7 Practice of 'total quality manufacturing' across PMUs

The maintenance function also benefits from these general advantages. In particular there is easier co-ordination and execution of maintenance work. In addition, human factors aspects (such as shop floor goodwill toward the management or an improved sense of equipment ownership) tend to improve.

The main general disadvantage in forming PMUs is the duplication of functions and equipment, which can result in a larger but diluted engineering staff. This is evident in many of the companies which have adopted the idea. In the example of Figure 7.6 it can be seen that the technical and engineering or maintenance expertise available within each unit is limited. This is a consequence of the dilution of centralized professional expertise and authority. It can result in each of the units going its own way in terms of maintenance strategy and engineering standards. The more successful examples of adopting PMUs guarded against this by clearly defining the responsibilities of the support teams and developing a clear understanding of the channels of communication between the support teams and the manufacturing units. In addition, considerable importance was given to the use of an *Engineering and Maintenance Procedures Manual*. Such a document was used in all the individual PMUs and was regarded as an extension of centralized engineering authority.

Review Questions

R7.1   A number of companies using process plant have changed the structure of their organization from a highly functionalized one of the type shown in Figures 7.1(a) and 7.1(b) to one of the type shown in Figures 7.8(a) and 7.8(b):
  (a) List the main changes that you consider have taken place.
  (b) Discuss the advantages of the structure shown in Figures 7.8(a) and 7.8(b) for the efficient and effective execution of maintenance work.
  (c) What would have been the advantages of retaining the functional structure.

R7.2   Define a PMU and explain the essential difference between a PMU and a so-called 'business unit'.

R7.3   When a company moves from a functional organization (see Figure 7.1(a)) to one based on manufacturing units (see Figure 7.8(b)), it becomes more difficult to carry out plant reliability control (PRC) (the identification and eradication of high maintenance cost/low-reliability hot spots). Explain why you think this is the case. What can be done to overcome this problem?

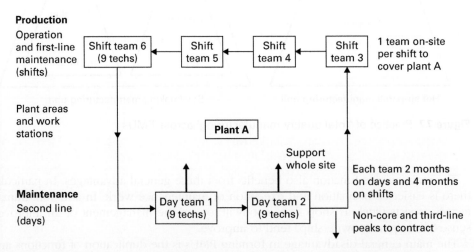

Figure 7.8(a) Modernized resource structure for plant A, petrochemical plant

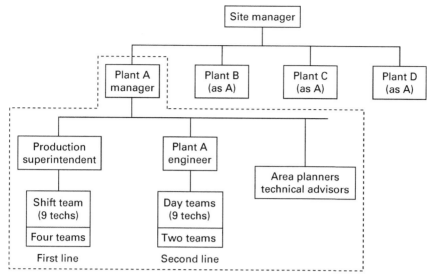

Note: Team leaders were previously operators. Thus advisors are electrical, mechanical and control specialists.

Figure 7.8(b) Modernized administration, petrochemical plant

7.6 Slimming the structure ('downsizing')

The company that exemplifies the principal maintenance organization developments of the last 1990s is Shell Chemicals, Carrington, UK. The move from a large traditional structure into one divided into PMUs (see Figures 7.8(a) and 7.8(b)) was accompanied by other significant changes, *viz.*:

- Reduction in the number of management levels from six to three (see Figure 7.9).
- Changing the role of the supervisor to that of a planner or technical adviser to self-empowered operator–maintenance teams.
- Amalgamating operators and artisans into a single-role group, *viz.* 'manufacturing technicians', who were assembled into process-oriented, shift-flexible, self-empowered teams – a single-team working as operator–maintainers for 4 months followed by 2 months as second-line maintainers. This was accompanied by extensive plant and process-oriented training. Each team had a leader whose core skill was in operations. The technical advisers were trade specialists.
- Putting non-core work (such as reconditioning or building services), and most of the major overhaul work, out to contract.

This restructuring was implemented as revolutionary change in the late-1980s but the structure, especially its flexibilities, has continued to evolve. In addition to the

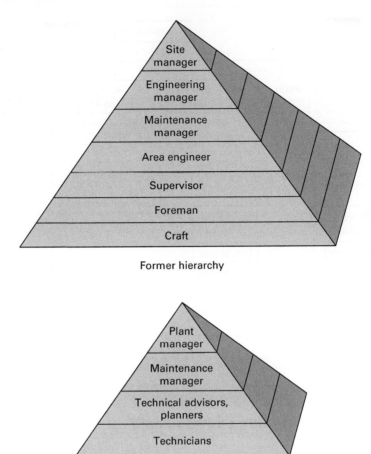

Figure 7.9 Reduction in number of levels of management, petrochemical plant

refocusing of the operator and maintainer effort, major gains in labor and management productivity were made.

Many other companies in the UK and Europe have implemented one or more of the above changes, usually as part of an evolutionary development. An interesting example is to be found in the power generation sector. Here, the organization has customarily been as shown in Figure 7.10, operation having responsibilities allocated *down* the process (i.e. by generating set) with maintenance having responsibilities allocated *across* (i.e. by equipment type: boilers, mills, etc.).

Several power stations have now set up structures of the kind shown in Figures 7.11(a) and 7.11(b); they have created PMUs by assigning maintenance workers down the process with the operations staff. In addition, considerable effort has been made to introduce self-empowered teams into these units.

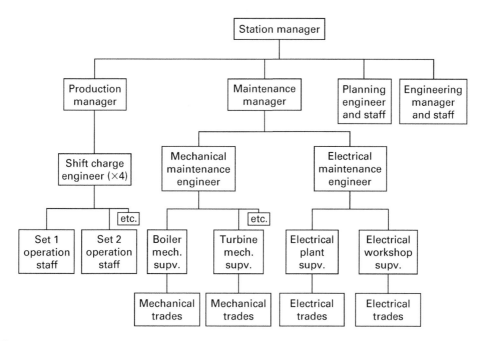

Figure 7.10 A traditional power station administration

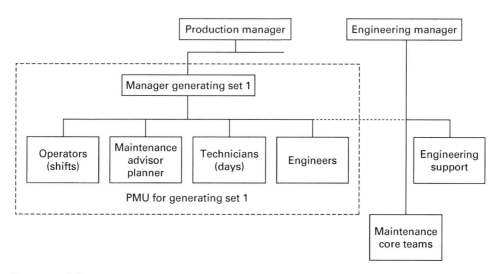

Figure 7.11(a) Power station administrative structure based on responsibility by generating set

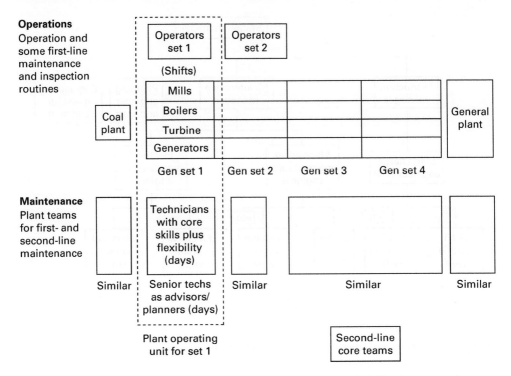

Figure 7.11(b) Power station resource structure based on responsibility by generating set

7.7 The movement toward self-empowered plant-oriented teams

The more advanced form of self-empowered plant-oriented teams (SEPOTs) possesses the following characteristics:

- It consists of approximately 10 shop floor personnel whose function is to operate and maintain a sub-process or area of plant (see Figure 7.12).
- Its members have various core skills but have been selected and trained to work flexibly in order to enable the team to tackle any job within its defined area of duty and responsibility (sometimes called 'vertical skilling').
- It has been empowered (allocated duties, responsibilities and authority) to carry out its day-to-day tasks with the minimum of *direct* supervision (sometimes called 'horizontal skilling').

The teams at Shell Chemicals, described earlier, clearly have these characteristics, as do the Nissan autonomous teams that were also discussed. In both cases the time needed for their introduction, not to mention the training cost, was considerable – but so were the rewards.

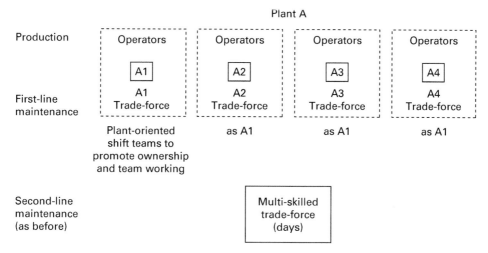

Figure 7.12 Plant-oriented teams

In Europe the movement toward self-empowered teams has been carried mainly on the back of TPM. Car manufacturers such as Rover (UK), Volvo (Belgium) and Renault (France) therefore feature strongly in its application. All have reported resultant large productivity gains.

Other than within the various TPM programs, the introduction of SEPOTs has been limited. This may be partly because of the setting up costs (mainly training), the running costs and industrial relations difficulties. In addition SEPOTs are not always necessary, in their advanced form at any rate. The size, type and characteristics of the teams will depend on the industry, the equipment and the workloads that they have to deal with (see Figure 7.13).

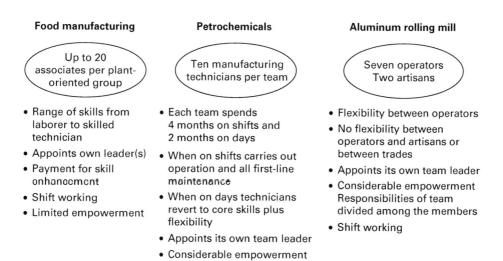

Figure 7.13 Alternative arrangements for plant-oriented teams

In food processing there is a high proportion of low-skill operator work and the composition of the plant-operating team reflects this, containing many low-skilled operators and only a very few (or even one) highly skilled manufacturing technicians, Sagit of Naples designate the one manufacturing technician in each of their teams as the *conduttore*, or leader. Mars Confectionery, Slough have a similar arrangement. In both cases considerable effort has gone into training schemes, both to integrate the skills of the team and to increase flexibility between the traditional trades of the second-line maintainer. Mars have introduced a motivational 'skill progression payment scheme', based on validated training and technical qualifications.

The aluminum rolling mill case of Figure 7.13 is an interesting example of SEPOT implementation. Although it was felt that inter-trade and operator–maintainer flexibilities were not essential, plant-oriented teams were needed. Each shift team operated without a supervisor but with a technical adviser on day shift. The normal duties of a supervisor were divided among the team members.

The idea of self-empowerment has not only been applied to plant-oriented teams. In the aluminum rolling mill case self-empowered teams, called the *core* teams, were also developed to carry out the second-line maintenance. The SEPOTs carried out the first-line maintenance on shifts but the core teams carried out the major repairs and preventive work on the weekly downday – the SEPOTs owned the plant, and the core teams owned the jobs. The core teams were given their duties and made their own decisions according to, and within, predetermined guidelines. Administrative tasks (concerning safety, co-ordination, etc.) were allocated on a rotating basis, 6 months at a time per team member (see Figure 7.14). This concept is known as 'STAR' (Self-Tracking And Regulation) team.

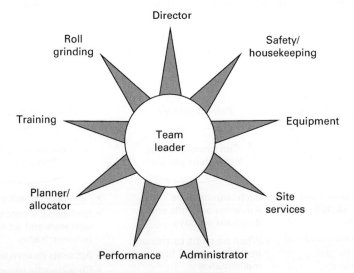

Figure 7.14 Star configuration of team responsibilities

Most examples of teams the author has come across have been set up on 'brownfield sites'. This is a much more difficult task than setting up teams on a greenfield site because of the 'IR and human factor' baggage that has to be carried across the team building procedure [1] (see Figure 7.15).

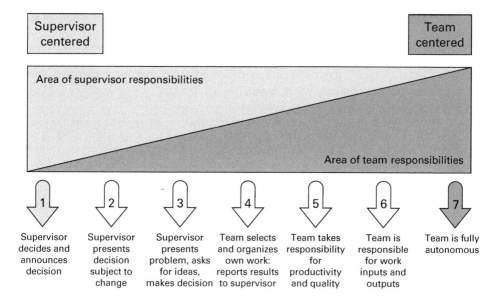

Figure 7.15 Team development continuum

Review Questions

R7.4   Explain what you understand by a 'SEPOT'.
R7.5   Explain why you think it might be more difficult to use SEPOTs in a power
station than in a car manufacturing plant.

7.8 Contracting, outsourcing and alliances

The employment of contract labor has been a commonplace feature of maintenance organization since the industrial revolution. The traditional use of *contractors* was discussed in Section 4.5.1 and the advantages and disadvantages of their use in Table 4.3. Over the last few years, however, the new 'buzzwords' in maintenance management have been 'outsourcing' and 'alliances'.

Outsourcing: has been defined as follows:

> Outsourcing takes place when an organization transfers the ownership and control of a company function/process, e.g. maintenance management, to a contractor [2].

The company tells the contractor what it wants and at what cost (laid down in a contract) and leaves him to decide how best to accomplish this. Generally speaking, those company functions that are outsourced are generally termed *non core*, i.e. they are not regarded as a part of the core competencies of the business.

Among the advantages of outsourcing are that it allows the company to:

- concentrate its business focus on its core operation;
- gain access to specialist contractors that bring in a high level of expertise and, through their size, bring economies of scale. This helps the company to control and reduce its operating costs.

However, it is not without its drawbacks, some of which are listed in Table 4.3 while others include the following:

- It is difficult to engender, among contractor personnel, a sense of equipment 'owner-ship'; at best they own a *job*. (The contractor would argue that this is counterbalanced by a contract which commits his personnel to achieving key performance indices on availability, cost, etc. or losing the contract.)
- The company loses knowledge of the equipment and expertise in maintaining it. (And some of this may be relevant to the core competencies as well as being difficult to re-acquire in the future.)

A company–contractor alliance has been defined as:

> **A transfer of the ownership and control of a company function (or part thereof) to a partnership made up of company and contractor personnel [3].**

The partnership can take a number of forms. For example, the two alliance companies may report to the same board, one company – a water utility, say – *owning* and *operating* the assets while another company *maintains* the assets (and probably the assets of other companies). (A more usual arrangement was modeled in Figure 12.16 of the Case study 6 – see Chapter 12 – and outlined in the accompanying text.)

The maintenance group was made up of personnel from the company and from the contractor, who reported via a steering group to the contract company. The main difficulty with alliances lies in setting up a partnership contract that achieves the objectives of both the company and the contractor. Whatever form the contract takes the essential ingredient of a successful alliance is to establish a culture of co-operation and mutual trust.

The key decision regarding an outsourcing alliance concerns the identification of core competencies.

Some electrical power utilities have decided that their core competencies should lie solely in the *marketing* and *selling* of electrical power; for the construction, operation and maintenance of their generating stations they have therefore arranged alliances with contract organizations. Likewise, universities, hotels, large public libraries and so on have identified maintenance as a non-core function and customarily now outsource it via similar alliances. Several airport authorities have set up alliances with contractors to operate and maintain their luggage handling equipment.

Some offshore gas and oil extractors have arranged alliances with other companies to build and maintain their platforms.

The key characteristics of each one of these examples are as follows:

(a) That maintenance is regarded as a non-core function.
(b) That the alliance partner brings considerable engineering and maintenance expert-ise – usually as a result of having designed, built, installed and commissioned the installation.

In the case of industrial companies (chemical processors, oil extractors, food proces-sors, etc.) who have owned and operated their plant for many years the situation is very different. Firstly, deciding whether maintenance is core or not is more difficult, and sec-ondly (and perhaps more importantly) the 'center of gravity' of asset-oriented engi-neering experience lies well toward such companies' engineers (rather than the alliance partner).

Review Questions

R7.6   Define outsourcing and company–contractor alliances.

R7.7   Explain why there are greater potential advantages in forming a company–contractor alliance to maintain the 'baggage handling facility' of a large international airport than a 30-year-old multi-plant chemical complex.

R7.8   Which of the following parts of the maintenance department of a large multi-plant chemical complex would you consider transferring to an alliance partner:
- First-line shift maintenance.
- Second-line area maintenance.
- Third-line shutdown maintenance.
- Maintenance workshops.
- Engineering and technical staff.
- Work planning.
- Stores.

In each case give your reasons.

7.9 Summary

The trends in maintenance management that have been outlined are summarized in Figure 7.16. From the 1960s to the mid-1990s industrial management used an internal labor force and engineering staff to carry out their maintenance. Contractors being used for shutdown work and external reconditioning. Over the period of time the main organizational aim was to improve the organizational efficiency of this internal labor force via various structural and human factor initiatives. The most influential were:

(i) The great improvement in trade-force flexibility, between trades, between production and maintenance, between areas of plant, in shift working and in the use of contract or temporary labor.

(ii) The gradual merging of the production and maintenance functions – moving from the situation in the 1970s, where there was total separation at company level, to that of the 1990s, where they were merged at plant unit level.

These trends were complementary; without improved flexibility it would have been impossible to achieve true SEPOTs. The move toward teams was the most important administrative trend.

In spite of considerable effort these changes met with only mixed success. The author will show later in Case studies 5 and 6 (Chapters 11 and 12, respectively) that teams and self-empowerment often did not work well. Management spent large sums on training and investing in new working practices and did not feel they were getting the necessary return on their investment. In particular the 'human factors' remained negative.

Perhaps for this reason the management of a number of industrial companies have set up company–contractor alliances to carry out their maintenance work. This move allows them to concentrate on their core functions. Such alliances have worked well in the case of building maintenance, offshore production platforms, airline baggage handling for many years. Industrial plant is very different and the 'jury is still out' on whether such alliances will be a success with industrial plant maintenance.

Trends in resource structure	1965	1975	1985	1995	2000
	Decentralized	Some centralization	Decentralized	Decentralized	• Outsourcing/alliances
	Multi-trade	Multi-trade	Inter-trade flexibility	Inter-trade flexibility	• Moves towards company–contractor alliances for second- and third-line work and stores management
	Numerous non-trades	Numerous non-trades	Reduction of non-trades and number of trades via consolidation	Production–maintenance flexibility of first-line work	• Production–maintenance flexibility for first-line work
	Strict demarcation	Strict demarcation			• Asset custodianship retained by company
	Poor resource flexibility	Poor resource flexibility	Improved resource flexibility including shift, inter-plant and use of contract labor	Increased resource flexibility, including: • Non-core to contract • Annualized hours • Inter-plant and cascade	
		Improved work planning systems, including work measurement			

Trends in administrative structure	1965	1975	1985	1995	2000
	Large structure	Large structure	Structured into business units	Structured into business units	• Condition-monitoring contracted out to a single preferred contractor
	Highly functionalized	Highly functionalized	Still functionalized	Use of plant-operating teams and other empowered teams	
	Maintenance and production separated up to general manager level	Maintenance and production separated up to general manager level	Maintenance and production separated up to business unit manager level	Maintenance and production joined at artisans level for first-line work	• Increased use of consignment stock in stores
	Centralized authority for maintenance	Centralized authority for maintenance	Introduction of plant operating teams	Extensive slimming of structure	• Moves towards companies sharing the holding – cost of strategic spares
	Single trade supervision	Single trade supervision	Multi-trade supervisors	Supervisor role changes to advisor/planner	
	Large chains of command	Engineering and/or maintenance ownership of equipment	Influence of TQM and TPM	Extensive influence of TQM and TPM	

Figure 7.16 General trends in maintenance organization

Exercise

E7.1   Outline the main maintenance organizational changes that have taken place in your own organization over the last 20 years. Identify how the changes have affected the maintenance organization.

E7.2   Now carry out Exercise 14.1 in Chapter 14 (the exercise guideline solutions are at the end of the Chapter 14).

References

1. Rose, L. and Scott, R., The maintenance organization – the new way, *Proceedings of the International Maintenance Conference*, Sydney, 1992.
2. Johnson, J., *Outsourcing*, Butterworth-Heinemann, 1997.
3. Bendor-Samual, P., Outsourcing Centre, www.outsourcing-faq.com
4. Petric, S., *The route to best maintenance practice*, Conference Communication, Farnham, 2000.

Review Questions Guidelines

R7.1   (a) The main changes are as follows:
- Introduction of PMUs.
- Reduction of management layers.
- Use of self-empowered teams to include inter-trade flexibility and operator–maintainer flexibility.
- Non-core work identified and contracted out.

(b) Improved 'esprit de corp' within the business units:
- Easier setting of manufacturing unit objectives.
- Fewer staff and reduced workforce.
- Improvement in production–maintenance team working, equipment ownership.
- Improved work planning within the business units.

(c) Numerous to include:
- Ease of maintaining the uniformity of engineering standards, objectives, mechanical knowledge, PRC.
- Uniformity and control of repair methods, documentation and work planning methods.
- Better ownership and maintenance of common services.
- Ease of communication of engineering knowledge between plants and with project engineering.

R7.2   A PMU (see Figures 6.6, 5.8 and 12.12 of the Case study 6) was defined in Review Questions Guidelines to 5.1(a). The difference between a PMU and a 'business unit' is one of scale. A business unit is shown in Figure 8.3 to match the plant layout of Figure 8.1. This business unit is essentially an autonomous business (to include sales, finance marketing as well as production and maintenance) operating under the umbrella of a large organization. A PMU is smaller and semi-autonomous in terms of production and maintenance.

R7.3   In order to change to a PMU from a functional organization it is typical for the central engineering function to be reduced to a rump and for the professional engineers/technical staff to be spread thinly through the PMUs, e.g. there is only one engineer in the PMU of Figure 7.8(b). In such situations the PMU engineer has little time to spend on PRC. To overcome this problem a number of companies using PMUs use the 'purge method' of PRC, i.e. periodically all of the PMU engineers are seconded into a centralized group to purge out the *top ten company-wide reliability problems*. (This will be discussed in more detail in Chapter 9.)

R7.4   One definition of self-empowerment is as follows:

> 'A team of employees who have day-to-day responsibility for managing themselves and the work they do with a minimum of direct supervision'.

> A 'SEPOT' can be described as a self-empowered team, made up of artisans, or operators with artisans, or manufacturing technicians (operator–maintainers) who are responsible for operating and maintaining (mainly first first-line maintenance) a designated area of plant or sub-process. The team is usually made up of about 10 members.

R7.5   Self-empowered teams are used extensively both in car manufacturing and in power stations. SEPOTs are used extensively in car manufacturing (the autonomous maintenance teams of TPM) but are much more difficult to use in power stations. A power stations maintenance resource structure is more likely to be centralized and the operators spend a high proportion of their time in the control room. In other words the operators are not distributed throughout the plant and various sub-functions of the process.

R7.6   Outsourcing takes place when an organization transfers the ownership and control of a company function, e.g. the non-core maintenance workload, to a contractor.

A company–contractor alliance can be defined as:

> A transfer of the ownership and control of a company function (or part thereof) to a partnership made up of company and contractor personnel.

R7.7   It is most likely that the 'baggage handling facility' has been designed, manufactured and commissioned by a single large engineering manufacturer. In addition the maintenance of such equipment is clearly non-core in terms of the main function of an international airport. Therefore, there are major advantages in forming a maintenance alliance with the equipment manufacturer, they have the technical knowledge and expertise.

The situation is different in the case of the chemical plant. Numerous engineering manufacturers have supplied units to the plant over its 30 years. The engineering expertise is clearly with the plant engineers and technicians. In addition, it is much more difficult to identify non-core maintenance work – first line is core/third line is non-core, but where does that leave the second line.

R7.8   Taking into consideration the comments in Review Question Guidelines to R7.7 it would be useful to rank the work/functions listed in R7.8 as follows:

High likelihood of transfer	Third-line shutdown maintenance
	Maintenance workshops
	Stores
Probable retain in company	Second-line maintenance
	Work planning
Definitely retain in company	First-line maintenance

PART 3

Maintenance organization case studies

8 Case study 1: Moving with the times

'If you always do what you've always done, you will always get what you always got.'
Dr Malcolm Gibson

Chapter aims and outcomes

To show via an industrial case study how a company has followed organizational trends over the last 15 years to the point where they have recently set up a company–contractor alliance to carry out their maintenance work.

On completion of this chapter you should be able to:

- understand the maintenance-management organizational trends that have developed over the last 15 years;
- understand how to identify the core and non-core maintenance work of an industrial company;
- appreciate the principles, concepts, advantages and disadvantages of company–contractor alliances.

Chapter route map

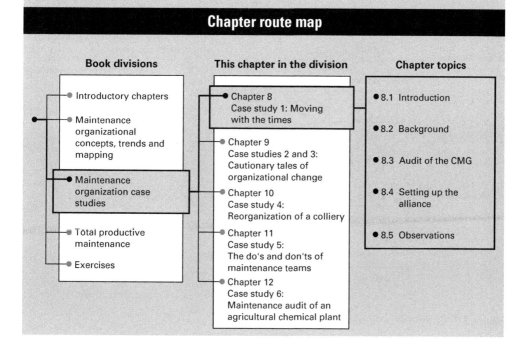

Book divisions	This chapter in the division	Chapter topics
Introductory chapters	Chapter 8 Case study 1: Moving with the times	8.1 Introduction
Maintenance organizational concepts, trends and mapping	Chapter 9 Case studies 2 and 3: Cautionary tales of organizational change	8.2 Background
Maintenance organization case studies	Chapter 10 Case study 4: Reorganization of a colliery	8.3 Audit of the CMG
Total productive maintenance	Chapter 11 Case study 5: The do's and don'ts of maintenance teams	8.4 Setting up the alliance
Exercises	Chapter 12 Case study 6: Maintenance audit of an agricultural chemical plant	8.5 Observations

8.1 Introduction

It will be instructive at this point to use a case study to illustrate how one company has followed the trends outlined in the previous chapter, culminating in a company–contractor alliance.

8.2 Background

Via several interlinked plants located on a single site (see Figure 8.1) Chemtow Ltd. make a wide range of chemicals. In the late-1980s the company had a traditional functional organization of the kind illustrated in Figures 8.2(a) and 8.2(b), i.e. all of the maintenance

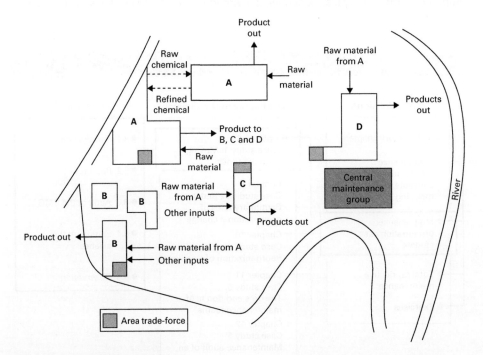

Figure 8.1 Chemtow, site layout

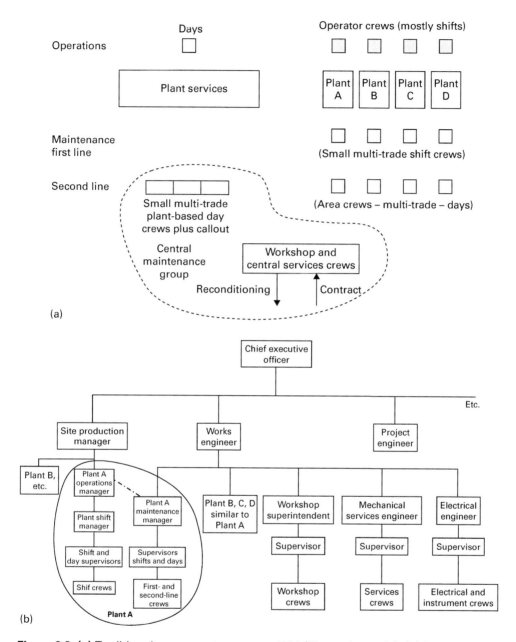

Figure 8.2 (a) Traditional resource structure, *c.* 1990 (illustration only). **(b)** Traditional administrative structure, *c.* 1990 (illustration only)

resources (centralized and plant-located) reported to the Maintenance and Engineering Department.

In 1991 the company reorganized itself into four autonomous business units (see Figure 8.3 which outlines the arrangement for one of them). Initially, the central maintenance group (CMG) was retained, to maintain the common site services (buildings,

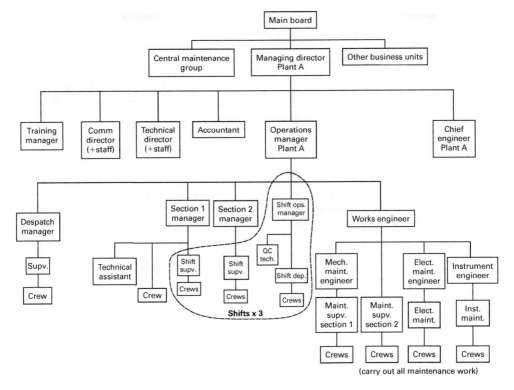

Figure 8.3 Plant A business unit administration (1995)

water, electricity, etc.) and to offer an 'internal contract' service to each of the business units. In addition, the CMG co-ordinated all the contract resources on site.

8.3 Audit of the CMG

In 1993, our consultancy group was retained to audit the site, in order to decide on the future size and composition of the CMG (a consultancy carried out jointly by A. Kelly and H.S. Riddell). The resource structure was then as shown in Figure 8.4 and the administrative structure as shown in Figure 8.5.

Following the horizontal axis of Figure 8.4, the services (and trade within each service) provided by the CMG were identified, and listed as in Table 8.1.

Also shown, across the top of that table (and stated more fully in Table 8.2), are the various criteria that were then applied in assessing whether each service was core or not. Finally, the last column of Table 8.1 shows (for each service) the appropriate resourcing arrangements that were proposed – and which were drawn from the following list of possibilities:

(a) Keep the present service with CMG but up-rate it to satisfy the customers.
(b) Identify the core resources of the service and retain it in the CMG, but disband the non-core resources.

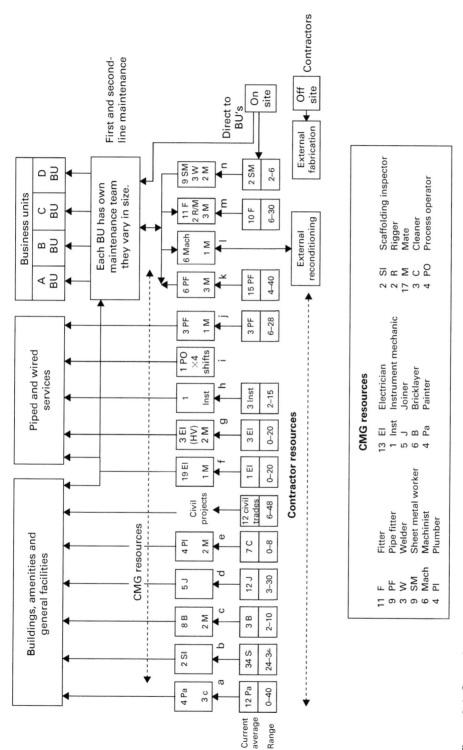

Figure 8.4 Central program group resource structure (1995)

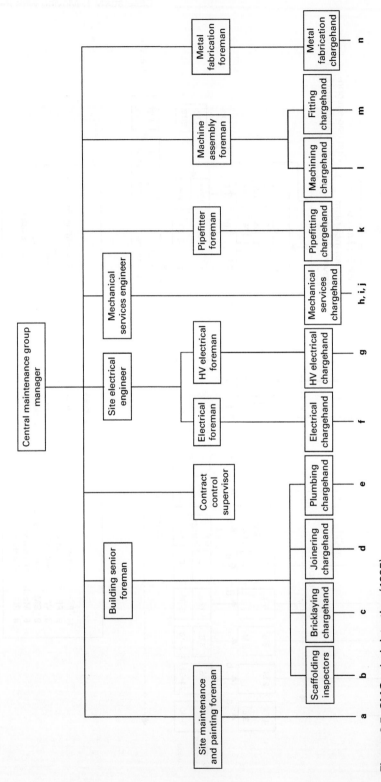

Figure 8.5 CMG administration (1995)

Table 8.1 Decision table to assist in the reorganization of CMG

CMG service	CMG resources		Criteria for retention						Recommendation	
	Trades	Numbers	Core service	Emerg. resp.	Special skills	Many small jobs	Local knowl.	User contact	Alternative resourcing code	Comment
Site-wide services										
Factory general services	Build EI PF/PI	4 2 2	No	Yes	No	Yes	No	No	D or B	Consider all to contractors. Meanwhile retain minimum Engage contractors for second line resources for first-line maintenance. and all project work.
site piped services	PF/PI Build F PO	5 5 1 4	Yes	Yes	No	Yes	Yes	Yes	B or C	Retain minimum resources for first-line maintenance, but consider transfer to BU 1. Engage contractors for second line and all project work.
Site wired services										
HT	HT EI	5	Yes	Yes	Yes	Yes	Yes	No	A	Retain minimum resources for all maintenance. Use contractors for all project jobs.
LT	EI Instr.	4 1	Yes	Yes	No	Yes	Yes	No	B	Retain minimum resources for first-line maintenance; use contractors for second line and all project jobs.

(Continued)

Table 8.1 (Continued)

| CMG service | CMG resources | | Criteria for retention | | | | | | Recommendation | |
	Trades	Numbers	Core service	Emerg. resp.	Special skills	Many small jobs	Local knowl.	User contact	Alternative resourcing code	Comment
Direct support to business units										
Capital work	PF/PI	5	No	No	No	No	No	No	D	Disengage from all capital work, use contractors.
	SMW	4								
	F	8								
	Mach.	1								
	EI	2								
	Build	4								
Maintenance support	PF/PI	7	No	No	No	No	No	Yes	D	Disengage, use contractors.
	F	7	No	No	No	No	No	Yes	D	Disengage, use contractors.
	Mach.	6	Yes	Yes	Yes	No	No	Yes	B	Retain minimum resources for reconditioning, critical repairs and specialized spares.
	SMW	10	Yes	Yes	Yes	No	No	Yes	B	
	Build	9	No	No	No	Yes	No	Yes	D	Disengage, use contractors.
	EI	3	No	No	No	No	No	Yes	D	Disengage, use contractors.
Total ERG		Resources	99							

Table 8.2 Criteria for determining a core mechanical service

- Service critical to the business units
- Provides a rapid skilled response to cover emergencies
- Provides a skill/knowledge which is not available from contractors
- Involves numerous short-duration jobs scattered across the site
- Close interaction with operation is essential

(c) As in (b), but transfer the core resource to the primary business unit.
(d) Disband the complete service and rely on contractors.

This analysis then informed the proposals for reorganizing the CMG which are modeled (in outline) in Figures 8.6 and 8.7.

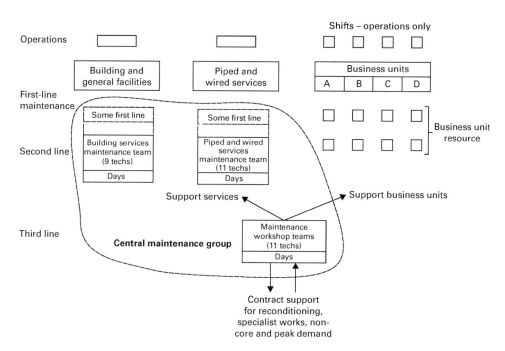

Figure 8.6 Proposed resource structure for CMG (1995)

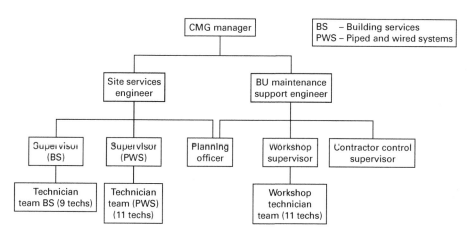

Figure 8.7 Proposed administration for CMG (1995)

8.4 Setting up the alliance

Chemtow accepted the recommendations of the 1993 audit and duly reduced the size of the CMG, which was reduced still further to 14 artisans/technicians over the period to 1999. In addition, the business units also moved their organization toward benchmark standards (as shown in Figure 8.8).

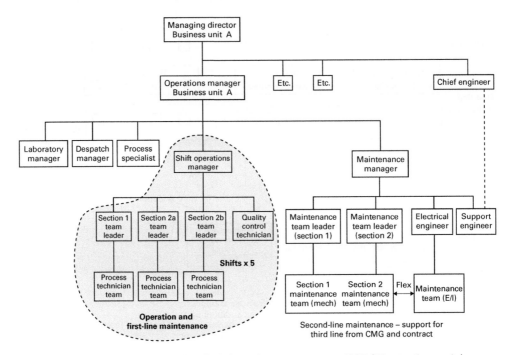

Figure 8.8 Typical business unit administrative structure at 1999 (illustrative only)

The production technicians (via training and recruitment of artisans within the team) operated as self-empowered teams and carried out first-line maintenance tasks. The maintenance technicians carried out the second-line work, their numbers being set at a minimum level – supplemented as necessary for second- and third-line work by the CMG or contract labor. Numerous contract companies were engaged with the contract arrangements being dependent on work type.

In 2000, we were again retained – to contribute to discussions aimed at deciding whether, and to what extent, the maintenance function should be carried out by a company–contractor alliance. The main points that came out of these deliberations were as follows:

- An alliance should be set up to carry out all the maintenance work except the first-line tasks undertaken by the production technicians.
- The alliance should be responsible for all the maintenance shop floor workers associated with maintenance work.
- The alliance should be responsible for spare parts management.
- Scheduling and planning of maintenance work and planning of resources would also be the responsibility of the alliance.

- It was agreed that the resource structure should include some second-line technicians located in each of the business units. Their numbers should be the minimum necessary to meet the essential second-line workload and it was important that they possessed a high level of plant-specific skills. The proposed resource structure is shown in Figure 8.9.
- The 'ownership' of the equipment should reside in professional maintenance support groups, one in each business unit (and who would be Chemtow employees – the asset custodians). Their responsibilities would include improving life plans, establishing workscopes, designing-out maintenance and providing plant-specific maintenance support. The size of each such group would be set at a minimum level and the group would be supplemented, wherever necessary, by specialist assistance from the contractor partner.

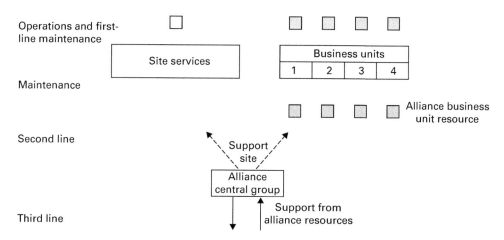

Figure 8.9 Proposed alliance resource structure (illustrative only)

An outline of the proposed administrative structure is given in Figure 8.10.

Exercise

E8.1   Carry out a brief literature search to establish a list of companies who have set up contractor–company alliances to carry out their maintenance work.

Review Questions

R8.1   Chomtow over a period of 15 years followed the maintenance organizational trends. List the main trends that Chemtow followed in chronological order.

R8.2   (a) Identify the key characteristics in successful examples of company–contractor alliances that are used to carry out the maintenance of physical assets.

(b) Would you consider forming a company–contractor alliance to carry out the maintenance work of the alumina refinery discussed in Chapters 4 and 5. Give the reasons for your answer.

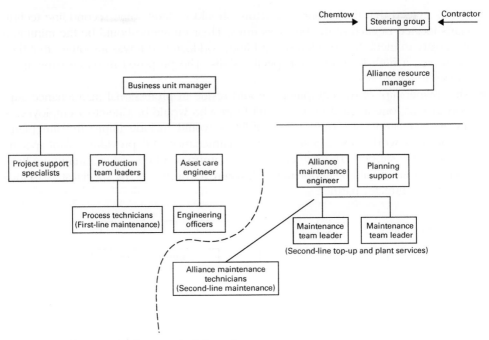

Figure 8.10 Proposed alliance administration

8.5 Observations

(i) In multi-product chemical plants it is very much more difficult to separate the maintenance function into core and non-core competencies than it is in, say, a hotel complex or even a power plant. Chemtow felt that the professional engineering and strategic maintenance side of the function was close to its core competencies and therefore they retained ownership of this activity. Their reasoning was that the plant process was specialized and in some areas unique, each of the business units using different process and process technology. The maintenance function also affected equipment availability, safety and the quality of product.

(ii) While the proposed alliance structure was agreed in principle Chemtow have yet (2001) to establish the details and dynamics of the operation of the arrangement. We envisaged, however, that the work planning system might be as outlined in Figure 8.11, which also shows how the division of responsibility between the Chemtow Asset Care Engineers (the asset custodians who decides what maintenance is to be carried out, and when) and the alliance (the resource owner who decides how the maintenance is to be carried out and executes it) might be allocated. Some of the responsibilities would need to be jointly owned and communication would need to be good in both directions.

(iii) In relinquishing control of all the shop floor maintenance resources Chemtow moved further toward a true alliance relationship than did Fertec (see Case study 6 of Chapter 12 and, in particular, Figure 12.16). However, the alliance is limited to the

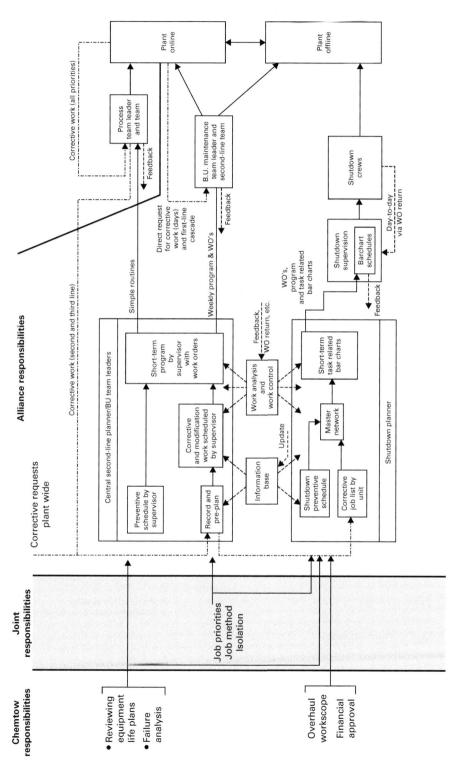

Figure 8.11 Division of maintenance responsibilities between Chemtow and alliance

responsibility for shop floor resources and, as such, the contract between the parties has to center on the cost of resources for a specified time to carry out a specified work program. Some kind of conventional term-contract could be used as a basis for such a contract. Setting it up, however, is not without complications, *viz.*:

- Plant condition may be such that considerable 'catch-up maintenance' might be required. Chemtow want to reduce costs but, initially, the cost may have to go up (see Figure 8.12).
- The level of maintenance work required in the future will be a function of the way the plant is operated, of the life plans and of the level of design-out maintenance, none of which falls within the responsibility of the alliance.

The point is that however carefully the contract is drawn up, considerable trust between the partners is going to be required. One way of monitoring the contract is through a series of indices/costs based on *organizational efficiency* (e.g. tradeforce utilization, maintenance cost, percentage of planned work, etc.).

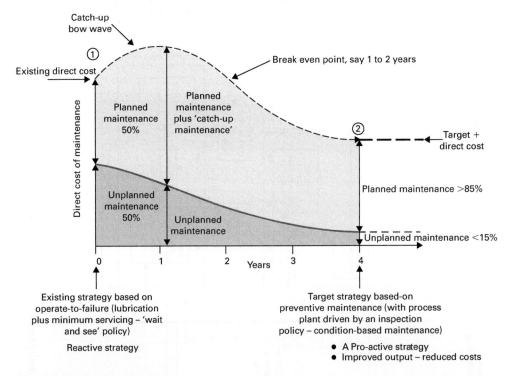

Figure 8.12 Catch-up strategy

(iv) Formulating the contract arrangements would have been much more straightforward if the alliance had covered the complete maintenance function. An incentive-based contract, derived from the statement of the maintenance objective, could then have been agreed – it could require specified improvements of various indices based on *maintenance effectiveness* (e.g. availability, safety integrity, plant condition) and on *organizational efficiency*.

Review Question

R8.3 (a) With reference to Figures 8.9 and 8.10 describe the way in which the responsibilities for maintenance work have been divided between Chemtow and its alliance partner.
      (b) Explain how this division of responsibilities for maintenance work affects the nature of the contract between Chemtow and its alliance partner.

References

1. Johnson, M., *Outsourcing in Brief*, Butterworth-Heinemann, Oxford, 1997.
2. Wireman, T., *Benchmarking in Maintenance Management*, Industrial Press, New York, 2004.

Review Questions Guidelines

R8.1 Early 1990s: Functional organization
      1993: Business units
      1995: Downsizing
      1995–1999: Self-directed, plant-oriented, operator–maintenance teams and self-directed maintenance teams
      1999–2000: Company–contractor alliance

R8.2 (a) The key characteristics in successful alliance arrangements are that the maintenance is regarded as non-core, and the alliance partner has considerable engineering and maintenance expertise relevant to the maintenance of the physical assets – often as a result of having designed and installed them.
      (b) Yes, but in a limited way – perhaps similar to the Chemtow alliance. The main reasons for this comment are as follows:
         – It is unlikely that any contractor would have a better engineering/technical knowledge of the refinery plant than the existing refinery professional engineers.
         – First-line maintenance would be regarded as core.

R8.3 (a) Chemtow have retained the responsibility for first-line maintenance through their operator–maintenance teams. More importantly they have retained the custodianship of the physical assets via their professional engineering and maintenance staff.
             The alliance has been made responsible for carrying out the second- and third-line maintenance work. This includes the planning of the work and the stores management.
      (b) This division of responsibilities means that the contract can only involve the 'cost of carrying out the maintenance work', e.g. the alliance maybe expected to reduce the cost of carrying out the maintenance over a period of 5 years.
             It is not possible to incorporate 'improvements in availability' into the contract because the alliance does not have control over the decisions that directly effect availability (e.g. life plans, shutdown workscope, etc.).

9 Case studies 2 and 3: Cautionary tales of organizational change

'Maybe I'm lucky to be going so slowly, because I may be going in the wrong direction.'
Ashleigh Brilliant, Artist

Chapter aims and outcomes

To show that while manufacturing units and plant-oriented teams are important they must be accompanied by a good maintenance strategy and sound maintenance systems.

On completion of this chapter you should be able to:

- appreciate that having a state-of-the-art organization does not guarantee cost-effective maintenance;
- appreciate that decentralization into manufacturing units and self-directed work teams improves human factors, such as ownership and plant familiarity, but such changes must also be re-inforced by good maintenance systems (life plans, documentation, etc.).

Chapter route map

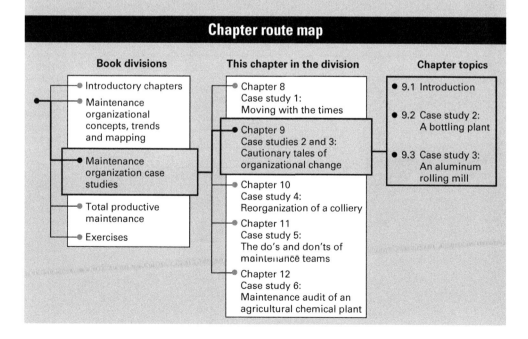

Book divisions

- Introductory chapters
- Maintenance organizational concepts, trends and mapping
- Maintenance organization case studies
- Total productive maintenance
- Exercises

This chapter in the division

- Chapter 8
  Case study 1:
  Moving with the times
- Chapter 9
  Case studies 2 and 3:
  Cautionary tales of
  organizational change
- Chapter 10
  Case study 4:
  Reorganization of a colliery
- Chapter 11
  Case study 5:
  The do's and don'ts of
  maintenance teams
- Chapter 12
  Case study 6:
  Maintenance audit of an
  agricultural chemical plant

Chapter topics

- 9.1 Introduction
- 9.2 Case study 2:
  A bottling plant
- 9.3 Case study 3:
  An aluminum
  rolling mill

9.1 Introduction

Case studies from my own practice will be used to show how two companies changed their functional organizations to organizations based on manufacturing units and teams. In each case the change created 'state-of-the-art' organizational structures and improved organizational efficiency but brought other problems in train.

9.2 Case study 2: A bottling plant

9.2.1 Background

BOTPLANT Ltd produced an alcoholic drink marketed internationally. A small process plant mixed the two main ingredients of the liquor, which was then put into bottles – of different sizes and variously labeled – in six production lines (see Figure 9.1). A seventh-line handled a new product, operating at reduced capacity and for short-production

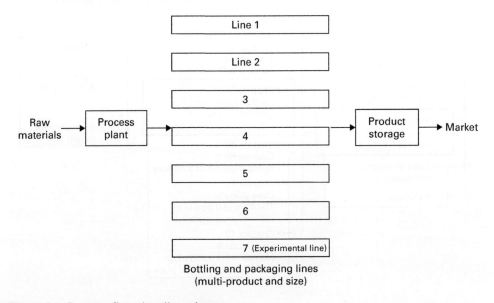

Figure 9.1 Process flow, bottling plant

runs until 1995 BOTPLANT had a traditional functional administrative structure with a centralized maintenance trade-force reporting via trade supervisors to a maintenance manager. The management then decentralized the maintenance resources in order to create line-oriented operator–maintainer teams. In 1997 the management were concerned that plant availability and general plant condition were beginning to suffer. They asked me to undertake a consultancy in order to identify the problems and to indicate their way forward. The audit was conducted over 1 day and involved interviewing five key personnel. Also, and prior to my visit, a questionnaire was completed to provide me with basic information about the organization structure.

9.2.2 The plant maintenance strategy and organization

The administrative and resource structures at the time of the audit are shown in Figures 9.2 and 9.3. The 1995 changes – dividing the plant into 'small manufacturing units' (e.g. centered around lines 1–3), and then into plant-oriented operator–maintainer teams for each such unit – were in line with international trends. The maintenance staff was reduced to the maintenance manager (mechanical) and the electrical engineer.

The role of the services technicians (promoted artisans) was envisaged to include development of preventive maintenance schedules and routines, investigation of failure causes, planning and co-ordination of major jobs, giving technical advice to the line-fitters, and collection and checking of plant history.

> It was decided for many reasons that at the time of the introduction of teams the situation was not right for the use of manufacturing technicians (operator–maintenance), e.g. the operator work was 'very unskilled' and the industrial relations climate was poor (it would have been difficult to retrain the existing operators and also to recruit artisans into the operator roles).

The artisans' role (see Figure 9.3) was to carry out the first-line maintenance (emergency work, change-overs and routine preventive tasks) for their own production line. The larger second-line jobs were undertaken by exploiting the potential for inter-line fitter flexibility while any necessary major overhauls were dealt with by a combination of internal labor and resources provided by the equipment manufacturer.

The artisans, in conjunction with the technicians, were also expected to develop the equipment life plans for their own line, and we noted that these were based on lubrication routines and an operate-to-failure policy. The documentation system (life plans, equipment register, spares lists, descriptions of standard jobs, history) had not been developed. In general, the maintenance strategy was based on a reactive approach, and the cost of maintenance was considered high (in comparison with that of other, similar, plants), a situation which appeared to have arisen because of the following:

(i) There were no maintenance systems in place before the 1995 reorganization, and afterwards, the key role that the technicians could have played in developing such systems, and the matching strategy, was not exploited because, in the main, they were used primarily to supplement the fitting resource.

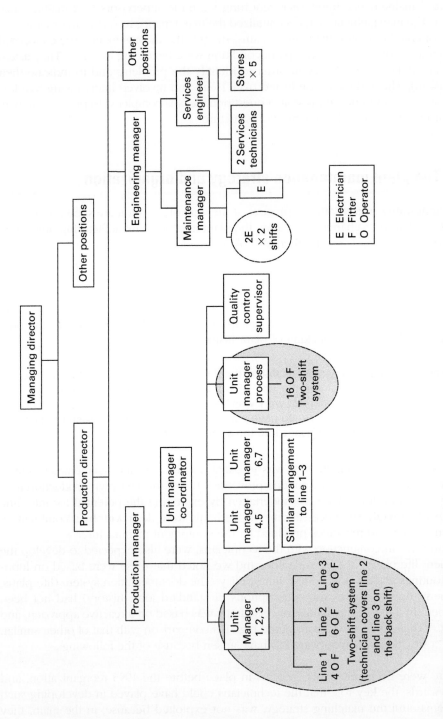

Figure 9.2 Administrative structure, bottling plant

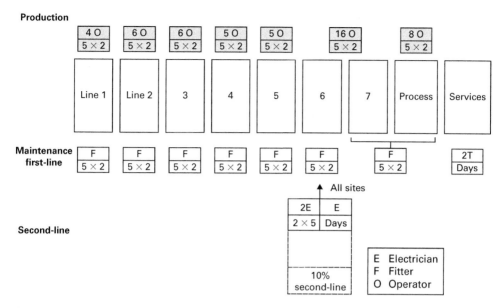

Figure 9.3 Resource structure, bottling plant

(ii) The line-fitters regarded themselves as a fire-fighting force responding, from a central workshop, to calls for emergency work and change-overs; they did not even carry out simple line patrol inspections.

(iii) As is invariably the case, relying on inter-line flexibility to resource larger jobs was difficult, there being a resistance to moving a fitter out of one plant-oriented team to assist another team (as a result, second-line work was either under-resourced or neglected altogether).

(iv) There was rigid inter-trade and operator-trade demarcation within the so-called teams, and the teams were not self-empowered.

(v) The unit managers had little engineering or maintenance knowledge and found their relationship with the fitters difficult.

(vi) An overtime culture existed throughout the maintenance department.

After just 1 day's visit I was left with the overriding impression that the management had not taken maintenance seriously. There is little point in setting up an organizational structure that meets international best practice when the strategy, systems and control are poor.

9.2.3 Organizational change: the way forward

Any changes to the organization to overcome its immediate problems had to bear in mind the following points:

● In the short term, the maintenance department needed to change if it was to provide the necessary technical resources for developing the essential documentation, strategy and systems. This could have been achieved via existing or additional personnel.

- The changes had to provide a resource for second-line corrective and preventive work. This in turn assumed that the plant would be released for such work, either because it would be done at weekends, or during production-agreed downshifts, etc. or because production could be sustained via redundant plant.
- It should be appreciated that the eventual aim will be to re-introduce plant manufacturing units and operator–maintainer line-oriented teams. Indeed, the ideal organization would be one in which fitters (i.e. manufacturing technicians) were recruited into the operating teams. This would have released the existing first-line fitters (or a major proportion of them) for second-line work (I have always felt that change-over work was production work rather than maintenance, which was the perception at this plant). Furthermore, such a change should only to be introduced after a careful study, on each line, of the workload profiles of operators and fitters, e.g. How do they co-ordinate? What level of training is required? Any re-introduction of line-oriented teams needed to be accompanied by self-empowerment and the introduction of an annualized-hours agreement to overcome the overtime culture.

9.2.4 Short-term actions

The following actions were therefore suggested:

(a) The first-line fitters' responsibility for the maintenance of individual production lines should remain and it is necessary to ensure (if needed, by recruiting additional fitters) that there were enough of them to cover such work, i.e. the work could be carried out without calling upon the assistance of the technicians. The line-fitters should report directly to the maintenance manager, their role should be clearly defined and should take in emergency maintenance, change-overs, line-inspection patrolling and the large preventive jobs. They should understand that most of their time was to be spent on the production line. Additional training, to upgrade their skills in change-over work, etc. should be given as necessary, and they should be moved to different production lines, from time to time, to broaden their knowledge and increase their flexibility.

(b) An alternative structure to that proposed in (a) is shown in Figure 9.4. This would retain the idea of the unit structure (the three lines) but would divide the maintenance resource into first-line shift-fitters and second-line day-fitters. Both groups would need to report directly to the maintenance manager, as in (a).

(c) The technicians should be released from fitting duties. Their main role would then be the development of maintenance life plans, documentation, standard job descriptions and lists of spares requirements. In addition, they should have a role in the scheduling, planning and resourcing of the large jobs. The maintenance life plans should be developed in conjunction with the line-fitters. In the short term, the technicians might need to be supplemented by contract technical or clerical resource.

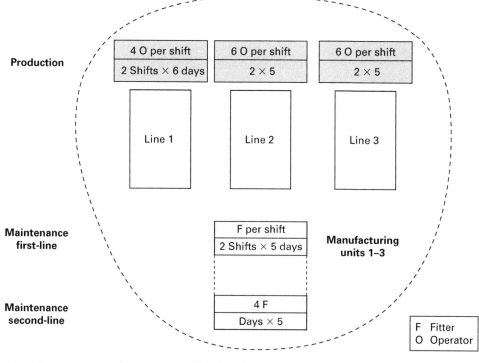

Figure 9.4 Resource structure modification, bottling plant

Review Question

R9.1   (a) Outline the 'maintenance advantages' BOTPLANT hoped to achieve by
           using the organization modeled in Figures 9.2 and 9.3.
       (b) Explain why BOTPLANT did not achieve these hoped for advantages.
       (c) What advice would you give to a company embarking on the kind of
           organizational change carried out by BOTPLANT to ensure that main-
           tenance systems and strategy are not neglected.

9.3 Case study 3: An aluminum rolling mill

9.3.1 Background

The company (ALROM Ltd) made aluminum products (from plate to foil) for an international market. The plant layout is shown in Figure 9.5 and its process flow in Figure 9.6.

Some 4 years before this audit was carried out, and in order to improve throughput
and quality of product, the company had updated the plant via a major capital investment
in state-of-the-art control equipment. At the same time, some of the main production
units were also replaced and others (e.g. the Hot Mill) retained and overhauled. There

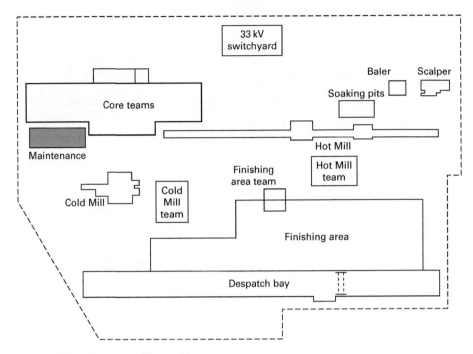

Figure 9.5 Plant layout, rolling mill

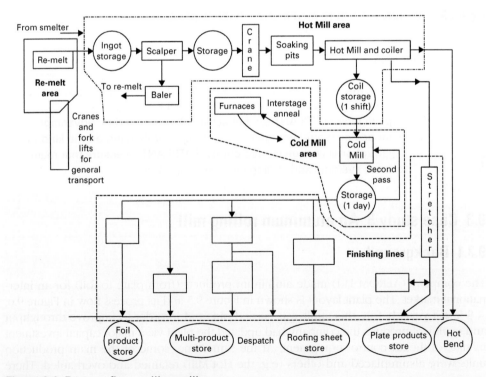

Figure 9.6 Process flow, rolling mill

was also a heavy investment in improving the skills of the workforce and improving the organizational structure up to international benchmark levels (e.g. by introducing plant-oriented self-empowered operator–maintainer teams). I was told that, as a result, the company had expected to increase sales to a level of 38,000 tons per annum, some 6000 tons of which was to be sold as Hot Mill product (Hot Bend) and the rest as products of the finishing area. However, at the time of the audit the Hot Mill output stood at only 30,000 tons per annum, which meant that considerable profit was being lost. The international benchmarks (see Table 9.1) indicated that the main reason for this was the low availability of the Hot Mill.

Table 9.1 International comparison of rolling mill maintenance performance indices

	ALROM	Plant X	Plant Y	Plant Z
Annual volume (tons)	30,176	104,223	50,812	44,567
Plant recovery (%)	65	65	64	63
Hot Mill				
Uptime/available time	47	82	79	66
Operation downtime	18	13	5	15
Maintenance downtime	18	1.0	1.8	9.1
Productivity foil stock (tons/hour)	18	27	25	14
Cold Mill				
Uptime/available time	81	75	74	64
Operation downtime	7.5	18	12	17
Maintenance downtime	5.4	0.6	4.8	8.5
Productivity foil stock (tons/hour)	10	7.3	9.0	4.6

I was asked to carry out a 2-day consultancy in order to identify firstly the reasons for the low Hot Mill availability and secondly actions for its improvement.

9.3.2 Plant-operating characteristics and objectives

The plant operated for 49 weeks per year, having a 3-week shutdown in December. The mills operated for 6 days per week on a three-shift basis, with Sunday offline, while the finishing area ran on a 3 day, 12 hours per day cycle (the re-melt plant operating continuously). As explained, the production objective and long-term plan was to increase the throughput of the Hot Mill to 38,000 tons per annum. I could find no corresponding maintenance objective or strategy.

9.3.3 Life plans and preventive schedules

Considerable effort had been put into the life plans for the main plant. The Hot Mill, e.g. had a comprehensive list of lubrication, inspection, cleaning and service routines, including vibration monitoring and lubrication oil analysis for motors and gearboxes. In the annual 3-week window the Mill underwent a partial or full overhaul, depending on its condition. Most of the routines were carried out during a weekly Hot Mill downshift (Sundays were not used for maintenance). In order to smooth the weekly planned maintenance workload the Hot Mill and Cold Mill came down on different days and the finishing area maintenance was also scheduled to avoid these Mill downdays.

The life plan for the Hot Mill was both comprehensive and detailed, and in spite of the high incidence of reactive work was mostly carried out. The Cold Mill was also well maintained. The finishing area life plans were, however, only 40% completed, but because of the spare capacity these were not considered important.

The following were typical comments by interviewees:

- 'The problem is not so much poor preventive maintenance but poor design. The modification of the Hot Mill finished up with some old equipment and some new equipment, they don't fit well together.'
- 'In the Hot Mill area we are snowed-under fighting fires, we have no time to look for improvement in life plans or to design-out problem areas.'
- 'What we would like to see is more engineering effort put into the Hot Mill area.'

I agreed. My overriding impression was that the reliability problems were being caused by poor design. In such cases even the best preventive procedures will not improve reliability. What was required was major investigative engineering to establish the causes and prescribe solutions.

9.3.4 An overview of the organization

Before modernization there had been a traditional functional organization, i.e. there were many single-trade maintenance teams reporting via supervisors to a centralized engineering manager (see Figure 9.7).

A centralized trade group was responsible for the maintenance of the workshops, building fabric and services. In addition, there were area trade groups responsible for first- and second-line maintenance of the production plant.

Figures 9.8 and 9.9 show the resource structure and administrative structure after modification, Figure 9.10 being a schematic model of the Hot Mill work planning system.

The essential characteristics of this updated organization are as follows:

- Manufacturing units were established (e.g. one based on the Hot Mill), each under its own manager and having its own unit engineer and process engineer. In the case of the Hot Mill there was also a control technician to ensure that the group held the correct mix of engineering skills (the mill engineer was a mechanical). Each shift team comprised six operators, an electrician and a fitter, were self-empowered and undertook a 'star configuration' of duties (see Figure 7.14). The function of the shift artisans was to carry out first-line maintenance. Each manufacturing unit had a degree of autonomy regarding its production and maintenance policy.
- The manufacturing units were supported by a centralized structure which included a limited engineering capability and two 'core' second-line maintenance teams. Because each plant area could be scheduled separately – for 1 day a week – for maintenance, the core teams, with the help of the local artisans, carried out all second-line work.

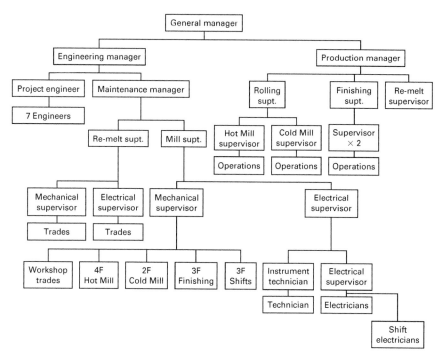

Figure 9.7 Rolling mill administration before plant modernization (illustrative only)

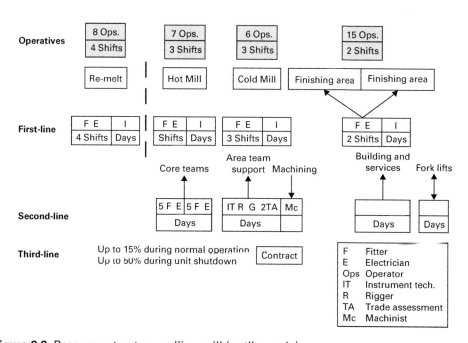

Figure 9.8 Resource structure, rolling mill (outline only)

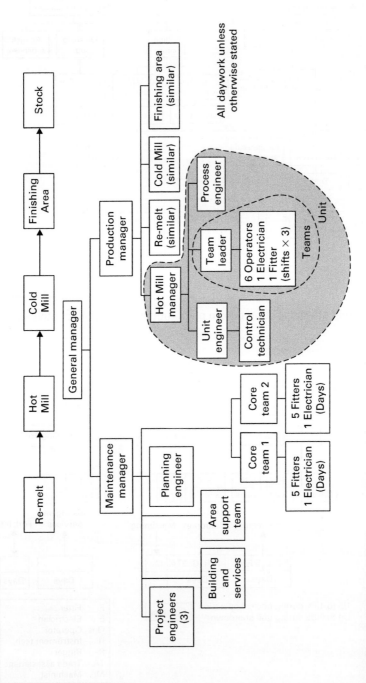

Figure 9.9 Administrative structure, rolling mill (outline only)

9.3.5 Maintenance systems

The operation of the work planning system (see Figure 9.10), was based on a multi-terminal maintenance documentation system. The system had a manual loop, i.e. work request to the unit engineer, he vetted it and entered it into the backlog. The downshift program was established at a Wednesday meeting and was in the hands of the core team planner on Thursday before the downday (the Monday).

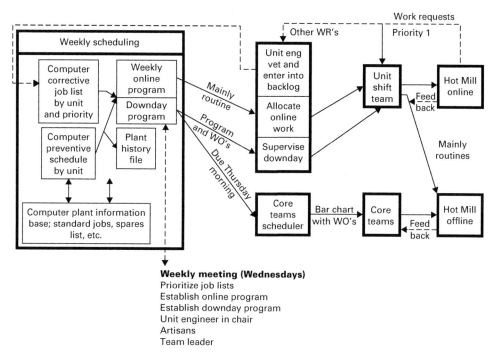

Figure 9.10 Planning system, rolling mill

Cost control maintenance documentation and spares management were briefly examined. They seemed to be generally satisfactory. The reporting of the top ten low reliability and high maintenance cost areas good. The quality of history recording compared well with that of the top quartile of maintenance departments I have audited.

Because of the Hot Mill problem, I concentrated my efforts on plant reliability control system (PRC). The overriding purpose of a PRC system is the identification and eradication of 'reliability hotspots'. Figure 9.11 shows the three levels of organizational effort necessary to carry this out. (PRC is discussed in depth in *Maintenance Systems and Documentation.*)

My comments on PRC at the rolling mill were as follows:

● Within the team procedures, a level 1 system was in operation. In terms of concept and philosophy it was a good system and worked well for all the teams, with the exception of the Hot Mill team. This was in part due to the reactive nature of maintenance which was preventing the unit engineer/team from concentrating on designing out unreliability.

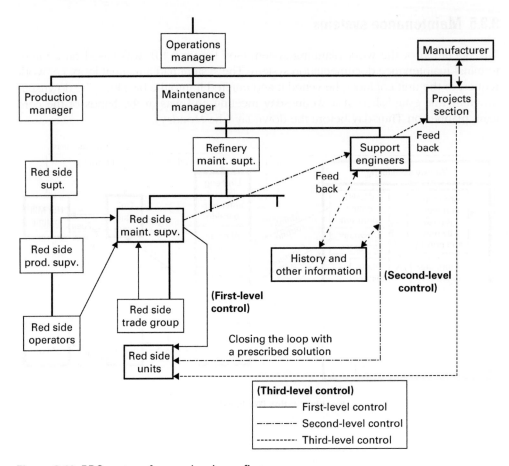

Figure 9.11 PRC system for an alumina refinery

- The level 2 and 3 systems were not operating in a satisfactory way, in particular in the Hot Mill area. This was caused by:
  - lack of definition of the PRC system and of the roles within the system;
  - lack of enthusiasm on the part of the project engineers for helping with maintenance problems, they felt they should concentrate on new projects;
  - too few professional maintenance engineers in the centralized maintenance group.

9.3.6 Observations and recommendations

The restructured organization (in particular the team concept) appeared to be working well, except at the Hot Mill, where the difficulties were exacerbated by the poor reliability of the electrical and control equipment. The Hot Mill Engineer came from a mechanical background and did not have the expertise to solve such problems. The control technician was just out of an apprenticeship and did not have the necessary experience or knowledge of the process. In addition, the Mill Engineer was finding difficulty in obtaining assistance from the project group and from other unit engineers.

> Difficulties of this kind are not uncommon when an organization restructures into manufacturing units. It is inevitable that the engineering and technical resource will inevitably be spread thin, leaving a limited central support, if any.

In such a situation it is not easy to operate the 'PRC system' in the conventional way – the search for reliability hot spots and their eradication, becomes very limited.

The following actions were recommended:

● A group should be formed, from within the company, of engineers and technicians who would have the necessary expertise (in control, electrical and mechanical disciplines) in Hot Mill operation and maintenance. They should be seconded, under the maintenance manager, in order to *purge* the Hot Mill of its reliability problems.

> This periodic assembling of a company's engineering expertise is one of the best ways of controlling plant reliability in a decentralized organization, it replaces the conventional second level system. (The purge method of PRC)

● The unit engineers from each of the manufacturing units need to improve their communication with each other and their sharing of knowledge.
● At least one additional professional maintenance engineer should be appointed under the maintenance manager.

Review Question

R9.2   ALROM carried out the same kind of organizational change as BOTPLANT but they had a good maintenance system in place before the change. Nevertheless they still had serious maintenance/reliability problems in the Hot Mill area due in part to a poor PRC system. A lot of companies' decentralizing into manufacturing units have problems with PRC:
  (a) Describe what you consider are the key reasons for these problems.
  (b) Outline what you consider is the best way of overcoming these problems.

Review Questions Guidelines

R9.1   (a) The BOTPLANT management changed a functional organization into an organization based on manufacturing units, they hoped the change would generate the following:
     – A sense of plant ownership from the operators and trade-force for their own lines.
     – Better team working.
     – Artisans with better 'plant specialized knowledge'.
     – Faster response for emergency work.
     – All of which should mean higher plant availability.

    (b) The maintenance systems were non-existent. They should have been in place before the organizational change took place. There were also 'industrial relations' problems that needed sorting out.

    (c) To make sure that excellent maintenance systems are in place before any such organizational change takes place and that there are sufficient centralized personnel to maintain these systems.

R9.2 (a) The key reason is that as a result of decentralization the professional engineers (and technicians) are distributed thinly across the organization into the various manufacturing units. They are under considerable pressure on day-to-day issues and find it difficult to carry out PRC within their manufacturing units. In addition, they can become professionally isolated.

    (b) The so-called 'purge procedure' of PRC. Periodically a group of engineers are seconded from their respective manufacturing units to form a 'company PRC team'. The team concentrates on the problem area of plant for a short period to purge out the reliability problems.

10

Case study 4: Reorganization of a colliery

Chapter aims and outcomes

To show how the models, procedures and concepts used for analyzing the maintenance of industrial plant can also be used for such analysis as regards other physical asset systems – in this case an underground coal mine.

On completion of this chapter you should be able to:

- understand how to apply the models, procedures and concepts of business-centered maintenance to map the maintenance operation in an underground coal mine;
- appreciate that the advantages of making maintenance supervisors and teams responsible for their area of plant are as important in a mining environment as in any other industrial context;
- appreciate how difficult it is to make strategic and organizational changes in a trade-union-dominated environment.

Chapter route map

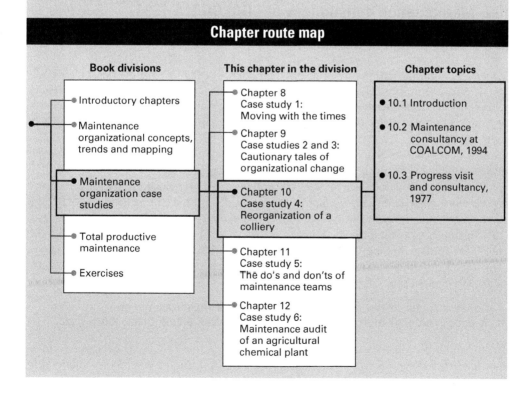

Book divisions	This chapter in the division	Chapter topics
Introductory chapters	Chapter 8 Case study 1: Moving with the times	• 10.1 Introduction
Maintenance organizational concepts, trends and mapping	Chapter 9 Case studies 2 and 3: Cautionary tales of organizational change	• 10.2 Maintenance consultancy at COALCOM, 1994
Maintenance organization case studies	Chapter 10 Case study 4: Reorganization of a colliery	• 10.3 Progress visit and consultancy, 1977
Total productive maintenance	Chapter 11 Case study 5: The do's and don'ts of maintenance teams	
Exercises	Chapter 12 Case study 6: Maintenance audit of an agricultural chemical plant	

Key words

- Demarcation
- Plant specific training
- Industrial relation problems
- Organizational power base
- Shift systems
- Mining unions

'Don't agonise, organise.'

Florynce Kennedy

10.1 Introduction

Over a period of 5 days in 1994, and working on my own, I carried out a consultancy of the maintenance and engineering departments at an underground coal mining company, COALCOM. Three years later, and also working alone, I carried out a 3-day consultancy to establish progress.

The COALCOM case study is introduced at this point to illustrate that the organizational models and concepts apply across a wide range of physical assets.

10.2 Maintenance consultancy at COALCOM – 1994

10.2.1 Background to COALCOM

COALCOM comprises three underground collieries – operating 3 shifts per day, for a 5-day week and for 50 weeks per year – and a coal preparation plant (see Figure 10.1).

The coal was taken to the preparation plant by truck and then by rail to the coal loaders some 200 miles away on the coast. The senior management structure is shown in Figure 10.2.

At this level each of the collieries and the coal preparation plant functioned as semi-autonomous manufacturing units. An engineering manager (with a secretary) had then just been appointed to assist in the co-ordination of the decentralized engineering departments, which carried out capital project work and had the responsibility for the off-site overhauls of major equipment (some of which is shared between the collieries).

The management commissioned the consultancy because they were concerned that the availability of their underground equipment was low and their maintenance costs high. They believed that the main problem was an inadequate structure for organizing maintenance and engineering. The consultancy was expected to answer the following question:

'What changes in the maintenance strategy and organizational structure were needed in order to improve equipment availability and reduce maintenance costs?'

Because all three collieries operated in a similar way and had similar problems *I decided to concentrate my main effort on Colliery A*. In addition, I interviewed the engineering

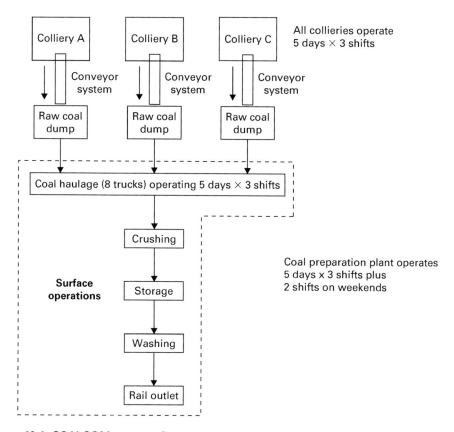

Figure 10.1 COALCOM process flow

manager and the other colliery-engineering superintendents in order to acquire understanding of the way the engineering effort across COALCOM was co-ordinated.

10.2.2 Equipment and operating characteristics

The layout of the tunnels and production areas of Colliery A – a drift mine, the main tunnel inclining down from the surface to three development areas and the longwall production area – is shown in Figure 10.3.

The main tunnel carried the trunk conveyor system and the personnel roadways. Continuous miners (diesel-driven vehicles, each with a front-mounted driller–cutter for creating the development tunnels through the coal measures) were used to develop the production areas and the tunnels for conveyor or worker access.

Coal extraction was achieved by 'longwall' cutting, an operation which employed a system comprising a shearer, armored face conveyor (AFC) (up to 100-m long), main conveyors and various services, such as an electricity supply (see Figure 10.4).

The shearer cut slices of the coal seam 2-m thick by moving across a 100-m block which had been developed between two tunnels by the continuous miners. The removed

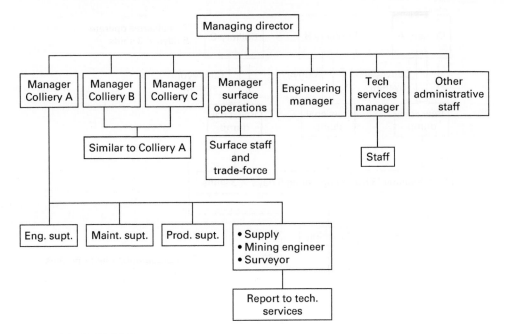

Figure 10.2 COALCOM senio management structure

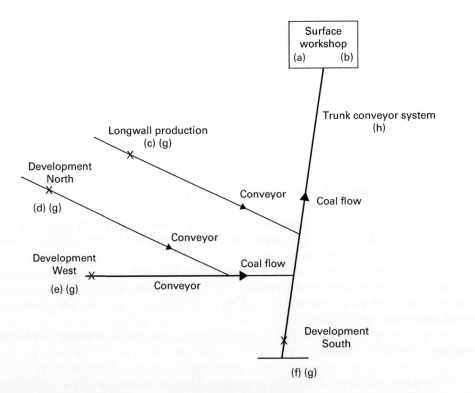

Figure 10.3 Layout of Colliery A, showing operating areas

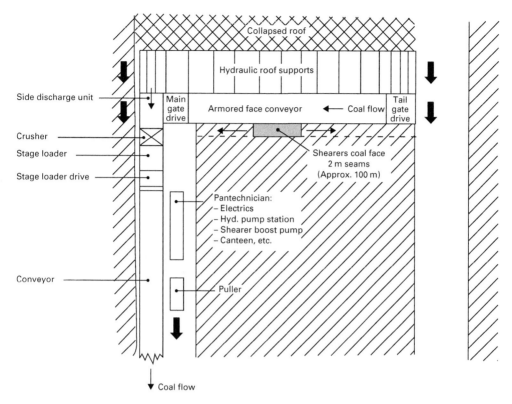

Figure 10.4 Longwall process

coal fell on to the armor-plated conveyor and was then moved outwards to the conventional conveyors. A balance had to be maintained between the rate of development work and of production.

The colliery operates a 5 day × 3 shift per day for 50 weeks per year.

10.2.3 Production and maintenance objectives

A production plan was being used to balance development and longwall production to meet target outputs. The mine was production limited. These target outputs were being used to set availability targets for the longwall. However, it was the impression that the engineering–maintenance department had not established equipment life plans to achieve these availability targets. Also, I could find no key performance indices for any area of organizational efficiency.

10.2.4 Life plans and preventive schedule

An outline life plan for the AFC of the longwall cutting system is shown in Table 10.1(a), Table 10.1(b) shows one of the job specifications.

Table 10.1(a) Outline of life plan for the AFC

Chain tension	1 week
Rudd link inspection	1 month
Oil test	1 month
Service	3 months
Code C service (statutory electrical)	3 months
Overhaul	At longwall change

Table 10.1(b) Example of a preventive job specification

Armored face conveyor	Plant no.	Weekly service (fitter)
Location:	Date due:	

	Complete the following and report condition (repair as required)	
Safety	Ensure correct isolation and tagging procedures are fulfilled before commencing. If working underneath equipment ensure it is adequately supported:	
Drives	Top up M/G drive box oil (p/gear heavy): Top up M/G slat box oil (p/gear heavy): Top up M/G drive sprocket (p/gear heavy): Inspect M/G drive sprocket for wear: M/G chain strippers – condition: : Security: Test operation of M/G slat box (including operation of interlock): Ensure M/G drive box mounting bolts are tight: Ensure M/G drive water cooling is operating correctly: Ensure all covers and guards are fitted & secure: Top up T/G drive box oil (p/gear heavy): Top up T/G slat box oil (p/gear heavy): Top up T/G drive sprocket (p/gear heavy): Inspect T/G drive sprocket for wear: T/G chain strippers – condition: : Security: Test operation of T/G slat box (including operation of interlock): Ensure T/G drive box mounting bolts are tight: Ensure T/G drive water cooling is operating correctly: Ensure all covers and guards are fitted and secure:	
Chains	Check chain tension – goaf side (10 → 13): Face side (10 → 13): Inspect chain & joiners for damage or wear: Inspect flight bars for damage or wear: Ensure all flight bar bolts are tight: Inspect for missing flight bars:	
Pans	Inspect for wide pan gaps or dropped pans – (this may indicate a broken dog bone): Rack bars – condition: : Wear: Rack bar pins – security: : Any Missing?: Spill plates – condition: : Security: Cable trough – condition: : Guide Rail Condition: Inspect all cables, hydrogen, water and air hoses for damage: Relay bar → AFC pan pin – condition: : Security:	
Work outstanding		

The minor work of the life plan is carried out underground while the major work (the overhaul) was undertaken off-site by contractors on the equipment manufacturer. This was typical of most of the underground equipment.

The minor maintenance of the equipment in the development areas was scheduled during the week into windows of opportunity provided by production changeovers. The work was scheduled to avoid clashes and also the weekly two-shift longwall down day, when minor maintenance (preventive and corrective) arising on the longwall was carried out. The major longwall maintenance took place during a longwall change (locating it to a new production area, which took about 3 weeks). Major units of long-wall equipment (e.g. the AFC, the shearer, etc.) are held as spares common to the three collieries, which minimized longwall overhaul and allowed the equipment to be recon-ditioned off-site.

There appeared to be no scheduled down day for the trunk conveyor and limited maintenance was carried out on it at the weekends. The engineering superintendent was responsible for all maintenance carried out off-site, including work specification and tendering, while the maintenance superintendent was responsible for all maintenance carried out within the mine.

Observations
- As regards the minor maintenance work, the development and longwall equipment life plans were satisfactory.
- The major off-site maintenance work was not being carried out satisfactorily. This was in partly due to the lack of communication and understanding, concerning its specification and quality control, among the engineering–maintenance departments.
- The life plans for the conveyor systems were satisfactory. However the offline pre-ventive and corrective work arising from the inspections was not being carried out. This was partly because of the absence of a downshift. The windows of opportunity (those provided by shift changeovers and those occurring at the weekends) were not being used for planned maintenance.
- Although the colliery was production limited the management preferred to use mid-week down days for longwall maintenance (a 13.5% availability loss) rather than sanction overtime or 7-day maintenance shift rostering for weekends.

Review Question

R10.1   In spite of being 'production limited', COALCOM used two mid-week down-shifts rather than the weekends to carry out the second-line maintenance. Why did they do this? Do you think this policy is acceptable?

10.2.5 Maintenance organization

Resource structure
Figure 10.5 shows the Monday-to-Friday maintenance resource structure, an inventory of the maintenance personnel being shown in Table 10.2.

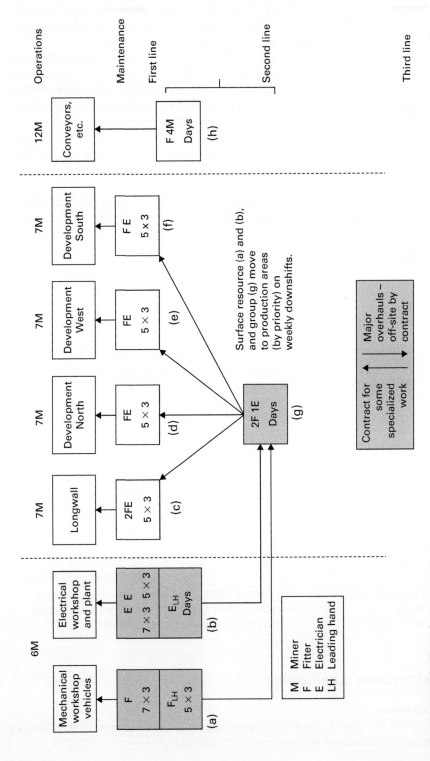

Figure 10.5 Colliery A resource structure

Table 10.2 Colliery A manpower inventory

Maintenance manager	1
Support engineers	5.5
Maintenance supervisors	10
Maintenance planner	1
Other staff	2
Total staff	19.5
Fitters	25
Electricians	22
Non-trades	4
Total	51

Only a small amount of labor was available for weekend work. The trade-force was plant specialized, to provide a first-line maintenance shift cover (e.g. the longwall had two fitters and an electrician – Group (c) – on each shift). A small centralized pool (g), working in conjunction with the surface resource (a) and (b), moved to supplement the first-line teams during mid-weekly downshifts.

During major underground maintenance work (mainly locating the longwall to a new production area) the resource was centralized as a shutdown group. Little or no contract labor was employed underground.

It should be noted that Figure 10.1 is the equivalent of an industrial plant process flow diagram (see, e.g. Figure 4.1) and Figure 10.3 is the equivalent of a plant layout diagram (see, e.g. Figure 4.2). In some cases Figure 10.3 is supplemented by a layout of the mine surface operations. Figures 10.1 and 10.3 are essential precursors to the construction of the resource structure shown in Figure 10.5.

Observations
- The first-line shift resource was poorly utilized.
- Demarcation was strong. Inter-trade and operator–maintenance flexibility were non-existent.
- Team working, involving both the miners and artisans in the development and production areas, was poor.
- Artisans and miners had little sense of equipment ownership.
- Plant-specific training was poor.
- The resource structure required modification. In the short term the second-line group (g) needed to be augmented by three fitters, at the expense of the under utilized first-line longwall group (c). In the longer term, increased skills training and flexibility (which was being introduced as a national initiative) would allow the operator teams (the miners) to take on some of the first-line work This would allow the further build up of group (g), which would provide better resourcing of the down days and, *via.* a staggered day shift roster would allow planned work to be carried out at weekends.

Administrative structure
The Colliery A administrative structure existing at that time is shown in Figure 10.6, which should be looked at in conjunction with Figures 10.3 and 10.5.

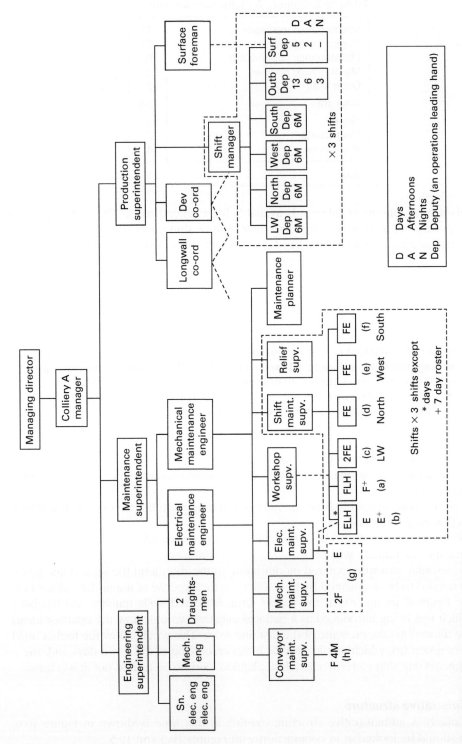

Figure 10.6 Colliery A administrative structure

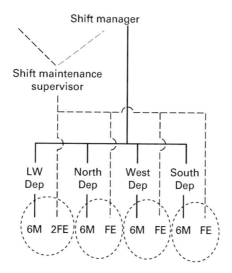

Figure 10.7 Colliery A shift reporting

The colliery manager is responsible for the process, equipment and manpower. Below this, administration is departmentalized at superintendent level into production, maintenance and engineering. It appears that the division of responsibility is as follows:

- Production superintendent: all aspects of the process, and in that sense is the owner of the equipment while it is in operation;
- Maintenance superintendent: maintenance of the equipment while it was on-site;
- Engineering superintendent: specification and procurement of new plant and major modification work; specification and quality control of major overhaul work; engineering support to the maintenance department; maintenance of the equipment drawing and documentation systems.

The maintenance and engineering superintendents were mainly managers – they only became involved in technical matters in a limited way. The main responsibility of the electrical and the mechanical supervisors was to organize the down days and major maintenance in conjunction with the process co-ordinators. The maintenance planner was used as a maintenance documentation clerk.

The electrical- and the mechanical-maintenance engineers provided an additional layer of management. The formers' function seems to be to support the 'management role' of the maintenance superintendent in the area of administration and industrial relations. ('I provide direct technical assistance for about 10% of my time'.)

The main feature of the maintenance–production administration was the shift reporting structure (see Figure 10.7). At supervisor and shop floor level it has resulted in a number of process-related small production–maintenance teams in each of the development and longwall areas.

Observations

- As regards satisfactory reliability and availability the most important activities were *the selection and procurement of equipment* and *the major maintenance work*. These were the responsibility of the engineering superintendents and were not done well.

- The first-line shift trade-force was poorly utilized.
- Relatively little progress had been made in creating operator–maintainer self-empowered teams. There was a considerable polarization (them and us) between the trade-force and the management.
- The responsibilities of the engineering and the maintenance sections – for the maintenance of underground equipment – were not clearly enough defined.
- At superintendent level a considerable polarization of attitudes and perception made communication difficult.
- The structure did not function as indicated in Figure 10.6. In practice, the electrical supervisors reported to the electrical-maintenance engineer and the mechanical supervisor to his mechanical counterpart.
- There appeared to be an 'organizational power base' at shift-manager level. Among other problems, this was causing serious polarization between production and maintenance.

10.2.6 Maintenance systems

I had been told not to spend much time on this area. A new computerized package had been bought and would shortly be installed and commissioned. Thus, the systems were audited superficially in order to obtain the complete picture.

The *work planning system* is modeled in Figure 10.8. Its main feature was that planning of the longwall down day needed to be better. One supervisor should have been responsible for the planning, scheduling and supervision of the down day.

Plant reliability control (PRC) was not satisfactory. There was no Level 1 system and the dominance of reactive work meant that the maintenance engineers and project engineer had little time to spend on support for the Level 2 system (see Figure 9.11 as an example of a PRC system).

Maintenance documentation was not satisfactory and would remain so with the new software unless considerable effort was made in improving the upkeep of spare parts lists, standard job specifications, history records, etc.

10.2.7 Recommendations

(a) For each of the collieries the adoption of the revised organization shown in Figure 10.9 was proposed. The main features of this were as follows:
  - A centralized engineering project group (EPG) should be formed with the following responsibilities:
    - To produce new equipment and perform other major engineering work.
    - To provide back up to the colliery maintenance departments for sophisticated technical problems, which might take the form of direct assistance or linkage with an outside third party.
    - To be responsible for the drawings master library and its updating system.

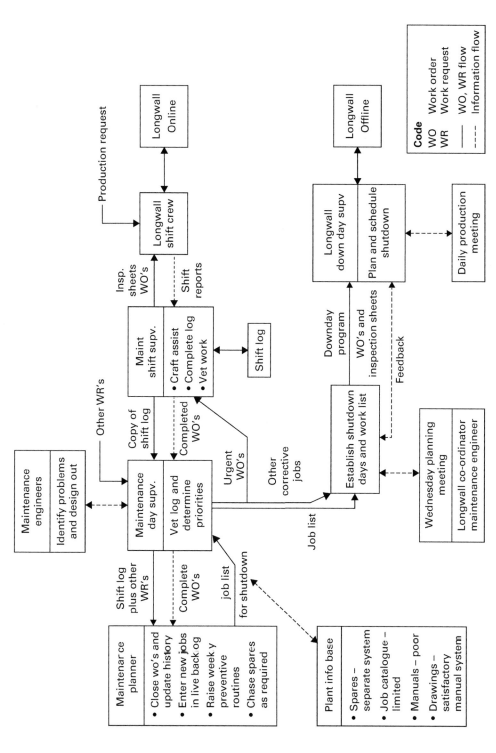

Figure 10.8 Colliery A work planning system

The EPG should not get involved in the direct execution of project or sophisticated engineering work that could be carried out cost effectively by contract. The size of the EPG should reflect such a policy and be set at a level which could cope with the lower limits of the workload. Contract engineers should service the workload peaks and deal with specialized tasks. Such a group could be made up of two or three engineers (transferred from the collieries) reporting to the engineering manager and should have a balance of expertise across the engineering disciplines and across the main colliery equipment. Although there should be a degree of specialization it would be essential that the individual engineers can work flexibly.

- Within each colliery a maintenance support group (MSG) should be formed from the existing maintenance engineers – supplemented by an engineer drawn from the engineering department as it then was. The group should include mechanical and electrical expertise and it should be devoted to supporting the maintenance department in improving equipment reliability.
- It was to be firmly understood that this recommended reorganization would only work if the roles and duties of the EPG and the respective MSG's were clearly defined – regarding areas of responsibility overlap, interrelationships and communication systems and so forth.
- The day maintenance supervisors should be made plant responsible (e.g. one should be responsible for the longwall). The second-line day shift resource should be increased as discussed in Section 10.2.5, and should report to the mechanical and electrical surface supervisors for day-to-day problems, and to the plant oriented supervisors during their down days.
- In the longer term the national exercise for improving flexibility and skill training might facilitate evolution of the shift structure – *via.* some intermediate stages – into self-empowered teams (see Figure 10.10).
- The second-line resource (see Figure 10.9) required a much improved planning and scheduling system – with greater emphasis on pre-planning of individual jobs and weekly work programs (see Figure 10.8) – if it were to be used effectively. This, in turn, would require the maintenance planner to be employed as his job title indicated rather than as a documentation clerk.

(b) The management of collieries needed to develop a policy of operating the longwall on a continuous 15 shift basis, which would mean that maintenance work on the longwall equipment and on the trunk conveyor system would have to be accomplished at the weekends. The maintenance life plans for all major equipment (miners, shuttle cars, etc.) would need to be updated, a project which would include:

- An audit of the existing condition of the equipment.
- Improvement of the online inspection procedures and the follow-up work.
- A review of the overhaul procedures – of overhaul frequencies, work specifications, contractor selection, standard job procedures, quality control, etc.

The ability to carry out recommendation (b) will depend on the implementation of (a). For example, the collieries would not have been able to move from reactive to proactive maintenance without the creation of the kind of second-line maintenance resource pool shown in Figure 10.9.

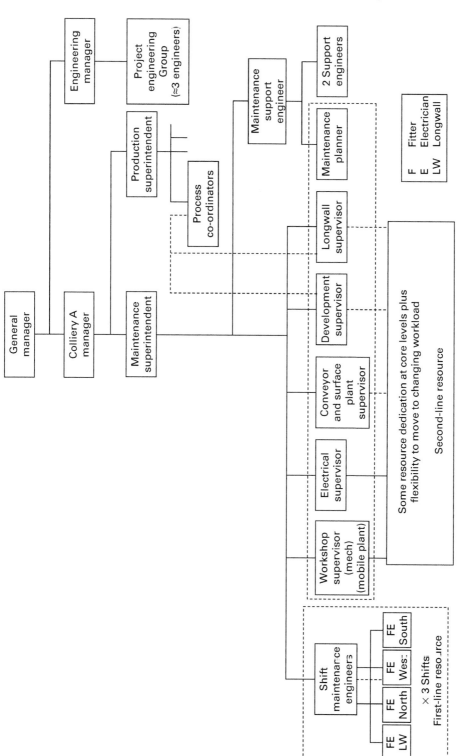

Figure 10.9 Proposed administrative structure.

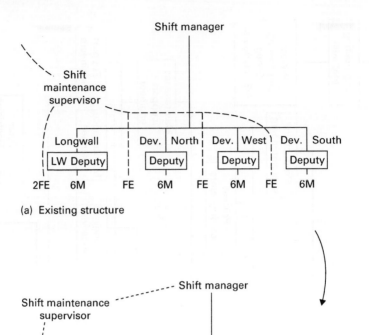

(a) Existing structure

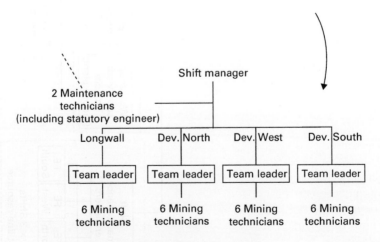

(b) Intermediate structure (Flexibility across F/E/M)

(c) Final structure (With self-empowerment)

Figure 10.10 Moves towards self-empowerment

Review Question

R10.2   List the main advantages that should stem from centralizing the engineering function of the three collieries.

10.3 Progress visit and consultancy – 1997

10.3.1 Introduction

In 1997 (3 years after the original consultancy) we were asked to revisit the colliery –
in order firstly to identify and appraise the changes that had taken place, and
secondly to identify any recommendations that had not been implemented and the reasons why. The Colliery A resource and administrative structures, and its manpower
inventory, at that later time are outlined and summarized in Figures 10.11 and 10.12 and
Table 10.3.

The following sections are a summary of the progress report's main observations.

10.3.2 Organization

(a) A centralized EPG was set up shortly after the 1994 audit was completed, was headed
by the engineering manager and three professional engineers transferred from the
colliery engineering section. The responsibilities were:
  (i) To procure new equipment and where necessary to assist in its installation and
  commissioning.
  (ii) To provide a project management service for capital and maintenance projects.
  (iii) To develop standards for underground equipment overhaul and to assist in
  standardizing the equipment maintenance life plans (e.g. for the longwall), and
  maintenance support agreements, throughout the collieries.
  (iv) To aid in ensuring that information (operation standards; areas of high maintenance cost; reliability problems and solutions) on common equipment is com-
  municated throughout the collieries.
  (v) To help the colliery support engineers in solving complex or technically
  sophisticated problems.
  (vi) To co-ordinate the use of shared equipment between collieries. The size of the
  group was set at a level which could deal with the core workload (arising from
  responsibilities (iii) to (vi)) and was increased as necessary (i.e. to handle responsibilities (i) and (ii)) by employing contract engineers.
  There was a consensus among those interviewed that over the 3 years since the formation of the EPG the engineering performance of the colliery equipment had
  steadily improved, particularly regarding the specification and control of quality of
  off-site overhauls. Projects were under way to move from 'buy and maintain' to
  'lease, and employ the original equipment manufacturer (OEM) to maintain'.
(b) It appeared that the appointment of supervisors dedicated to specific equipment had
been a success. For example, in the longwall production group it was felt there had

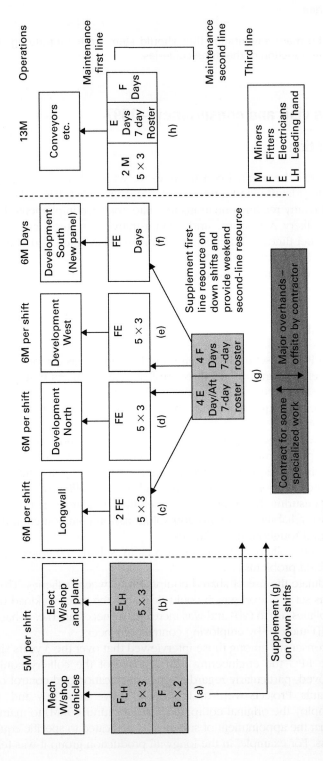

Figure 10.11 Resource structure (1997 audit)

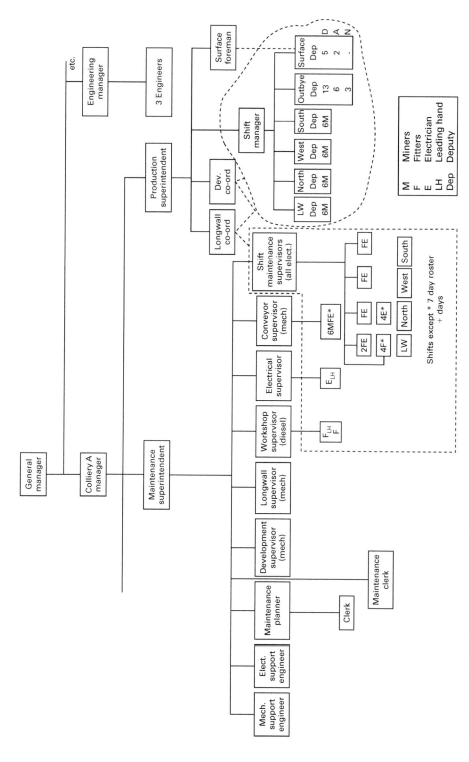

Figure 10.12 Administrative structure (1997 – audit)

Table 10.3 Manpower inventory change audit to reaudit

	Reaudit (97)	Audit
Maintenance manager	1	1
Support engineers	2	5.5
Maintenance supervisors	8	10
Maintenance planner		1
Other staff	1	2
Total staff	13	19.5
Fitters	22	25
Electricians	21	22
Non-Trades (miners)	6	4
Total	49	51

    been a considerable improvement, especially in the planning of the down days and of longwall changes.

(c) The only change to the resource structure had been an enlargement of the second-line group (g) and their rostering on a staggered day shift to cover the weekend work. However, the development and production areas remained at the same resource levels of resource, which were under utilized.

(d) The main difference between the 1997 administrative structure and that proposed in the original audit was that all the trade-force reported directly to the shift supervisors (who were regarded as the resource owner). To arrange resources, the equipment supervisors had to proceed *via*. the shift supervisors. In some cases, the equipment supervisors had become planners and had lost touch both with the trade-force and with a knowledge of equipment condition – they spent limited time underground.

(e) There had been no movement towards the longer term improvements illustrated in Figure 10.10.

10.3.3 Life plans and preventive schedule

(f) The two mid-week downshifts were still used for longwall maintenance, even though the second-line resource worked at weekends *via*. a staggered day shift. The reason given for this was that the coal-shearing unit, and some others, would not operate the full 15 shifts without maintenance (although they do in the USA mines).

(g) There had only been a marginal improvement in the underground equipment life plans and no improvement whatsoever in the identification and design out of items exhibiting low reliability or high maintenance cost.

10.3.4 Recommendations – 1997

In the light of points (b) to (e) the structure could be modified, in the short term, to operate as indicated in Figure 10.13, this being essentially what was recommended in 1994 but with some clarification in order to overcome the problems identified in point (d).

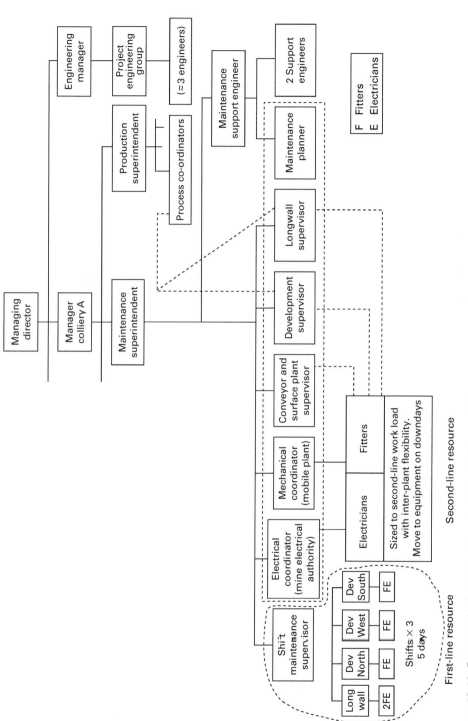

Figure 10.13 Proposed administrative structure (1997 – audit)

The first-line resource should continue to report to the shift supervisors and the second-line resource to the electrical supervisor and workshop supervisor (mechanical). These positions should, however, be renamed electrical co-ordinator and mechanical co-ordinator. When allocated to a downshift, both the shift resource and the second-line resource should report to the equipment supervisors responsible for the downshift (e.g. longwall downshift resources should report to the longwall supervisor on all matters associated with the longwall). This would be a matrix reporting structure, and if it is to function satisfactorily the supervisors must work as a team and link closely with the process co-ordinators – a development which, for its success, may well call for the running of a team-training exercise, off-site and also involving the shift managers. It would be essential that the equipment supervisors develop, for their own areas, improved life plans, spares lists and information systems.

Because of the importance of the longwall, an interdisciplinary team (a project manager plus representatives from engineering, maintenance, production, technical services and, where necessary, the operations workforce and trade-force) should be formed to carry out the following tasks:

● Identification of the reasons for loss of cutting time and low performance. This may well be a combination of poor maintenance, poor design and operation.
● Formulation of actions to overcome the listed problems.
● Formulation of a schedule for the implementation of the identified actions.

This should be a precursor to improving PRC at first level (involving operators, artisans and equipment supervisors), at second level (involving equipment supervisors and support engineers) and third level (involving support engineers and the CEG).

Many of the recommendations arising from the first audit had not been carried out because of shop floor industrial relations problems (see points (c) to (f) of the reaudit review above). The management's difficulties with problems of this kind were understandable. However, if the company wished to compete internationally then it was essential that these recommendations be pursued. At the time of the reaudit availability and cost performance were well below international benchmark standards for underground coal mining.

Review Questions

R10.3   The consultancy proposed the administrative structure shown in Figure 10.9. Particular emphasis was placed on making the supervisors equipment responsible and setting up a kind of matrix structure, *viz.*

Under normal operation the shift trades report to the shift supervisor and the day trades to the respective workshop supervisors. During down days all trades report to the equipment supervisor, e.g. longwall supervisor.

The progress report showed that this approach had not been adopted. Examine Figure 10.12 and explain what structure was being used and why it was not working well. Do you consider Figure 10.13 clarified sufficiently the way I expected the administration to work.

R10.4   Many of the key recommendations of the snapshot audit had not been adopted, e.g. the recommendation incorporated in Figure 10.10. Discuss what you consider were the main reason(s) for this.

Review Questions Guidelines

R10.1   Two main reasons were given. Firstly the longwall 'coal shearer' would not last 15 shifts without maintenance and secondly the management did not want to pay overtime rates at the weekend.

         The auditor felt that the shearer could be made to run 15 shifts with proper care and/or improved design-out effort. The 'overtime reason' did not make sense when compared with the lost profit of 2 shifts.

R10.2   The main advantages are:

- The utilization of the engineers should improve as a result of combining the engineering workload of the three collieries and the surface plant. It was recommended that the size of the group should match the core workload and contract engineers used for the peaks, e.g. project work.
- Standardization of equipment and overhaul procedure across the three collieries.
- Establishment of a master drawings library, master manuals library and updating system.
- Co-ordination of equipment shared across the collieries.

R10.3   Instead of adopting the matrix arrangement outlined in Figure 10.9 the Maintenance superintendent had allowed all the underground resource to report (at all times) to the shift supervisor. The equipment supervisors, e.g. longwall supervisor had become planners and did not spend much time underground even on the longwall down days. The shift supervisor owned the resources and 'called the shots'.

         Figure 10.13 tries to clarify how I considered it should work. The shift maintenance supervisor was responsible for all maintenance shift trades other than when they were involved in the down days. The day shift trade group ((g) of Figure 10.11) would report to the electrical and mechanical co-ordinators other than when they were involved on down days. During down days, e.g. the longwall down day, the down day trade group would report to the longwall supervisor.

R10.4   Two of the most important consultancy recommendations were:

- Operating the longwall for 15 shifts per week and carrying out the maintenance at weekends.
- Move towards operator–maintenance and self-directed work teams, see Figure 10.10.

Both of these recommendations were not acted upon because of potential industrial relations problems.

11 Case study 5: The do's and don'ts of maintenance teams

'Small enough to care but large enough to cope'

Anon

Chapter aims and outcomes

To identify the characteristics that can influence the successful operation of self-empowered maintenance teams.

On completion of this chapter you should be able to:

- identify the characteristics that make for the successful operation of maintenance teams;
- identify the characteristics that hinder their successful operation.

Chapter route map

Book divisions	This chapter in the division	Chapter topics
Introductory chapters	Chapter 8 Case study 1: Moving with the times	11.1 Introduction
Maintenance organizational concepts, trends and mapping	Chapter 9 Case studies 2 and 3: Cautionary tales of organizational change	11.2 Characteristics of teams at Fertec B
Maintenance organization case studies	Chapter 10 Case study 4: Reorganization of a colliery	11.3 Characteristics of teams at Cario
Total productive maintenance	Chapter 11 Case study 5: The do's and don'ts of maintenance teams	11.4 Improving team operation at Fertec B
Exercises	Chapter 12 Case study 6: A maintenance audit of an agricultural chemical plant	11.5 General comments on maintenance teams

Key words
• Maintenance team leader • Maintenance facilitator • Annualized hours • Greenfield site • Human factor profiling • User-friendly • Brownfield site • Trade-force skill profiling

11.1 Introduction

I recently carried out a major consultancy exercise for a company making industrial chemicals. They had two main plants, Fertec A making agricultural chemicals (the subject of Case study 6) and Fertec B making industrial explosives. Both Fertec A and Fertec B had for several years been using operator–maintenance teams and self-empowered maintenance teams. The consultancy exercise revealed that the teams were not working well – in particular those of Fertec B which is the subject of this case study. However, a sister plant Cario, within the same organization, and also making industrial explosives, was reported to be using teams successfully. I decided to carry out a simple benchmarking exercise, to compare the practices and characteristics of the teams of Fertec B with those of Cario.

The purpose of the study was to advise Fertec B on how to improve the operation of their teams. However, it will be instructive to use the case study to draw more general comments about the negative and positive factors that can affect the successful operation of maintenance teams.

11.2 Characteristics of teams at Fertec B

Fertec B is an integrated chemical complex made up of six plants. The administrative structure was decentralized and each plant considered as a distinct manufacturing unit. Figure 11.1 shows the administrative structure for one of the main plants and Figure 11.2 the corresponding resource structure.

The self-empowered teams had been introduced some 5 years earlier using the conventional wisdom of the time (see, e.g. Figure 11.3 for the guidelines for moving from traditional supervision to self-empowerment).

A team manager (see Figure 11.1) was brought in, mainly to help to resurrect the training process in the process teams. The following were some of my principle observations regarding the team operation:

- Twenty-five percent of the process teams were skilled maintenance artisans.
- The process teams undertook no first-line maintenance tasks despite this being a part of their responsibilities.

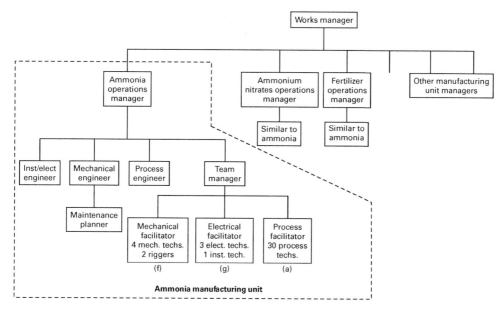

Figure 11.1 Administrative structure, ammonia manufacturing unit

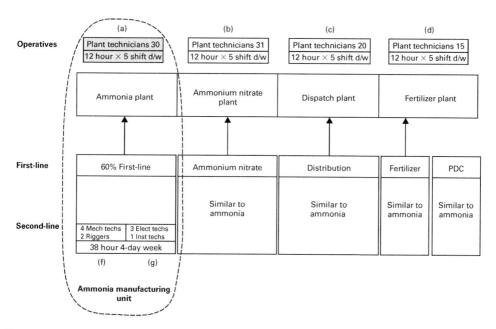

Figure 11.2 Resource structure, Fertec B

- The process teams seemed to be a law unto themselves with very negative human factors characteristics.
- The ratio of managers, planners and facilitators to 'on-the-tools' maintenance technicians in the maintenance teams was 2.8 to 1.

- The planner was introduced when a new computer system was installed; it was regarded as user unfriendly and the associated training was poor.
- The maintenance teams did not operate as self-empowered. They have reverted to the traditional structure (where the facilitator is in effect the supervisor).
- The facilitators and planner positions were permanencies.
- There was a genuine confusion over the roles of the planner, facilitator and some of the technicians. In addition, there was no a clear understanding of the roles of the plant engineer and process engineer and their relationship to the teams. Job descriptions were not used or were not available.
- The teams did not monitor themselves nor did they get involved in continuous improvement activities.
- Flexibility between mechanical trades, and between instrument and electrical trades, was good. Demarcation remained strong, however, between the two technological cultures (mechanical and electro-instrumentational).
- The maintenance technicians were rotated, on a 2 yearly basis, around the teams of the different plants.
- Maintenance technicians were on an annualized hours scheme; the process technicians were not (which did not help co-ordination when work was required out of hours).
- The plant was some 30 years old and gave rise to a great deal of first-line high priority maintenance. Because of their involvement with this, the maintenance teams (on days) only carried out 50% planned work per period – and it was the preventive routines that, as a result, were omitted.
- Out of hours emergency work was by a call-out system that was regularly used.

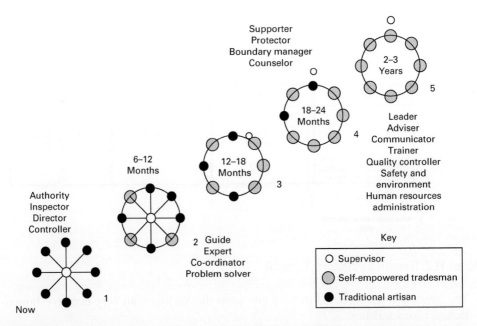

Figure 11.3 The five steps from traditional supervisors to self-empowered team with facilitator

- Team working had been introduced into a 'brownfield' site where there was a considerable history of industrial relations problems. There was no 'human factor profiling' in the selection of the team members. A considerable level of training was used at first but this rapidly fell away.

11.3 Characteristics of teams at Cario

Cario used a similar process to Fertec B but the plant was only 6 years old. The administration is shown in Figure 11.4 and the resource structure in Figure 11.5. As regards its team operations:

- Some 40% of the process teams were maintenance tradesmen.
- The process teams carried out production work plus minor preventive work (lubrication, inspection) and small emergency corrective jobs.
- The process teams (on shifts) had a good relationship with the maintenance teams and human factors were mainly positive. They were the highest paid of the shop floor workers.
- In each team there was a planner, team selected every 3 months, who spent little time on the tools. Overall, the ratio of planners to on-the-tools tradesmen was 5 to 1.
- The planners and tradesmen had been trained up to a high level of competence in the use of the computer system – which was far from being the most advanced of its kind and was not installed enterprise-wide (it *was* user-friendly, however, and *was* therefore used).
- The maintenance and process teams were self-empowered, accountability for duties and responsibilities being shared across each team.
- The two planners (electrical and mechanical) worked out of the same office. In effect, the planners became the facilitators and worked closely with the day shift production planner (PP) to co-ordinate plant outages, etc.

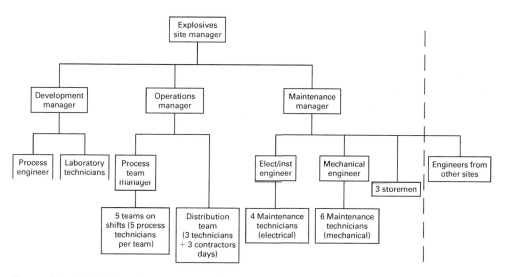

Figure 11.4 Administrative structure, Cario Ltd. explosives plant

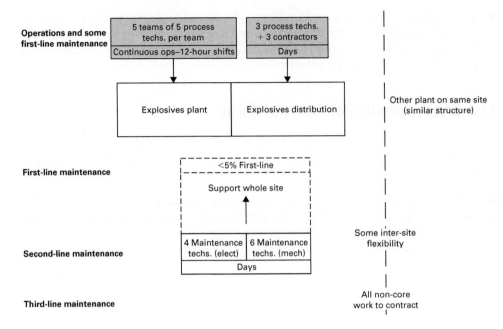

Figure 11.5 Resource structure, Cario Ltd. explosives plant

- The PP was a volunteer from shifts, for a 1-year period and without losing shift allowance, being replaced on shifts by a maintenance technician (with the necessary experience), and who in turn was replaced by a contractor. This exchange helped to break down the barriers between maintenance and production.
- The roles of the team, planner and engineer had been clearly identified and written up as job descriptions. The engineer considered himself to be very much part of the team.
- The teams spent a proportion of their time on design-out maintenance and improving life plans, these tasks being carried out in conjunction with the engineer.
- The electrical and mechanical teams worked separately but gave each other considerable assistance when needed.
- The payment scheme is the same for both the maintenance and the process teams.
- The plant was 6 years old and gave rise to very little high priority maintenance.
- Ninety-five percent of the teams' workload was planned. In fact, one of their objectives was have 'no call outs – ever!'.
- The teams had been formed during the commissioning phase of the plant. Profiling of skills and human factors was used to select the team members. Once the teams had been set up, a group from the company (including team members) were given the equivalent of 6 months full time training at a similar site overseas that was regarded as a world benchmark.

11.4 Improving team operation at Fertec B

Any conclusions drawn from this exercise must take into consideration that Cario was a relatively new plant (6 years old) and the 'teams' were set up on a green field site.

Fertec B is some 30 years old and the teams were set up around the same time as the Cario teams but on a brown field site. The maintenance workload profile of an old plant is very different from a new plant (lower level of high priority corrective work). Setting up teams on a green field site is much easier (and usually more successful) than on a brown field site where considerable 'human factor baggage' has to be taken across the organizational change.

It must also be pointed out that this was not a full benchmarking exercise. Only a limited number of benchmarks were used, *viz.*:

- percentage of artisans in operator–maintainer teams,
- ratio of planner–facilitators to 'on-the-tools' tradesmen,
- maintenance team planned work (expressed as a percentage of each period),
- maintenance team emergency work (expressed as a percentage of each period).

Even taking these points into consideration the 'performance gap' between the teams at Cario and those at Fertec was considerable.

Fertec B process teams were not working well and were refusing to carryout first-line work. Consequently, the day maintenance teams were carrying out all such work, which was *disrupting their planned* work. The preventive work was being neglected, causing more corrective work and a downward spiral of plant condition. We recommended that a key action would be to *insist* that the process teams carried out first-line work. This would need a careful study of the process teams work profile and a resurrection of the skills training. It might also be necessary to restructure the teams, perhaps removing the 'bad apples' – all of which might have worsened industrial relations, which was the reason these actions had not been taken sooner.

An additional recommendation was that the duties, responsibilities and accountability of the teams, and their relationships with other members of the administration should be clearly defined. These recommendations had little to do with problems of 'team structure and operation'; *they were associated with poor general management.*

In the longer term other recommendations were made, e.g. bringing operations and maintenance into the same payment system; improving computer training so that the facilitator does the planning, etc.

11.5 General comments on maintenance teams

Before setting up teams it is important to:

- Study the workload and skills profile of both the operators and the first-line maintainers to ensure an appropriate size and skills match.
- Study the 'human factor' profile of team members to ensure compatibility with the required team ethos.
- Ensure that the team members have been trained to use the necessary maintenance systems, e.g. documentation, stores.
- Ensure that the duties, responsibilities, accountability of the team and the relationship of the team with other personnel have been clearly defined.
- Ensure that the teams have been trained in the mechanics of team operation, e.g. division of responsibilities and duties, team and individual decision-making, planning, objective setting and performance control, discipline, continuous improvement, etc.

For teams to operate successfully the following points should also be bourne in mind:

- It is advisable to use a common form of payment system (shift allowances, overtime, annualized hours, etc.) across operation and maintenance.
- Ensure that the operation, structure and standards of team performance are seen to be monitored by management.

Reference

1. *Lee, C., Background Teamwork, *The Training Journal, New York*, 1990.

Review Questions

R11.1   Fertec B clearly had problems while Cario was operating well. It could be argued that Fertec B was always going to find it more difficult to operate teams successfully than Cario. What was the 'key difference' between these companies that might justify this statement. Do you consider this 'key difference' flawed the benchmarking exercise?

R11.2   Some teams operate with permanent, management appointed team leaders and other with fixed term, team appointed team leaders. List the advantages and disadvantages and indicate your preference.

R11.3   A paper by Lee [1], describes the characteristics of a self-directed work team as follows:

(a)   They usually have 8–15 members who are responsible for producing a well-defined output – either a product or a service.

(b)   Team members learn all the tasks their team must perform, and each person rotates from job to job. As a result, most organizations that adopt 'work teams' implement some sort of pay-for-knowledge system.

(c)   As the team matures, it takes over supervisory and support responsibilities such as scheduling, hiring, firing, training, troubleshooting, maintenance, ordering materials, and so on.

(d)   Because the team takes on supervisory, and in some cases management tasks, the number of management layers decreases until the organization takes on a flattened, informal structure.

Most of the maintenance teams and operator–maintenance teams the author has investigated have not worked well. This includes Fertec A (see Case study 6 of Chapter 12), Fertec B and more recently teams used by a large cement plant. The main problems seemed to be associated with the characteristics listed in (c) and (d) above. Using the work of this module coupled with your own experience outline explain why you think this is the case.

Exercise

E11.1   Now use the information from this chapter, in conjunction with Chapter 1, in order to answer Exercise E14.2 in Chapter 14 of this book. (The answer to Exercise E14.2 is at the end of Chapter 14.)

Review Questions Guidelines

R11.1 The essential difference between the two companies was that Fertec was setting up teams on a 'brownfield site' with considerable industrial relations history. Cario was a green field site. This key difference limited the possible
benefits of the benchmarking exercise. However, Fertec B was still able to learn
much from the exercise, e.g. the need to clearly define the responsibilities and
relationship of the team with other members of the ammonia plant administrative structure.

R11.2 The author has come across some companies 'who swear by permanent team
leaders' and others 'who swear by a rotating team leader'.

   I would regard the fixed period, team appointed team leader as part of the
true team ethos and culture. When the team has been properly structured and
the team members carefully selected, taking into consideration human factor
characteristics, the team appointed team leader works well. The problems with
this arrangement is when there are human factor problems and/or skill deficiencies within the team (which seems to be mostly the case), e.g. the team
leader may have to discipline an individual who subsequently may become
team leader.

   The point being made is that in a Fertec B situation it might be advanta-
geous for the management to select and appoint the individual team member
who they feel will be the 'best team leader'. It could then be argued (rightly)
that this is moving back someway towards the traditional supervisor. Perhaps
in the situation of Fertec B find themselves this may well be a possible course
of action.

R11.3 The answer to this question is linked in part to the answer to R11.2. If the team
has one or more members who are poor tradesmen and/or have human factor
problems then without discipline, advice and guidance the team can become a
'law unto themselves'. Management can, and do, lose control of the team (the
author has noted that it is often after such an experience that management set
up a company–contractor alliance).

12 Case study 6: Maintenance audit of an agricultural chemical plant

'A man convinced against his will, is of the same opinion still.'

Lawrence J. Peter

Chapter aims and outcomes

The main purpose of this case study is to show how the business-centered maintenance methodology can be used to audit the maintenance strategy and organization of a large complex chemical plant. Whilst the actual audit covered all aspects of maintenance management at the chemical plant concerned, this study will focus on the maintenance strategy and on the mapping, modeling and re-engineering of the maintenance organization.

The case study is also used as a vehicle for review questions arising from the preceding chapters.

Chapter route map

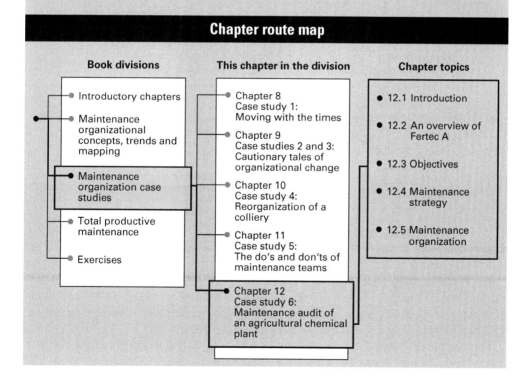

Book divisions
- Introductory chapters
- Maintenance organizational concepts, trends and mapping
- Maintenance organization case studies
- Total productive maintenance
- Exercises

This chapter in the division
- Chapter 8
  Case study 1:
  Moving with the times
- Chapter 9
  Case studies 2 and 3:
  Cautionary tales of organizational change
- Chapter 10
  Case study 4:
  Reorganization of a colliery
- Chapter 11
  Case study 5:
  The do's and don'ts of maintenance teams
- Chapter 12
  Case study 6:
  Maintenance audit of an agricultural chemical plant

Chapter topics
- 12.1 Introduction
- 12.2 An overview of Fertec A
- 12.3 Objectives
- 12.4 Maintenance strategy
- 12.5 Maintenance organization

12.1 Introduction

This case study concerns a full audit of Fertec A, a company manufacturing fertilizers for the agricultural industry. Fertec is made up of two plants: Plant A and Plant B located in different cities. This audit was carried out on the maintenance department of Plant A. Fertec is owned by a parent company Cario.

12.2 An overview of Fertec A

The plant layout of Fertec A is shown in Figure 12.1 indicating the location of the main process areas and the maintenance resources (labor and parts store). The labor resources are identified by a letter code that carried through to the organizational models.

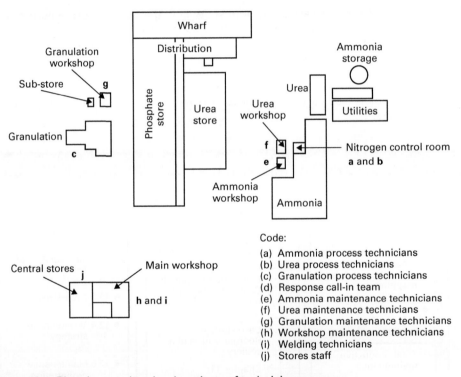

Code:
(a) Ammonia process technicians
(b) Urea process technicians
(c) Granulation process technicians
(d) Response call-in team
(e) Ammonia maintenance technicians
(f) Urea maintenance technicians
(g) Granulation maintenance technicians
(h) Workshop maintenance technicians
(i) Welding technicians
(j) Stores staff

Figure 12.1 Plant layout showing locations of technician resource

An outline process flow diagram is shown in Figure 12.2. The ammonia plant is production critical since it supplies the other plants with ammonia and CO_2. There is some inter-stage ammonia storage. The plant can also be supplied with imported ammonia, which is much more expensive than that produced internally.

The complex is some 30 years old but has been up-rated especially in the areas of instrumentation and control systems. The urea plant is currently being up-rated. The cost of energy (natural gas) is a very high percentage of the ammonia-plant-operating

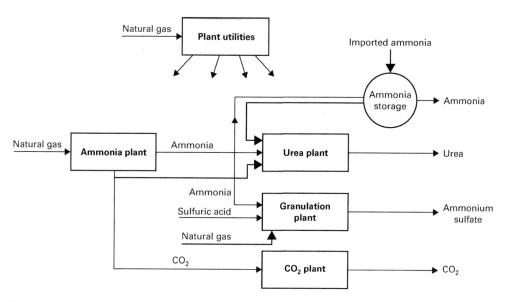

Figure 12.2 Outline process flow diagram of Fertec Ltd

cost. The energy efficiency of the ammonia plant is low compared to the worlds best because it has 'old technology'. The reliability of the plant has a major influence on energy efficiency and needs to be improved.

Fertec is one of a number of companies that belong to the parent group Cario. The senior management structure of Fertec A and its relationship with Fertec B and its parent group is shown in Figure 12.3. It should be noted that the Reliability Manager has responsibilities that cover both Fertec Plant A and Fertec Plant B.

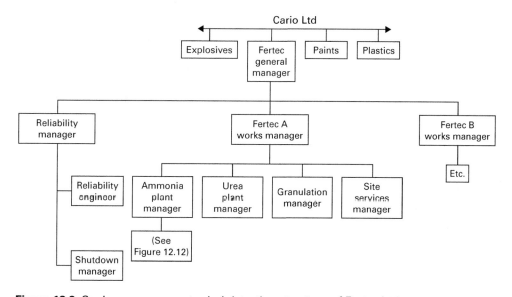

Figure 12.3 Senior management administrative structure of Fertec Ltd

A number of the senior positions in Fertec A had recently changed and had been filled with a young forward-looking team. The new team commissioned the audit because they felt that in order to remain competitive they needed to improve plant reliability and at the same time reduce maintenance costs. In addition, they considered that there were 'attitude issues' that needed resolving both with respect to 'trade-force performance' and 'maintenance management standards'. The new management of Fertec A wanted answers to the following fundamental questions:

- Taking into consideration the ageing nature of the plant 'How effective is the maintenance strategy' (life plans, preventive schedule, etc.) in giving Fertec what they want in terms of reliability and output?
- How organizationally efficient is the maintenance department in providing this service at 'best cost'.

12.3 Objectives

An outline of the process of setting objectives and business plans is shown in Figure 12.4. This is a form of management-by-objectives (MBO) closely allied to the authors business-centered maintenance approach.

The Fertec A senior management group (to include the group Reliability Manager) establish a 'works objectives and performance statement'. Objectives at this level are concerned with manufacturing performance. Maintenance objectives are set for those areas that directly affect manufacturing. For example, an objective is set to improve the availability of the ammonia plant from its current level of 88% to match the world best at 96%. Objectives are also set to improve energy efficiency.

At plant manager level the works objectives are translated into local plant objectives through three separate but linked objective/action statements, *viz.* the people plan (concerns organizational efficiency objectives), the performance plan (concerns effectiveness objectives) and the safety plans. For example, in the case of the performance plan reliability improvement objectives are set for the critical units of the ammonia plant (e.g. the syn-gas compressor, SGC). In addition a series of tasks are identified to achieve these improvements, e.g. introduce the use of 'reliability centered maintenance'. These actions are allocated to specific engineers and supervisors.

The actions are reviewed by the plant manager at 3-monthly intervals. Similarly the works objectives and actions are reviewed by the senior management group at 3-monthly intervals.

In addition, to this procedure each of the managers, engineers and supervisors are set annual objectives within which are included many of the objectives/actions of Figure 12.4.

12.3.1 Comments on objectives

The auditors were impressed with the objectives and the objective setting procedure. It had only recently been set up and required time to 'bed in'. The main criticism was that

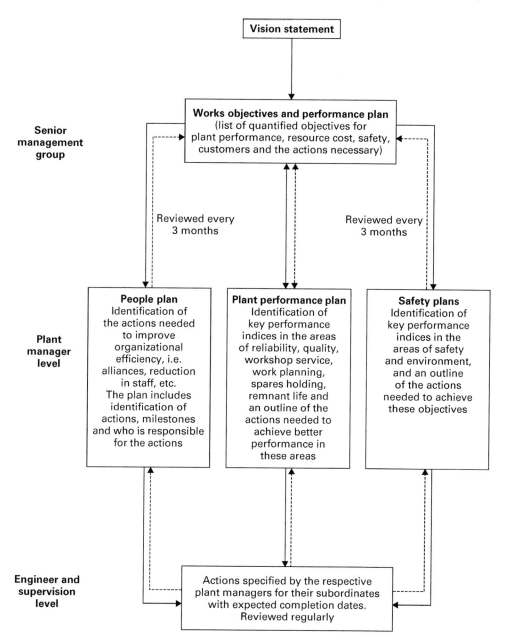

Figure 12.4 MBO at Fertec Ltd

the procedure had not been brought down to the 'self-empowered teams'. The auditors were told that this would have to wait until the 'negative human factors' of the process teams improved.

12.4 Maintenance strategy

12.4.1 Plant-operating characteristics

The outline process flow diagram for the Fertec A complex was shown in Figure 12.2. The ammonia plant is the rate determining process, it is production limited. Ammonia plant failures can only be made up via imported ammonia (which is costly). The auditors were given the figure that a 1% loss of annual availability translates into many hundreds of thousands of pounds. The ammonia storage tank gives some protection (days) to the ammonia plant in the case of urea plant downtime. Failure of the ammonia plant also brings out the urea and CO_2 plants. The granulation plant is largely independent of the rest of the complex. In terms of downtime cost the following is the rule of thumb:

| Ammonia plant downtime costs | >> | Urea plant downtime costs | >> | Granulation plant downtime costs |

This section of the audit will be limited to the ammonia plant (the audit covered the strategy for the full complex).

An outline process flow diagram for the ammonia plant is shown in Figure 12.5. At unit level it can be seen that plant is a series process with limited redundancy. There are many units whose failure can affect the output of the ammonia plant and those that present the highest risk of failure are regarded as *critical*, e.g. the SGC.

12.4.2 Ammonia plant maintenance strategy

The current strategy is to operate the ammonia–urea–CO_2 complex for a 4-year period before a 4-week shutdown. This operating period is a function of statutory inspection of the pressure vessels (now self-regulating) and the need to inspect/repair/replace other plant units whose reliability falls off after 4 years. The timing of the shutdown is set to coincide with low annual urea demand.

The 4-year operating period has been determined by the reliability group based mainly on an empirical study of the 'risk of failure factor' vs the period of operation of pressure vessels before inspection (i.e. how long can we operate the plant for without affecting safety integrity?). They have established that the critical 20% of units carry 80% of the 'risk factor'.

Continuous vibration monitoring is used on the large machines mainly for operational safety but also for maintenance prediction. A number of other online monitoring techniques are used both on the large machines and the pressure vessels to aid condition-based maintenance.

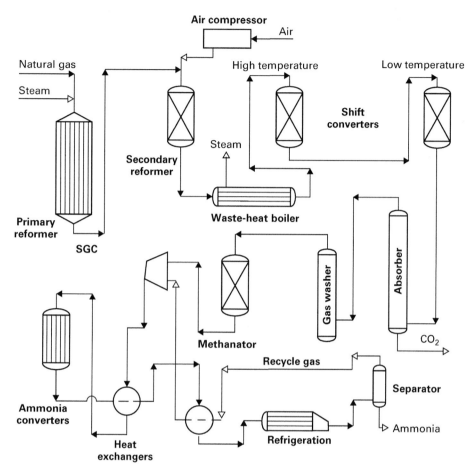

Figure 12.5 Outline of process flow model of the ammonia plant

The ammonia plant strategy has its center of gravity well toward condition-based maintenance. While the plant is operated for a 4-year period the shutdown workscope is mainly based on the work predicted from:

- online inspections;
- offline inspections from previous shutdowns;
- history from previous shutdowns.

The duration of the shutdown is normally 4 weeks which includes a 'dead-week' needed for shutdown and start-up. The critical path during the shutdown is the reformer inspection (pressure vessel) and the SGC (large machine).

In terms of maintenance characteristics the plant can be categorized into large machines, pressure vessels, ancillary equipment (e.g. duplicate pumps and electrical/instrumentation equipment).

Life plan for the SGC

A schematic diagram of the SGC is shown in Figure 12.6 which includes details on spare parts holding. The condition-based maintenance carried out on the machine is shown in Table 12.1. The machine is expected to operate continuously for 4 years. The shutdown workscope is established from previous shutdown history, deferred corrective maintenance

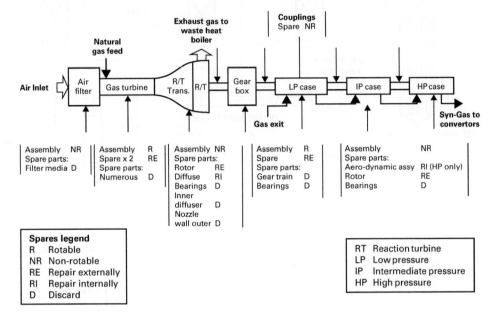

Figure 12.6 Schematic diagram of a SGC

Table 12.1 Syn-gas compressor condition-based maintenance

Bently Nevada system
● This sophisticated system records various data and has the ability to combine inputs to produce multidimensional displays.
● It produces data in real time plus long and short trend patterns.
● Items measured include:
– Radial shaft displacement
– Axial shaft displacement
– Bearing temperatures: radial and thrust
– Accelerometer readings (gearbox and gas turbine only)
– Shaft orbit readings (multidimensional)
– Shaft phase angle (multidimensional)
● In addition to the above approximately 200 process variables are monitored.
● All the above have alarm points and key items have shutdown settings.
Oil analysis
● Routine oil analysis.
Seal bypass test (compressor only)
● Routine seal accumulator drop test.
Oil debris analysis (gas turbine only)
● Online continuous monitoring.

and the online monitoring information. Additional work is identified as a result of the offline inspection during the shutdown (unplanned).

Standard job procedures are in use, e.g. inspection-overhauls of the high-pressure case. These are comprehensive and detailed. The machine history records have not been formalized, are hard copy and reside in a number of locations looked after by a number of different people. The life plan has not been formally documented.

Although not shown in Figure 12.6 there is an automatic lubrication system for the SGC. There are simple documented service routines associated with this system which have been computerized.

Life plan for pressure vessels

The generic life plan for pressure vessels is based on condition-based maintenance. The maintenance carried out during the shutdown is based on condition prediction from previous shutdown history and on any online non-destructive testing (NDT) monitoring performed between the shutdowns. Additional work is identified from inspections carried out (open and closed) during the shutdown.

There are variations on the life plans to suit specific vessels. Those that are high on the 'risk factor analysis' (see Table 12.2 for the basis of the calculations) are subjected to an in-depth analysis to up-rate the life plan. Every pipe, weld and hot support that might give rise to failure is examined to develop the most appropriate NDT technique and inspection methodology (see Figure 12.7 for an example).

This inspection-based life plan is backed up with a comprehensive computerized information base, the pressure systems database which includes for each vessel the following information:

- Process and mechanical data sheets.
- Inspection history.
- Inspection procedures and test plans (see Figure 12.7).
- The vessel life plan (which has involved risk assessment and remnant life analysis).
- Hard copy reports of previous shutdown case studies.

This computerized database is independent of the recently purchased company-wide computerized enterprise system.

Ancillary equipment*

The life plans of such equipment is based on 'service routines' which are embedded in the main computerized maintenance system (linked to other company systems). A typical routine would be as follows:

> *Pump preventive routine*: 3 monthly frequency
> - Oil change
> - General inspection
>   - Check coupling
>   - Lift-bearing cap, etc.

---

*For example, pumps, pressure relief valves, control valves, etc. – equipment that can be maintained outside of the main shutdowns.

Table 12.2 Assessment of criticality ranking for a pressure vessel

Pressure vessel CF601 sulfur drum		
Likelihood of failure		
Is there a known active metallurgic damage mechanism?	No known damage mechanism	0
Is there a known active mechanical damage mechanism?	Vibration fatigue	2
Have the inspections been effective?	Ineffective, no confidence	5
What is the frequency of inspections?	More than 30 years	4
How reliable are the control systems + operating parameters?	Poor	1
Are the vessel limits exceeded in plant upsets?	Yes	1
Are the vessel's limits exceeded in normal operation?	No	0
Have process conditions changed (but still within design)?	Yes	1
Are the vessel limits exceeded in plant startups or shutdowns?	Yes	1
Are the vessel's protective systems effective?	No	1
As detection of damage previously warranted further investigation?	Yes	1
Have repairs been required in the past?	Yes	1
How old is the vessel?	Over 30 years	3
Is the vessel original design to current standards?	No	1
Is the vessel material specification to currently acceptable?	No	1
Total		23
Consequence of failure		
Is the vessel contents . . .?	A lethal gas?	7
What is the temperature of the vessel contents?	Above 500°C	3
Are the contents flammable if they leak?	Auto ignites	3
Would a failure promote consequential damage elsewhere in plant?	Yes	5
Would emergency services help be required to contain a situation?	Yes	3
What is the vessel pressure?	Above 10 MPa	3
What is the volume of worst rating contents in the vessel?	Over 1000 m^3	8
Will a leak cause secondary damage to other equipment?	Yes	1
What is the distance to internal personnel?	Less than 10 m	2
What is the distance to the general public?	Less than 10 m	4
What is the business impact of a vessel failure?	Over £10,000,000	11
Total		50
Criticality risk ranking number = 23 × 50 = 1150		

EQUIPMENT NUMBER: T503   PRESENT CLOSED FREQUENCY: 4 years   PRESENT OPEN FREQUENCY: Yearly   INSTALLATION DATE: 01-01-1968

DESCRIPTION: Ion Exchanger   VOLUME:

OPEN INSPECTIONS

Equipment item	Visual	Ultrasonic	Radiography	Mag/part	Dye/pen	Thermovision	Vibration	AE	Attenuation	Metallographic	Other
2RK65 to Tray Ring Weld	Yes				x						
Alignment	Yes										
Associated piping	Yes		O/head line only								
Davit/Lifting devices	Yes	Prior to S/D		Prior to S/D							
Earth connection	Yes										
Heads	Yes	Bottom									
Instrumentation	Yes	Evidence of bulging									
Insulation	Yes										
Internal liner	Yes	4 per petal			To Bot Tray						
Manway and bolting	Yes	Manway plant									
Nozzles	Yes	Manway liners		Internal							
Platforms/handrails	Yes										
Pressure relief devices	Yes										
Protective coating	Yes										
Shell	Yes	Lower 1.5/m			Liner welds						
Supports and bolting	Yes										
Thermowells and sockets	Yes				x						
Vessel bolting	Yes										
Vibration	Yes										
Welded joints	Yes										

Figure 12.7 Open inspection test plans for exchanger

These routines were established some 20 years ago and are in need of review. Many of the routines have been put into the new computer system without review. Vibration monitoring is also used for the rotating equipment in this category (mainly portable instruments but some periodic permanently wired systems).

In general the monitoring procedures have not been tied into the routines.

In addition to the routines a 'contract lubrication system' has been introduced operated by one of the large oil companies.

The auditors noted that the operating procedure for units with duplicated drives was as follows:

- Electric motors: change over weekly
- Electric motors and steam turbine: use the electric motor and proof test the turbine weekly.

Electrical/instrumentation equipment

The life plans are based on clean, inspect and calibrate where necessary. These preventive routines were set up many years ago and need review. It was noted that much of the more recent equipment, e.g. PLCs, were not included on the routines and had not been reviewed. The large electrical machines had no documented life plan. More importantly the whole of the electrical/instrumentation equipment had not been reviewed in terms of 'spares criticality'. The information base data (job specification, modification and plant history, etc.) was either on hard copy (in a number of different locations) or held in peoples' memory.

Comments and recommendations on strategy:

(i) When auditing maintenance strategy the auditors ask the interviewees their opinion of preventive maintenance in use in their plant. The following are some of the comments:

> *The main shutdowns are carried out well – this is where most of our preventive work is carried out.*
> *We must tie up the preventive routines with vibration monitoring.*
> *Routines are used as fill in work – they are not regarded as important.*
> *The electrical routines are in peoples heads – they must be documented.*
> *The refrigeration units in the plant services are in poor condition and are operation critical – we must sort out our spares.*
> *We should rethink our operating period – the USA plants do it differently and at lower cost.*
> *Our condition monitoring is heading toward international benchmark levels.*
> *We should be replacing old equipment – mono pumps out and granfar pumps in.*
> *Our life plans for large machines are not right yet – we should seek help from the original equipment manufacturer (OEM).*

(ii) The auditors observed that the operating period of the plant has been extended from 2 to 4 years and will shortly extend to 4½ years. This is due to the considerable efforts of the reliability group in the area of pressure vessel maintenance (NDT techniques, good computerized information base, criticality and remnant life analysis, metallurgic knowledge).

However, it appears from ammonia plant failure data that the main production losses occur as a result of problems with the large machines. The data shows that the large machines fail more often and more randomly than the pressure vessels with a mean-time-to-failure (m.t.t.f.) < 4 years. This is not surprising since they are up to 30-years old and are a complex arrangement of many rapidly moving parts. Over the years as a result of numerous overhauls, often carried out without standard job procedures, their condition appears to have fallen away from the OEM standard specification. This leads to the following comments:

(a) If the company are to get the best out of a 4½-year operating period they will have to bring the condition of the large machines back to an 'as new standard' – perhaps with the assistance of the OEM. Since the machines are old this is almost equivalent to a life extension decision and relates to the probable remaining life of the plant.

(b) It is recommended that the company use the top-down–bottom-up approach TDBUA [1] to review the life plans of the large machines. This should include a criticality analysis of the spares holding. In addition the large machine 'plant information base' should be brought up to the same standard as the pressure vessel database.

(iii) The auditors are aware from discussions with the company engineers that companies in the USA operate a different maintenance strategy than that outlined above. For example, some companies use an operating time of 2-year and a 2-week duration shutdown.

Many factors affect this decision to include:

- The period for statutory pressure vessel inspection (now self-regulating).
- The shortest expected running time of other critical units before requiring maintenance (e.g. the large machines).
- The remaining life of the plant (remnant life), in this case 7 years (the existing gas contract is 7 years) and uncertain.
- The market demand (assumes the plant is production limited).
- The shutdown duration needed to complete the workscope. This must take into consideration a 1-week dead period for shutdown and start-up. (Thus a 2-week shutdown with a 2-year operating period has only 66% of the maintenance time of a 4-week shutdown with a 4-year operating period, see Figure 12.8.)

The maintenance objective for this situation can be expressed as follows:

Minimize Σ Planned downtime costs + unplanned downtime costs

This is a complex problem involving information not available to the auditors, e.g. Why is the dead period apparently shorter in the USA? Can the 4-week shutdown duration be reduced by shortening the reformer critical path? If so, how much would this cost? Do the large machines need realignment/offline inspection at 2 years?

In spite of this (and without the use of statistical/cost modeling) it is the auditors opinion that if the company comply with the points listed in (ii)a and (ii)b they are moving toward an optimum maintenance strategy.

(iv) It is recommended that 'opportunity scheduling' should be used to compliment the existing strategy, i.e. when a failure of a plant unit occurs unexpectedly all other

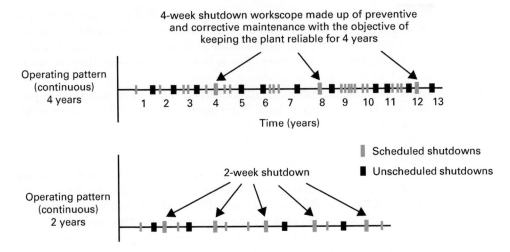

Figure 12.8 Illustration of strategy based on 4- and 2-year operating periods

outstanding work should be looked at with a view to carrying it out in the 'opportunity window'. The auditors accept that the planning system will also have to improve if opportunity scheduling is to be used.

(v) Both mechanical and electrical/instrumentation routines are in need of review and update. Such a review should use the TDBUA to focus the routines on necessary and worthwhile tasks. In addition to modify as necessary the policy and frequency of routines, e.g. the changing of replace/repair of pumps/motors from fixed time to condition based.

12.5 Maintenance organization

12.5.1 Introduction

The methodology model (see Figure 1.1) showed that the maintenance organization is best understood by analyzing it into its resource structure and administrative structure.

12.5.2 The maintenance resource structure

A model of the resource structure for Fertec A is shown in Figure 12.9 and the inventory of resources is shown in Table 12.3. See also the plant layout of Figure 12.1 which indicates the location of the trade groups. The following are the main characteristics of the structure:

- Each of the maintenance and process group, e.g. the ammonia maintenance group, are intended to be self-managed and co-ordinated by their facilitator.
- The process groups include 25% artisans and are expected to carryout some first-line maintenance. In fact these groups carryout little or no maintenance.

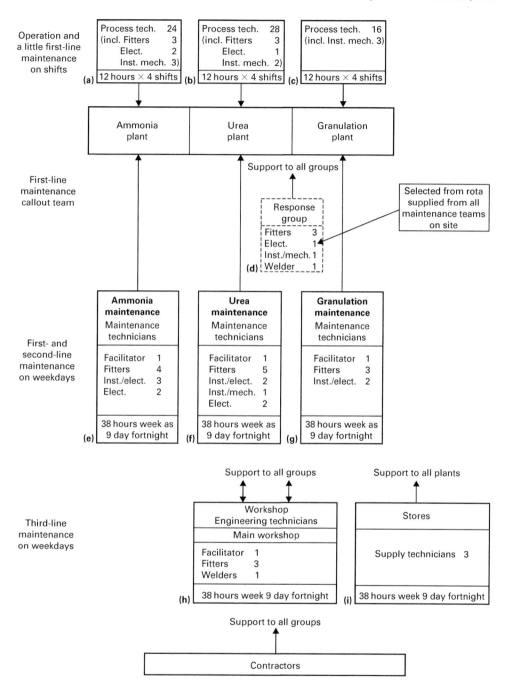

Figure 12.9 Fertec A resource structure

Table 12.3 Maintenance resource inventory

Resource categories	
Technicians	
Maintenance facilitator	4
Fitter	15
Instrumental/electrical	7
Instrumental machinist	1
Electrician	4
Welder	2
Semi-skilled	
Stores technicians	3
Subtotals	
Total maintenance facilitators	5
Total technicians (less facilitators)	29
Total semi-skilled resources	3
Total skilled and semi-skilled resources	32
Total maintenance resources	37
Total process technicians	68
Ratios	
Operators per maintenance employee	1.85
Percent semi-skilled of maintenance resource	8%
Total skilled and semi-skilled resource facilitators	6.5
Total skilled technicians/facilitators	5.8

- The out of hours priority maintenance is carried out by the response group (d) supplied on rota by all engineering technicians on site. These maintenance technicians are on an annualized-hours agreement and do not get paid for callouts. The average overtime is about 5%. In order to enable all maintenance technicians to support the response group they are rotated across plants on a 2-yearly periodicity.
- The plant located maintenance day-groups, e.g. the ammonia maintenance group carry out most of the first- and second-line maintenance work in their own areas. They are supplemented by an average 25% contract labor to ensure the higher-priority second-line work is complete. In spite of the use of contract labor the lower-priority corrective and the preventive routines are neglected.
- Inter-plant flexibility is encouraged by the management to cover the smaller over-hauls. In general such sideways movement is resisted by the technicians.
- The area maintenance groups are supported in terms of fabrication, machining, recon-ditioning and spares by the workshop facilities, stores and external contract work-shops (see Figure 12.10 for the reconditioning cycle).
- The workshop technicians also provide a maintenance service to non-manufacturing facilities.
- The 4-yearly shutdown (third-line work) involves an influx of many hundreds of arti-sans for a 4-week period to supplement the internal labor. The resource structure changes to a 'shutdown structure' for this period.

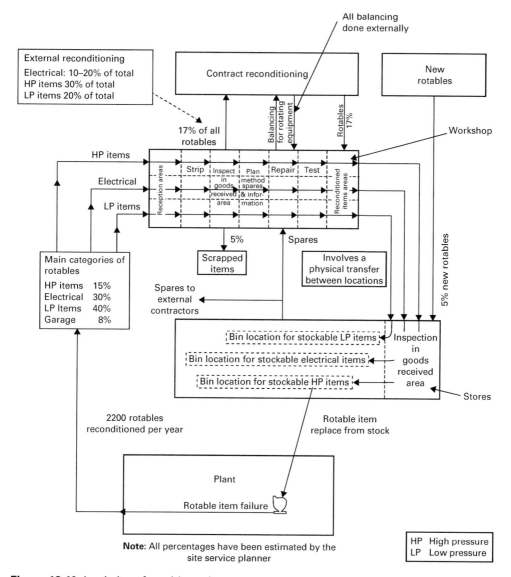

Figure 12.10 Logistics of rotable maintenance

- The management has recently recognized the need for 'engineering skills training' and introduced a comprehensive list of 'goal-oriented learning' units.
- A number of surveys were carried out to include the following: Production perceptions of maintenance service, in general the maintenance service was regarded as just satisfactory.
- Maintenance technicians' – 'human factors', moral and goodwill toward management was low and equipment ownership less than satisfactory. There was a feeling of strong vertical polarization.

- An alliance between the company and an internationally known contractor has been proposed to carry out all non-core maintenance activities. This will include all workshop services, spare parts management and other non-maintenance activities.
- There is little or no skills flexibility between the mechanical trades and the electrical/instrumentation trades in spite of the two groups having a common facilitator and planner.

Recommendations

Taking into consideration the resource structure comments the auditors recommended the following alternative modifications to the existing structure.

Proposal A

The existing structure is retained with a transfer of as much of the first-line work as possible to the process technician teams. This will involve a study of the workload of both the maintenance and the process teams. The existing plant-based maintenance teams would handle the residual first- and the second-line work. In addition improvements should be sought in the following areas:

- Increase in skills flexibility between the mechanical and the electrical/instrumentation trades.
- Improved use of inter-plant flexibility across ammonia/urea/granulation via improved work scheduling.
- The maintenance team facilitators should act as facilitator-planners.
- The workshop and other non-core maintenance to be carried out by a contractor alliance.

Proposal B

The existing structure is changed to that shown in Figure 12.11. For the ammonia and urea plants the first-line work is carried out by a combination of the process technician teams and a skeleton plant-based first-line day maintenance cover. The second-line work is carried out by a nitrogen area group (ammonia plus urea) backed by the workshop contractor alliance.

The above modifications should be proceeded by a study of the workload of both the process technician teams and the maintenance technician teams (What is the true level of the maintenance first-line work? What kind of work should they do?)

This would enable the identification of the level and type of maintenance work that the process technician teams should be able to carry out effectively after appropriate training. This in turn would allow the correct manning levels for the first-line skeleton cover and the second-line maintenance teams to be established. In the longer term in Proposals A and B it may be that the process teams could cover all of the first-line work. *In addition the possibility of linking the second-line groups into the proposed alliance should be considered.*

12.5.3 The maintenance administrative structure

The senior management administrative structure for Fertec A was shown in Figure 12.3. The administrative structure for the ammonia plant is shown in Figure 12.12. The (urea

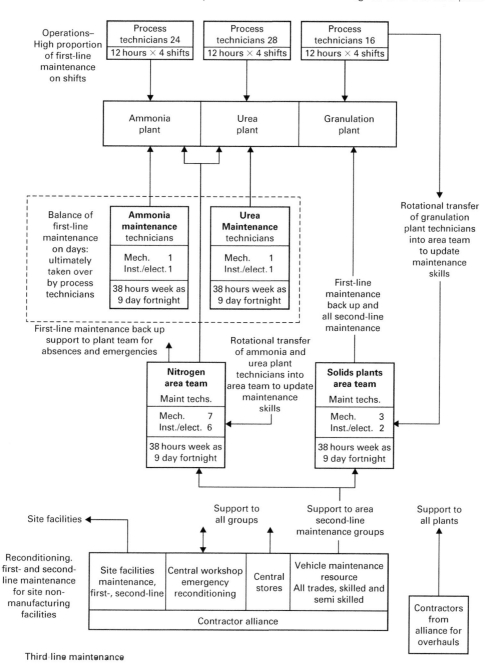

Figure 12.11 Proposal for modified resource structure

and granulation structures are similar) site services is shown in Figure 12.13 and the reliability group is shown in Figure 12.14. An inventory of the staff is shown in Table 12.4. These structures should be looked at in conjunction with the resource structure of Figure 12.9, the plant layout of Figure 12.1 and the trade-force inventory of Table 12.3.

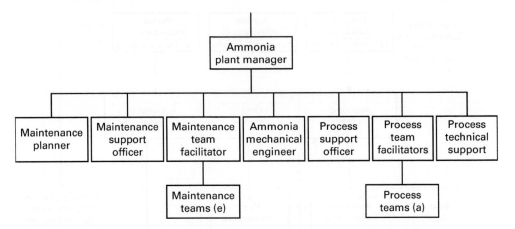

Figure 12.12 Ammonia plant administrative structure

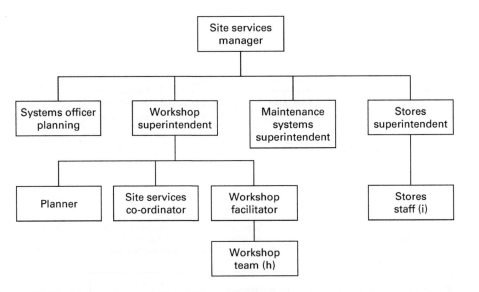

Figure 12.13 Site services administrative structure

The following are the main characteristics of the structure:

- The structure is built around the idea of semi-autonomous manufacturing units, e.g. the ammonia manufacturing unit (see Figure 12.12). Each of the Plant Managers report to the Fertec A Works Manager who is solely accountable for all operational activities on site.
- The manufacturing units are supported (in both Fertec sites) by the Reliability Department via a matrix structure (see Figure 12.15). In general the auditors found the co-ordinating mechanisms across this matrix to be satisfactory.

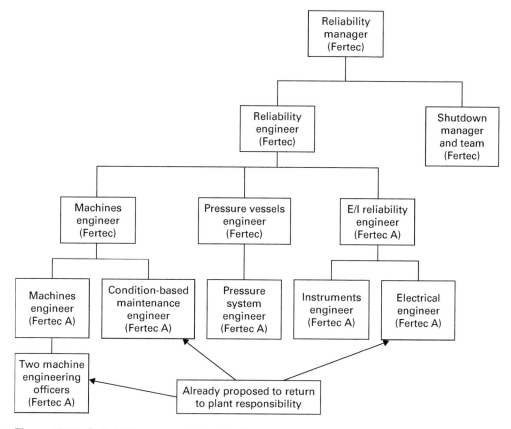

Figure 12.14 Reliability group administrative structure

- Within the manufacturing units (e.g. see Figure 12.12), the process technicians (to include 25% artisans) report via their Facilitator to the Plant Manager.
- The maintenance technicians also report via their Facilitator to the Plant Manager. In the case of the ammonia plant the team is made up of 10 artisans. The operation of the teams has reverted to the traditional structure with the Facilitator acting as the supervisor and the planner carrying out the clerical duties. In addition technical support comes via the mechanical engineer and mechanical support officers. The electrical/instrument technicians feel vulnerable since no electrical engineer is employed within the works structure.
- The site services were only looked at in outline because a decision had already been taken to carry this function out via a contractor alliance.

Recommendations

Taking into consideration the comments on the administrative structure above and the resource structure proposals, the auditors recommend the following two alternative structures.

Table 12.4 Maintenance staff inventory

Staff categories	
Plant or site services manager	4
Mechanical engineer	4
Maintenance support officer	2
Maintenance planner	4
Maintenance team facilitator (in team)	4
Workshop superintendent	1
Maintenance systems superintendent	1
Systems officer planning	1
Site services co-facilitator	1
QA officer	1
Total maintenance staff	23
Subtotals	
Total managerial staff	4
Total supervisory	5
Total planning staff	5
Total engineers (non-managing)	4
Total special duties	5
Ratios	
Supervisors per manager	1.5
Supervised per planner	7.4
Engineering technicians (skilled) per planner	5.8
Engineering technicians (skilled) per engineer	7.2
Engineering technicians (skilled) per maintenance staff	1.3
Maintenance resources per maintenance staff	1.6

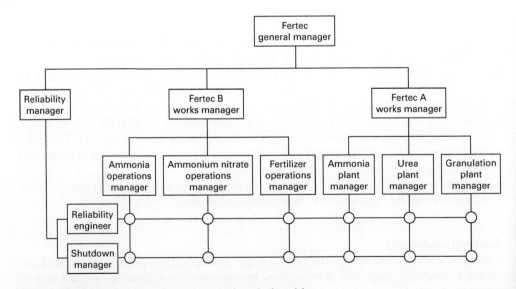

Figure 12.15 Senior management matrix relationships

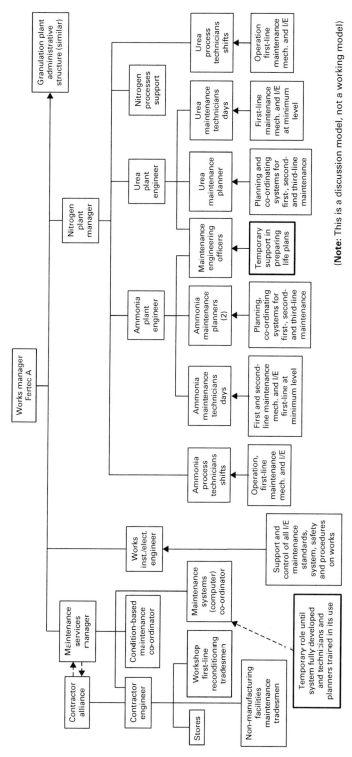

Figure 12.16 Modified administrative structure: Proposal A

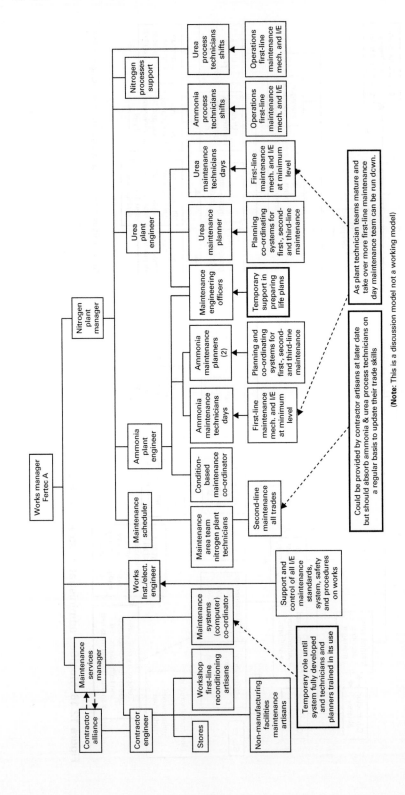

Figure 12.17 Modified administrative structure: Proposal B

Proposal A

The existing resource structure is retained (see Figure 12.9), incorporating the recommendations outlined. The modified administrative structure to tie up with this is shown in Figures 12.16 and 12.17. The main changes incorporated into this structure are as follows:

- The management of the ammonia and urea plants is combined at Plant Manager level.
- A professionally qualified electrical engineer is appointed within the works structure.
- The existing planners and facilitators act as a planner-facilitator. Training in the use of the existing computer system must improve before this proposal can be implemented.
- The maintenance teams report directly to the plant maintenance engineer with a link (as necessary) between the electrical/instrumentation technicians and the professional electrical engineer.
- All workshop and other non-core work is carried out by a contractor alliance.
- A benchmark should be sought for the operation of self-empowered maintenance and operation teams. The performance gap should be established and corrective actions identified.

Proposal B

The resource structure proposal shown in Figure 12.11 (Proposal B of the resource structure alternatives) is accepted and the administrative structure is modified as shown in Figure 12.17. The main changes incorporated in this structure are as follows:

- The management of the ammonia and urea plants is combined at plant management level.
- A professionally qualified electrical engineer is appointed within the works structure responsible for supporting and controlling all electrical standards, systems and safety.
- The first-line maintenance technicians report to their respective plant engineer with a link (as necessary) between the electrical instrument technicians and the electrical engineer.
- A condition-based maintenance co-ordinator is appointed to be responsible for all condition monitoring equipment and procedures within the works. He reports to the ammonia plant engineer.
- A maintenance scheduler is appointed (one of the existing planners) to report to the nitrogen plant manager. The function of the maintenance scheduler is set up to the weekly program of work (in conjunction with the ammonia plant and urea plant maintenance planners) across these two plants.
- The second-line nitrogen area team reports to the maintenance scheduler. The area team will have an 'on the tools' facilitator.
- All workshop and other non-core work is carried out by a contractor alliance linking with the maintenance services manager. This might extend later to cover second-line work.
- The planners report to their respective engineers in the ammonia, urea and granulation plants. Their function is to plan the work coming from the plants (priority check, method, spares, carnage, specification, etc.) as well as provide administrative support to the local maintenance team. The planners will work closely with the maintenance scheduler and area group co-ordinator.
- A plant teams development officer is appointed to assist the plant technicians in maturing into self-directing groups and acquiring and using appropriate trade knowledge and skills for first-line maintenance work. This task should be aided by benchmarking the teams against a 'best practice team'.

PART 4

Total productive maintenance

13 Total productive maintenance: its uses and limitations

'We fear what we don't understand.'

Aesop

Chapter aims and outcomes

To define total productive maintenance (TPM), its history, its application and its limitations.

On completion of this chapter you should be able to:

- define TPM and describe its history;
- understand the concepts, principles and structure of TPM;
- appreciate the extent of the application of TPM in European industry and the reasons for its success;
- understand the limitations of TPM.

Chapter route map

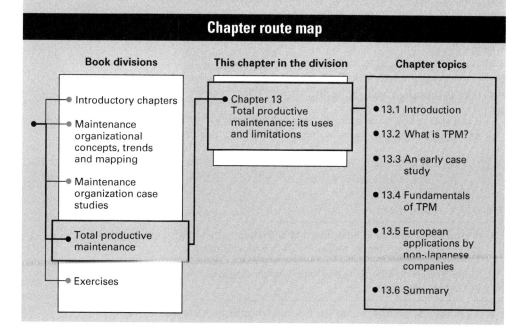

Book divisions

- Introductory chapters
- Maintenance organizational concepts, trends and mapping
- Maintenance organization case studies
- Total productive maintenance
- Exercises

This chapter in the division

- Chapter 13
  Total productive maintenance: its uses and limitations

Chapter topics

- 13.1 Introduction
- 13.2 What is TPM?
- 13.3 An early case study
- 13.4 Fundamentals of TPM
- 13.5 European applications by non-Japanese companies
- 13.6 Summary

Key words
• TPM • Autonomous teams • Just-in-time • Total quality management (TQM) • Overall equipment effectiveness • Kaizen • Participation

13.1 Introduction

One of the major trends in European industry is the adoption of the Japanese technique (and underlying philosophy) of TPM. Its main users are the motor manufacturers and associated industries, although there are some applications of its use in the process industries. This development is of such significance that the devotion of a chapter to its review is more than justified.

13.2 What is TPM?

This question is not easy to answer since every company seems to have its own interpretation. It is a technique which has been developed by Japanese manufacturing industry in order to provide both effective and efficient (and hence *productive*) maintenance in response to the needs of Just-In-Time (JIT) manufacturing and Total Quality Management (TQM). Indeed, it has been said by one of its originators that JIT and TQM are just not possible without TPM. It was recently introduced in a conference as follows:
    'There is nothing earth-shattering about TPM'.

> It is a sub-set of 'genba kanri' (workshop management), using a people-oriented approach to resolve maintenance and reliability problems at source.

A more formal definition and concept was given by Suzuki [1] (see Table 13.1 and Figure 13.1). The technique first surfaced in Japan in their manufacturing industry in the

Table 13.1 TPM definition

1. Is aimed at maximizing equipment effectiveness – by optimizing equipment availability, performance, efficiency and product quality.
2. Establishes a maintenance strategy (level and type of preventive maintenance) for the life of the equipment.
3. Covers all departments, such as planning, production and maintenance.
4. Involves all staff, from top management down to shop floor.
5. Promotes improved maintenance through small-group autonomous activities.

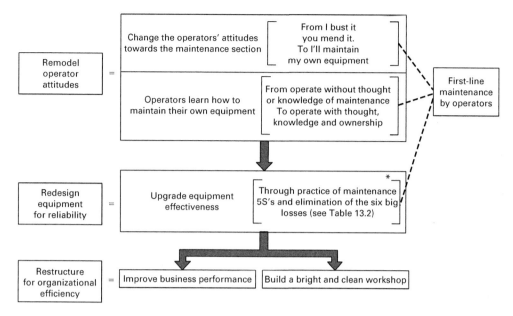

* Refers to systematic housekeeping practices–seiri (orderliness), seiton (tidiness), seiso (purity), seiketsu (cleanliness) and shitsuke (discipline).

Figure 13.1 TPM concept

early 1970s – the first application being carried out at Nippondenso. It is now used throughout that country but is most strongly represented in the manufacturing sector (especially in Toyota-based companies). More recently it is being introduced, in a modified form, in their process industries [2]. Over the last few years it has been developed and implemented in some of the larger European companies – in both the manufacturing and the process sectors [3–5].

13.3 An early case study

The author's first contact with TPM was in 1977. Then the Japanese Institute of Plant Engineering (JIPE) sent a maintenance management study tour to Europe. As part of this the group spent a few days at Manchester University exchanging views on maintenance management and, among other things, presented an explanatory case study of the ideas of TPM, based on the experience of the Toyoda Gosei Company Ltd., medium-sized suppliers of plastic injection and rubber moldings to the car industry [6].

In the early 1970s the company was expanding rapidly, had neglected preventive maintenance, and was in the classic 'maintain it when it fails' situation, which is expensive in downtime and which engenders ineffective use of resources. In order to improve plant availability, product quality and resource utilization, the management decided to use TPM.

In order to incorporate the ideas of TPM into its existing organization the management used a 'small group circle' approach (see Figure 13.2).

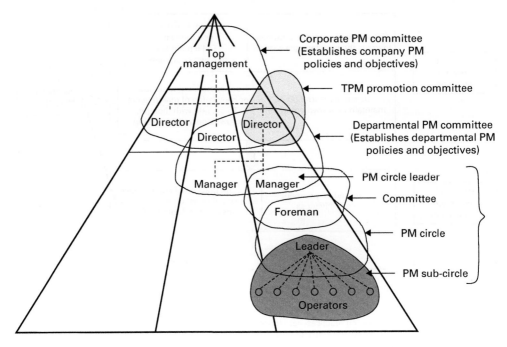

Figure 13.2 A system for promoting TPM within an existing organization

The TPM promotional activities were administered via a TPM promotions committee. The first step was to form a corporate TPM committee – which would decide on maintenance objectives and strategy – and departmental TPM committees – which would interact with the corporate committee and the voluntary small group circles of the shop floor. (This type of small group activity is a major feature of Japanese organizational culture. At one time the Toyota Motor Company, e.g. had over 4000 such circles in operation.) Each of the committees and the circles had a membership which cut across departmental boundaries.

The committees suggested the aims and themes of the circles and also acted in supporting roles. Each circle (or sub-circle) appointed its own leader (who would then be a member of a higher group) and established its aims (within the theme set for it). The group was expected to find ways of achieving these aims and was given help and support as necessary.

One of the first conclusions of the senior committee was that the maintenance department should be more closely linked with production. This was carried out in two stages, as shown in Figure 13.3.

The engineering department was responsible for procurement of new equipment, setting technical standards and maintenance policy, and major shutdown planning. The production manager was given the responsibility for the production and maintenance of his plant and had the maintenance supervisor reporting directly to him.

Within this new plant-oriented maintenance organization the most important change was the creation of a new role for the plant operators, who were now expected to

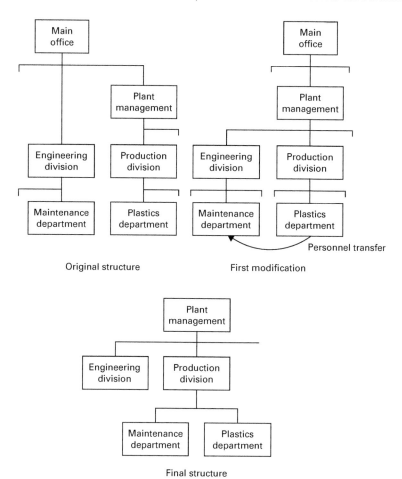

Figure 13.3 Organizational modification for TPM

'maintain normal operating conditions of machinery'. *This meant that they had to operate the machinery, carry out inspection and cleaning routines, perform simple maintenance tasks and assist artisans as required.* This necessitated expenditure of considerable effort to upgrade the operators' understanding of their machines and their maintenance 'know-how'. The small group circles were successfully used to help this training activity and also for the promotion of a closer relationship between mainte-nance artisans and plant operators.

The TPM committee introduced a new maintenance policy, the thrust of which was based on the following:

● Mandatory daily and weekly inspections carried out by the plant operators (consid-erable effort was put into improving the plant for ease of condition monitoring).
● Improved corrective maintenance techniques (considerable effort was put into upgrading the artisans' maintenance know-how).

- Identification and correction of those plant abnormalities that caused low availability or high maintenance costs or poor quality, and feedback of such information to design for plant modification.

The TPM committee also emphasized the most important change of all: *'that the new plan was to be carried out through the positive participation of all concerned'*. The following example illustrates that such co-operation was indeed achieved.

A suggestion from a small circle, for reducing die-replacement time on molding machines was implemented as a joint project by engineers from the die department, maintenance department and production division. Over a period of 2 years this reduced the replacement time from 49 minutes to 40 seconds.

The success of the efforts of the management and workers of Toyoda Gosei will be appreciated from the fact that, over a period of 2 years, the failure rate fell to 25% of its original level (see Figure 13.4).

This impressive case study, and the accompanying discussion, revealed that the main concepts, principles and characteristics of the TPM technique were as follows:

- The company decided at corporate level to revolutionize its traditional maintenance strategy and practice.
- The industrial relations environment allowed the company to make such a change.
- The small group activity was an essential part of the technique. In this case it was used in particular for design-out-maintenance (in the search for 'zero failures').
- Operators were given responsibility for the first-line maintenance of their own equipment and were given appropriate training.
- Equipment effectiveness was defined and downtime categories were identified.

At this stage in its development (1977) the author considered that the main advantages of TPM over the then UK maintenance practice appeared to lie in the area of human factors rather than in systems or strategy.

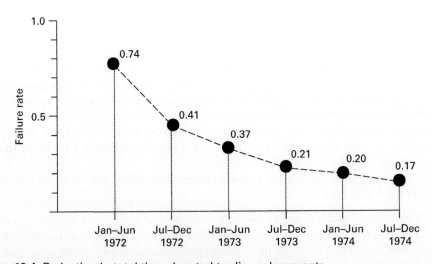

Figure 13.4 Reduction in total time devoted to die replacements

Review Question

R13.1   A number of companies in the 1990s announced that they were using TPM. On inspection the author found that they were *only* using a form of autonomous maintenance teams (AMT). List the main characteristics that you would expect to find if a company was using TPM.

13.4 Fundamentals of TPM

Over the last 15 years the JIPE has been involved in promoting and consulting on TPM in Japan and worldwide. As a result, the technique has developed further and a number of JIPE-based books, and related papers, explaining its philosophy and application have been published [2,7]. These, and various direct discussions with the JIPE, have led the author to an interpretation of the fundamentals of TPM as outlined below.

The basic philosophy [7]: Is to improve the way maintenance is carried out by improving its corporate image. Radical improvements based on new ideas and concepts are needed and are introduced by breaking away from past traditions and practices. One of the most important characteristics of TPM is that it must be accepted by the company as a whole – *it is a total company-wide maintenance philosophy.*

The maintenance objective or goal: Is not stated directly. However, it is implied that the main aim is to maximize overall equipment effectiveness (OEE) where:

$$OEE = Availability \times Performance\ rate \times Quality\ rate.$$

This is accomplished via the elimination of the six major losses (see Table 13.2) – reduction of downtime losses increasing availability, of speed losses increasing performance rate and of defect losses increasing quality rate.

Suzuki [2] goes further and implies that the effects obtained by using TPM (and therefore the objectives aimed for) are those indicated in Table 13.3.

Table 13.2 The six main losses

Downtime losses	1. Failures: losses caused by unexpected breakdowns.
	2. Set-up and adjustments: losses due to actions such as exchanging dies in press and plastic injection machines.
Speed losses	3. Idling and minor stoppages: losses caused by the operation of sensors and by blockages of work on shutes.
	4. Reduced speed: losses caused by the discrepancies between designed speed and actual speed of the equipment.
Defect losses	5. Defects in process: the production of defects and the reworking of defects.
	6. Reduced yield: losses that occur between the start up of a machine and stable production.

Table 13.3 Some of the results of applying TPM

MEASURABLE IMPROVEMENTS			
(A, B, C, etc. refer to Company A, Company B, etc.)			

Productivity		*Quality*	
Total efficiency of equipment	97% (D) 92% (N)	Fraction of defectives	60% decrease (A) 90% decrease (T)
Labor productivity	2.2 times (A) 1.7 times (I)	Number of claims	0 (T) 1/9 (D)
Number of problems	1/20 (I) 1/15 (S)	Cost for work-in-process	1/4 (Y) 1/2 (N)
Productivity of added value	1.5 times (T)	Lot out	0 (T)
Cost		*Delivery*	
Cost decrease	50% (R) 30% (A)	Inventory decrease	40% decrease (T) 50% decrease (S)
Energy saving	1/2 (I and D)	Lead time	1/2 (A)
Maintenance cost	40% decrease (A) 60% decrease (K)	Turnover rate	1.3 times (I and T)
Manpower saving	1/2 (I)	Direct shipment rate:	60% (T)
Safety		*Morale*	
Holiday accidents	0	Number of patents	37 (I) 28 (O)
Accidents with no rest	0		
Labor accidents	0		
		Number of suggestions for improvement	30 times (I) 5 times (T)
		Number of national qualified experts	7 times (N) 2 times (N)

'INVISIBLE' IMPROVEMENTS
Human resources   ● Confidence that we can do what was thought not possible.   ● Staff takes care of their equipment through self-maintenance activity.   ● Leaders upgraded by practicing 'progress and harmony' again and again through the positive activities of group leaders.

Table 13.3 (*Continued*)

Equipment
- Safe operation with decreased breakdowns and fewer unexpected small line stoppages.
- Realization of 'Streaming Factory' with less work-in-process and improved physical distribution through progress toward line production.

Management
- Improvement of the objective achievement rate after center for assessment and policy development (CAPD) is activated.
- Do and report.
- 'Competitive consciousness' between the staff of plants by sharing the same goal and activities of a company.
- 'Sense of unity' among them by participating in and exchanging inspection visits.

Company image
- Improves the image of business partners and the group companies by getting them to know about the introduction of TPM, by word of mouth in the area and/or inspection visits.

Exercises

E13.1   I have indicated that one of the aims of TPM is to maximize OEE. I have not given a full definition of OEE. Carry out a simple search of literature and define OEE in full.

E13.2   Extend your literature search to see if you can establish a TPM version of a maintenance objective(s). How does this objective(s) compare to the maintenance objective defined in Chapter 1.

The maintenance policy: Can be considered to be made up of the following interrelated elements:

(a) Improving the effectiveness of the plant via an analysis of the OEE of each piece of equipment. In each case attempting to eliminate the six major losses and aiming for zero defects.
(b) Establishing a 'capital asset management' system with emphasis on the procurement, design and installation phases so as to ensure minimum maintenance life cycle costs.
(c) Establishing, for existing and new equipment, a cost-effective maintenance life plan. This should include maintenance, spares holding and documentation policies.

Maintenance organizational characteristics: No one particular design of administrative structure seems to be recommended – in spite of the changes indicated in the introductory example (see Figure 13.3). However, the following major organizational characteristics are an essential part of the technique:

(a) The establishment of company-directed small teams of operators who also carry out first-level maintenance activities – the so-called Autonomous Maintenance Teams (AMT). An essential characteristic of these is the sense of plant ownership for their own area. The maintenance workers are also structured into groups of 20 and then into smaller teams (of up to 7), each with a leader.

Table 13.4 The seven steps for establishing operator–maintenance groups

1. Initial clean-up	All-round clean-up of dust and dirt, centering on the equipment proper, and implementation of lubrication, and machine parts adjustment; the discovery and repair of malfunctions in equipment.
2. Measures against sources of outbreaks	Prevention of causes of dust and dirt and scattering, improvement of places which are difficult to clean and lubricate. Reduction of the time required for clean-up and lubrication.
3. Formulation of clean-up and lubrication standards	Formulation of behavioral standards so that it is possible to steadily sustain clean-up, lubrication and machine parts adjustment in a short period (necessary for indicating a time frame-work that can be used daily or periodically).
4. Overall check-up	Training in check-up skills through check-up manuals; exposure and restoration of minor equipment defects through overall check-ups.
5. Autonomous check-up	Formulation and implementation of autonomous check-up sheets.
6. Orderliness and tidiness	Standardization of various types of on-the-job management items and complete systemization of upkeep management. • Standards for physical distribution in the workplace. • Standards for clean-up, check-ups and lubrication. • Standardization of data records. • Standardization of die management, jigs and tools.
7. All-out autonomous management	Development of corporate policies and goals, and making improvement activities routine. MTBF recording and analysis, and consequent equipment improvements.

(b) The use of small group activities – superimposed on the existing structure to promote, set up and monitor the use of TPM within the company (see Figure 13.2). This facilitates the top-down promotion of company TPM activities as well as the bottom-up generation of ideas for the shop floor group's activities.

(c) The mounting of a major effort in education and training. The small teams of operators, e.g. go through the training steps indicated in Table 13.4, the last of which is aimed at engendering continuous improvement (or '*kaizen*'), i.e. the groups are encouraged to look for ways of assisting the maintenance teams or engineers in their pursuit of zero defects. Each of the groups also sets its own objectives and targets, and monitors and records these results on an activity board for all to see.

13.5 European applications by non-Japanese companies

Several non-Japanese companies have used the ideas and concepts of TPM in an attempt to improve maintenance performance.

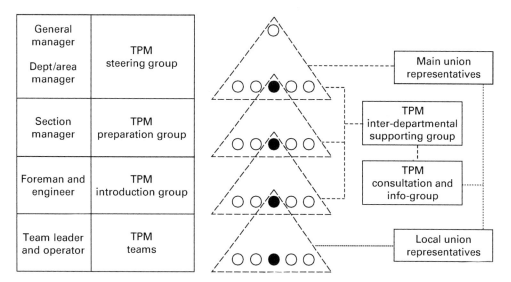

Figure 13.5 Overlapping small groups at Volvo

The Volvo car assembly plant at Ghent has carried out a major reorganization which involves the establishment of small self-managing teams of operators responsible for quality, operation and first-line maintenance in individual production process areas. These teams have followed the standard TPM training steps indicated in Table 13.4, focusing on continuous improvement.

The maintenance department carries out second- and third-line maintenance with major emphasis on planned preventive maintenance programs. Thus, TPM in this plant lays stress on the idea of small self-managing teams of operators. In addition, the whole reorganization was implemented via classic overlapping small group activities (see Figure 13.5). As a result, the plant has seen considerable improvements in production, quality and reliability. It appears that Volvo used their own management to design and undertake the implementation.

A process plant example of TPM is that of Hoechst, in France, who used the JIPE as consultants and advisers [5]. They concentrated on the following three areas:

1. Improvement of the reliability and maintainability of new equipment – via company and manufacturer analysis and systems. Hoechst called this the AMEDEC procedure – making new investments reliable.
2. Improvement of OEE – via the analysis of the six major losses for existing critical units. Hoechst called this the time-resolved spectroscopy (TRS) technique. They showed, as an example, how it had improved production output of a critical unit by 30%.
3. The formation of small groups of operator-first-line-maintainers (they called this 'automaintenance'). Although considerable effort was put into this area, through restructuring and training, Hoechst were not convinced of its success.

TPM has also been used in a more conventional way in the steel company Usinor Sacilor [8] and in the car manufacturers Renault, both in France [3,8]. Both companies are satisfied with the improvements in production, quality and reliability thus obtained.

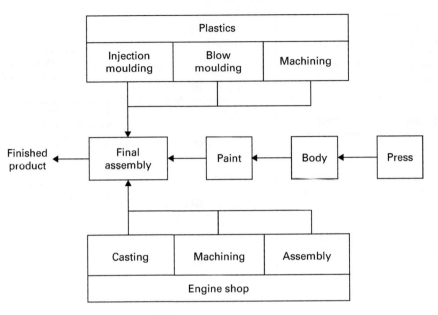

Figure 13.6 Plant layout, Nissan (UK)

Review Question

R13.2   The Total Productive Management (TPM) and Autonomous Maintenance
Teams (AMT) are similar (if not the same) as the self-empowered plant-
oriented teams (SEPOTs) described in Section 7.7. AMTs appear to work
extremely well in Japanese industry while SEPOTs have been much more
difficult to operate successfully in European/Australian companies. List
some of the main reasons that might account for this.

TPM the Nissan (UK) way [9]: Nissan Manufacturing (UK) (NMUK) was established in
1984 as Nissan's foothold in the European market. By 1993, the total investment in
NMUK was around £670 million, employing 3500 people, and producing some 200,000
cars per year. The plant was located on a greenfield site in Sunderland and is a fully
integrated car manufacturing facility (see Figure 13.6). NMUK has negotiated a single
union agreement with the AEEU – about 28% of the workforce having membership.

The resource structure outlined in Figure 13.7(a) shows that each major plant has its
own trade-force located in its own workshop, the operators undertaking the first-line
maintenance. The trade-force work on shifts and back up the operators' first-line maintenance during normal running. In addition they carry out, where possible, limited second-
line work during normal running and also weekend-planned maintenance. Figure 13.7(b)
shows that the administration is functionalized at the top – into Production, Engineering,
Sales, etc.

This structure is further functionalized, under the Production Director, into Production
and Maintenance and remains thus divided down to shop floor level – in many respects
a 'traditional' large structure comprising many departments and a number of levels of
management.

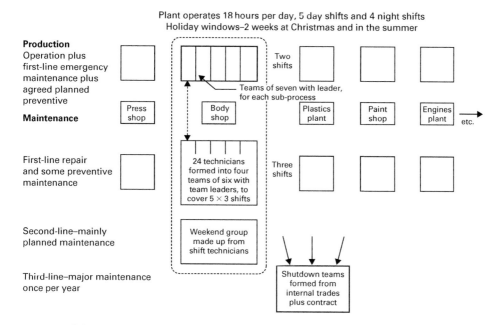

Figure 13.7(a) NMUK resource structure

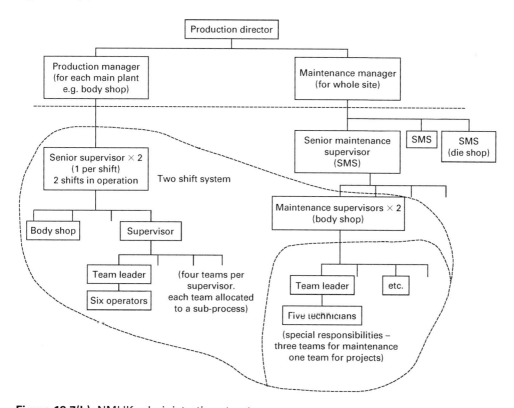

Figure 13.7(b) NMUK administrative structure

Perhaps the key organizational characteristic is the way the first-line supervisors and shop floor are structured into groups. Figure 13.7(b) shows that both production and maintenance supervisors are responsible for groups of about 20 workers. In the case of production the groups are further divided into three teams, each with six or seven operators and a leader. The supervisor is responsible for a zone (a process area) and the team leader for a sub-process. Two maintenance supervisors (one of whom, per shift, links with production) are responsible for the body shop. They have four teams, each with a leader, to cover 15 shifts – Monday to Friday. The function and training of these groups and teams, and the systems employed, are essential to the Nissan way of management.

Each group has a degree of autonomy. The supervisor is the focal point for recruitment, training and solving industrial relations problems. The team leader helps to train the group and looks after day-to-day planning. There is considerable peer pressure within each group and there is undoubtedly a sense of plant ownership within each operation team. They carry out the maintenance tasks shown in Figure 13.8 and are also heavily involved in continuous improvement (*kaizen*) projects.

Each group also puts considerable effort into the ideas of visual management, it being expected to produce and display regularly updated charts of the key group-performance indices – of attendance, quality, output and so forth. These are on display near where the group works and for all to see.

The maintenance teams carry out the planned preventive activities, respond to production first-line maintenance requests and train the operators in their TPM tasks. In addition, they get involved in group analyzes of maintenance problems.

TPM is an essential part both of NMUK's general managerial philosophy (genba kanri) and of its procedures, features of which are as follows:

- Objectives are set at corporate level and translated down to the shop floor groups. Every employee has a copy of his or her objectives on a personalized card.

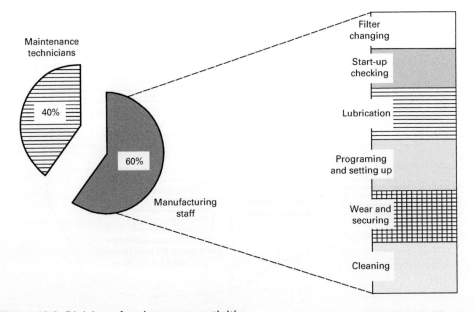

Figure 13.8 Division of maintenance activities

- *Kaizen* is not only a part of TPM, but is promoted through small group activity at all levels of the organization.
- *Ad hoc* and company-led team working is used for ongoing vertical or horizontal communication and for the initiation and development of special projects.
- The 5S's housekeeping approach (see Figure 13.1) is used to foster optimal working conditions on the shop floor.
- A major program of education and training provides high-quality personnel.
- Standard operating and maintenance procedures are established.
- Management control systems are adopted which, in the case of the maintenance department, include the following:
  - measurement of line operating ratio,
  - achievement reports,
  - audits of work standards,
  - review of preventive maintenance procedures.

13.6 Summary

During the last 10 years the author has studied TPM implementations in a range of companies, some European and some Japanese owned. He has been asking the following questions:

- What is TPM?
- How is it different from other techniques?
- Has it been used successfully, and if so why?

Regarding the first of these a response has been attempted in this section. The others are a little more difficult to answer.

How is it different? In terms of management procedures and maintenance systems there is nothing new:

- *The capital asset management approach*: Was pushed hard in the UK in the early 1970s and there were some particularly successful applications of the idea [6].
- *Maintenance strategy*: Many UK and European companies have an excellent approach, especially as regards condition-based programs.
- *First-line maintenance by operators and inter-trade flexibility*: Many Western examples could be given, notably Shell Chemicals, Carrington, which is a center of excellence in this matter.
- *Self-empowered groups*: Zeneca (pharmaceuticals) and many others have successfully have adopted this idea.
- *Small group activity*: Is based on the work of Rensis Likart [10] and has been applied in many Western organizations.
- *Continuous improvement*: For many years the author has advocated the approach similar to this has been shown in Figure 9.11. It has been adopted by several Australian companies.
- *Computerized documentation systems*: In this area the USA and the UK are in a particularly strong position, having some of the most advanced and innovative systems.

So, to reiterate in the systems area there is nothing new in TPM. Indeed, most of its concepts and systems have long been established in the USA and in Europe, various companies having employed a number of the above techniques in combination. Although this knowledge *has* been available to them, most European and USA companies cannot, however, be regarded as having *pro-active* maintenance departments. They usually function only *reactively* – because of the human factors problems of their conventional organizations.

In the UK the problem of vertical polarization – especially between the shop floor and the rest – is endemic and management rarely has the goodwill of the shop floor. This problem is often exacerbated by the division between first-line supervision and professional engineering staff. In addition, there is almost always a horizontal polarization between the production and the maintenance departments – 'we bust it, you repair it'. Superimposed on this is the corporate attitude that maintenance is a 'fixed overhead'. This, in conjunction with a rigid budgeting and costing system makes for short-term as far as maintenance decision-making is concerned. In such an environment it is therefore hardly surprising that most maintenance initiatives come from within the maintenance department and are unlikely to succeed fully because of the lack of support of other organizational and functional groups. Even when such initiatives come from corporate management they can fail because of the lack of a promotional procedure in a context of organizational resistance to change.

Has it been successful, and if so why? TPM has clearly been successful when applied in Japan and also to a lesser extent in its application in the European car manufacturing industry.

It appears that TPM succeeds not because of its strategy or systems or techniques, but because of the following:

(i) A belief by corporate management in the importance of maintenance and the realization that some resources have to be expended for long-term gain.

(ii) The use of the small circle approach, superimposed on the existing organization to initiate, and foster the acceptance of, the ideas of TPM. Or, as the Japanese say, 'it will not work without the participation of all concerned'. This approach was illustrated in Figures 13.2 and 13.5 and an example of it, for a large manufacturing company, is shown in Figure 13.9 [2].

(iii) The traditional features of Japanese organization, that tends to break down organizational polarization and create the ideal environment for TPM, i.e.:
   – overlapping groups to enhance horizontal and diagonal communication,
   – empowered shop floor groups, further subdivided into teams,
   – an extraordinary level of 'company values indoctrination' and conventional training.

On the negative side, although TPM is a strategic approach to maintenance management, it is presented as a recipe of structures, techniques and procedures that:

If applied in the way that we say will improve your maintenance organization.

In addition, the recipe is slanted towards the manufacturing industry (in particular car manufacturing) of its birth and development. For these reasons the author has not come across many examples of the successful application of TPM outside of the manufacturing industry.

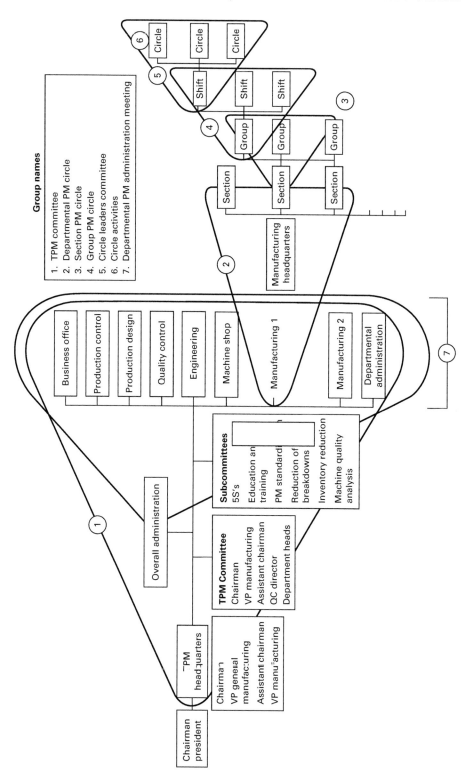

Figure 13.9 A TPM promotional structure

In spite of these last comments it is in the area of human factors management that we have most to learn from the Japanese. On his visits to Japan in 1978 and 1979 the author was impressed by many of the maintenance systems he was shown, including TPM. At that time he did not feel they could be applied in the UK because of that country's industrial environment. In addition, he felt that even if industrial relations improved, the UK culture was so different from the Japanese that the techniques would not be transferable. The experience of Nissan, Renault and Volvo shows that he was wrong.

Review Question

R13.3   Explain:
(a) Why TPM is unlikely to be the 'universal approach' to the establishment of a maintenance strategy?
(b) The essential differences between TPM, reliability-centred maintenance (RCM) and business-centered maintenance (BCM).

References

1. Suzuki, T., *New Directions for TPM*, Productivity Press, Cambridge, MA, USA.
2. Suzuki, T., *New trends for TPM in Japan*, Total Productive Maintenance Conference, MCE, Brussels, April 1992.
3. Grossman, G., *TPM at Renault*, Total Productive Maintenance Conference, MCE, Brussels, April 1992.
4. Poppe, W., *Autonomous maintenance, autonomous quality*, Total Productive Maintenance Conference, MCE, Brussels, April 1992.
5. Bisson, F., *Managing the production process*, Total Productive Maintenance Conference, MCE, Brussels, April 1992.
6. Kelly, A., *Maintenance Planning and Control*, Butterworths, UK, 1984.
7. Nakajima, S., *TPM – maximising overall equipment effectiveness*, Paper published by the Japanese Institute of Plant Maintenance, Minato-Ku, Tokyo, Japan (undated).
8. Barbier, C., *TPM in the steel industry*, Total Productive Maintenance Conference, MCE, Brussels, April 1992.
9. Fernie, A., *MEng thesis*, University of Manchester, 1992.
10. Likart, R., *The Human Organization: Its Management and Value*, McGraw-Hill, 1967.

Review Questions Guidelines

R13.1   The main characteristics of TPM are listed on Section 13.4 under the headings of philosophy, objectives, policy and organization. Autonomous teams is only part (a) of the organizational characteristics.

R13.2   Some of the main reasons are as follows:
   ● Japanese industry (especially the top companies) have until recently had a very small labor force turnover and could afford to select the best and invest heavily in training.
   ● The Japanese trade unions and culture are more conducive to team working in an industrial environment.

R13.3   (a) This is explained in part in the summary in Section 13.6. TPM is regarded as a maintenance strategic approach, but in the literature it is presented as a recipe. In addition, the recipe is slanted heavily towards the manufacturing industry of its birth and development. Therefore it is difficult to consider it as a universal approach.

   (b) TPM is a strategic approach slanted towards the manufacturing industry. BCM is also a strategic approach but stems from business objectives and is based on the fundamentals of management. It has a general application across a wide variety of industry. RCM is not a strategic approach. It is a powerful technique that is most useful when applied to problem units of plant to identify the failure modes and identify the most appropriate maintenance tasks.

Exercise Guidelines Solutions

E13.1   OEE = Availability × Performance rate × Quality rate
   ● Breakdown losses
   ● Idling and minor stoppages
   ● Quality defect and rework
   ● Set up and adjust losses
   ● Reduced speed
   ● Startup losses

E13.2   During my literature search I could find no clear statement (or starting point) of TPM maintenance objectives. However, numerous papers on TPM listed various forms of maintenance key performance indices (KPIs) (or the equivalent) (see e.g. Table 13.3).

   Compare this approach with the business-centered approach where the objective statement was:

   to achieve the **agreed** operating pattern, product output and quality, within the accepted plant condition and safety standards, and at **minimum** resource costs.

PART 5

Exercises

14 Course exercises

'Practice makes perfect.'

a Celtic proverb

Chapter aims and outcomes

Two exercises are presented to allow the reader the opportunity to test his knowledge of the organizational principles that have been developed in this book.

Chapter route map

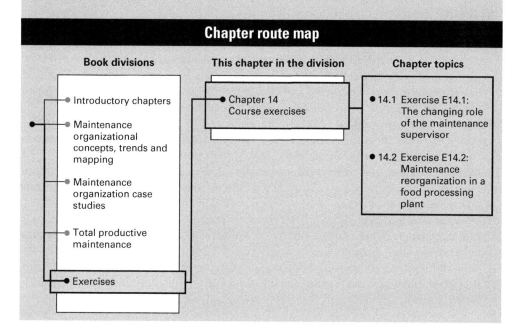

Book divisions	This chapter in the division	Chapter topics
Introductory chapters	Chapter 14 Course exercises	14.1 Exercise E14.1: The changing role of the maintenance supervisor
Maintenance organizational concepts, trends and mapping		14.2 Exercise E14.2: Maintenance reorganization in a food processing plant
Maintenance organization case studies		
Total productive maintenance		
Exercises		

14.1 Exercise E14.1: The changing role of the maintenance supervisor (Contributed by Dr. H.S. Riddell)

14.1.1 Background

This exercise will involve the concepts and principles incorporated in Riddell's work-role grid shown in Figure 5.11, which categorizes the duties and responsibilities of the traditional supervisor.

14.1.2 Part A: The supervisor's role in a traditional organization

The administrative structure of a petrochemical company is shown in Figure 14.1. The operating policy of the company is to run its plant continuously, at its rated output, for three shifts per day, 330 days per year, the plant being shutdown each August for a 5-week major overhaul. The maintenance supervisor and their teams (all on days) carry out first-line and second-line work within their respective trades and areas. Emergencies arising outside normal daywork hours are covered by a callout system for each trade and area. The plant teams are supported by the workshop for minor reconditioning and fabrication and by contract labor for work overloads and during the annual shutdown.

All of the supervisors have at least 6 years' experience, have been promoted from the artisans' ranks and have been well trained in supervisory duties. In general, they are respected by both trade-force and management. Their ages have a wide spread, with a mean of about 45 years.

Questions

(a) For a typical supervisor in Figure 14.1 develop what you consider to be a full set of the duties and responsibilities falling into each of the categories upward-facing technical (UT), upward-facing personnel (UP), downward-facing technical (DT), downward-facing personnel (DP) defined in Figure 5.11. Your approach should be based on your own experience and on Figure 5.11. Your answer should recognize that the supervisor has no clerical, planning or technical assistance.

(b) Estimate of the proportion of time that the supervisor should spend on each of the duties in each category. From this, estimate the total proportion of time spent in each category and draw a grid of the type shown in Figure 14.2.

(c) Do your lists and grid show a balance in the supervisors range of duties and in the time allocation between working as a junior member of the management team (UT + UP) and as a leader of his own team (DT + DP)?

(d) Do your lists and grid show a balance in his range of duties and in the time allocation between being responsible for technical and plant matters (UT + DT) and being responsible for personnel matters (UP + DP)?

(e) How different are the personal behavioral characteristics needed by the supervisor to successfully carry out 'upward-facing' duties from those needed for 'downward-facing' ones?

14.1.3 Part B: The role of the supervisor after a 'downsizing' exercise

After a downsizing exercise the administration outlined in Figure 14.1 was changed to that outlined in Figure 14.3 where it can be seen that the levels of management have been reduced (by the removal of the engineers and operations managers) and the spans of control (in particular that of the supervisor) increased. The supervisors increased span of control has been balanced by the introduction of planning officers to provide him with planning, scheduling and clerical support. The technical and plant knowledge of the planning officers is no greater than that of the supervisor.

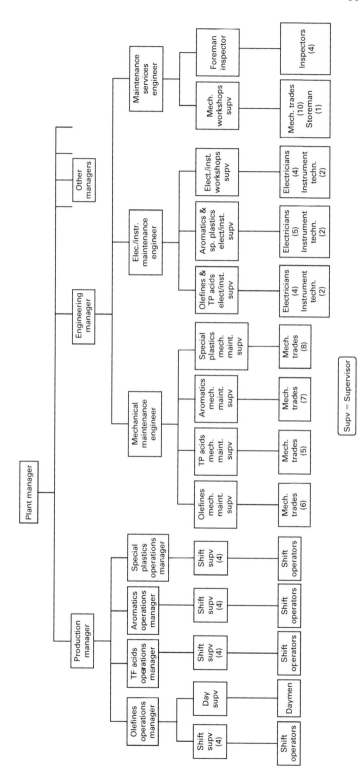

Figure 14.1 Administrative structure, petrochemical company

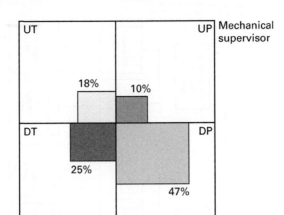

Figure 14.2 Proportion of maintenance supervisor's effort spent in each category of duties

Questions

(f) Re-examine your initial categorized list (question (a)) in the light of the organizational changes outlined in Figure 14.3. Revise your time estimates and draw a new grid of the type shown in Figure 14.2.

(g) To what extent do you consider that the increase in the supervisors DP and UP duties (resulting from his increased span of control) is likely to be compensated for by a decrease in his DT – and possibly UT – duties as a result of the support he now has from the planning officer?

(h) What other changes could be made in the maintenance organization to support the supervisor in coping with management's drive for flatter structures.

14.1.4 Part C: Introduction of self-empowered work teams

Management are now considering to introduce a program of change leading to the establishment of self-empowered teams (SETs) involving both operators and maintenance artisans.

Questions

(i)　(i) Use your answer to question (a) to identify the first batch of UT, UP, DT and DP duties which you consider should be transferred to the SETs.

(ii) Identify those of the remaining duties in each of the four categories which, in your opinion, should be transferred and suggest a time scale for the transfer.

(iii) Are there any duties remaining that still need to be carried out but which you do not consider appropriate to transfer to the SETs?

(j) When the SETs have been set up how would you change the job descriptions of the following personnel:

(i) maintenance manager,

(ii) maintenance supervisor,

(iii) artisan.

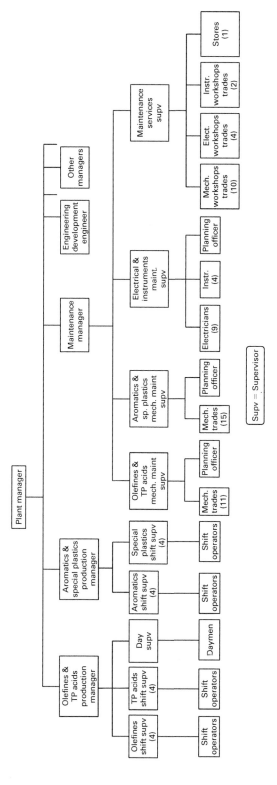

Figure 14.3 First change in administrative structure, petrochemical company

(k) What part should the maintenance supervisor take in the initial introduction of SETs?
(l) What role (if any) do you see for the maintenance supervisor after the SETs are fully implemented?

14.2 Exercise E14.2: Maintenance reorganization in a food processing plant*

14.2.1 Background

A food processing plant occupies a site with an area of some 50,000 m². It comprises 10 biscuit-making lines, 4 chocolate lines, a chocolate refinery, mixing and preparation plant and plant services (see Figure 14.4). The maintenance establishment numbers 95, 21 of whom are staff.

To a large extent, each production line is independent – although there are some common services at the front end of the plant. The chocolate-making lines (see Figure 14.5) are far more sophisticated than those for making biscuits. Each of the chocolate-making lines makes a different product and are not interchangeable. In general, they are made up of units in series (to include the raw material input streams, such as the caramel line), the failure of any one unit closing down the line. The chocolate lines, however, have some spare capacity (e.g. as shown, only two out of the three wafer lines are needed to keep the main line in full production). The plants operate three

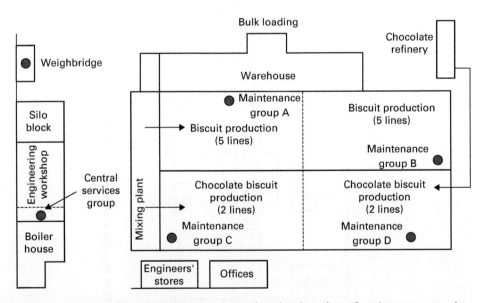

Figure 14.4 Layout of food processing plant, showing location of maintenance trade groups

---

*A similar exercise was carried out in the food processing plant of Chapter 1.

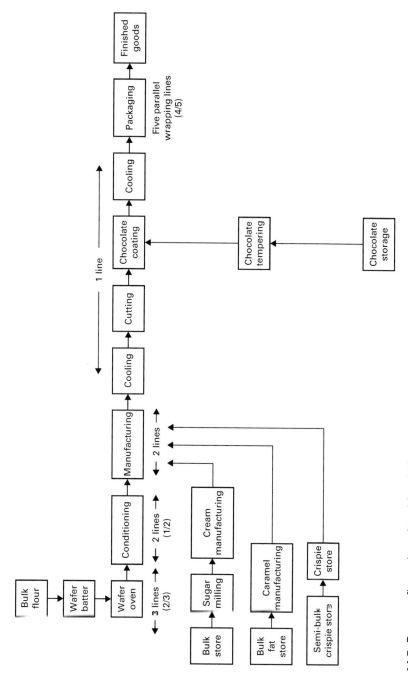

Figure 14.5 Process flow, chocolate biscuit line

shifts per day, 5 days per week, 50 weeks per year. The weekends are used for pro-duction cleaning and maintenance.

The major maintenance is carried out during the annual fortnight's shutdown in the summer. In general, all the lines operate throughout the day (08.00–16.00 hours) and evening shifts (16.00–22.00 hours), and about 30% of them throughout the night shift (22.00–06.00 hours) (the night shift is used to cover the peaks of production).

14.2.2 Company organization and maintenance strategy

The location of the maintenance 'plant groups' is shown in Figure 14.4, the mainte-nance resource structure in Figure 14.6. The trade-force is divided into five semi-autonomous groups, each carrying out the total maintenance workload for a designated number of lines (called plant sections) and the plant services, i.e.:

Group A: five biscuit lines (Section A).
Group B: five biscuit lines (Section B).
Group C: two chocolate lines (Section C).
Group D: two chocolate lines (Section D).
Group E: the common services.

Each group carries out first-line maintenance to cover the weekday production shifts, the second-line work at weekends, approximately half of each group coming in at the weekend for the latter purpose. The third-line work is carried out during the annual shutdowns, when each group is supplemented by contract labor. *Each group remains plant-specialized and to a large extent operates autonomously; there is only very limited movement between the groups.* It should also be noted that the 'wrapping fitters' work only in the wrapping area of each plant section, reporting to the section supervisors for industrial relations purposes but receiving technical advice as necessary from 'wrap-ping supervisors'. There is little or no inter-trade flexibility and none at all across the operator–maintainer divide, strict trade demarcation rules applying within the company, which has a poor history of operator and trade-force training.

In addition, to the above plant-specialized groups there is a centralized night shift-group that carries out first-line maintenance (overspill from the day and evening shifts) plus some inspection routines and other minor planned work.

The *company* administrative structure, shown in Figure 14.7, indicates that at senior management level there is a traditional functional division of responsibility. At superin-tendent level the division of responsibilities and duties is by plant area/product with complementary responsibilities across production and maintenance, e.g. Section D production superintendent and Section D maintenance superintendent are both respon-sible for the same five biscuit lines – they are also located in adjacent offices in that plant area.

The *maintenance* administrative structure is shown in Figure 14.8 and should be looked at in conjunction with Figures 14.6 and 14.7 or each of the plant-specialized groups a basic work planning system for online and offline work is used, although the majority of work from Monday to Friday is unplanned. The rather limited planning and scheduling for the weekend and shutdown work is carried out by the section mainte-nance superintendents.

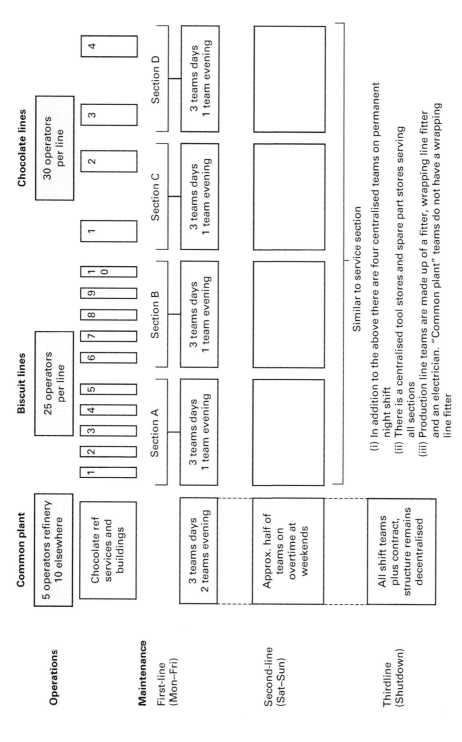

Figure 14.6 Resource structure, food processing plant

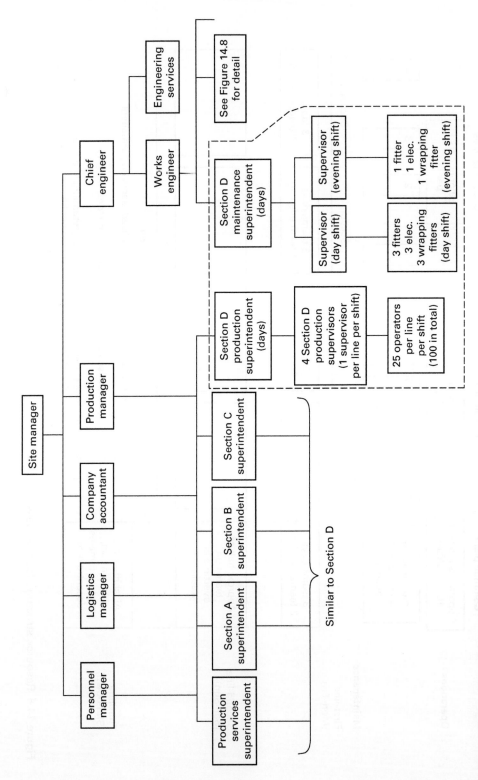

Figure 14.7 Company administrative structure, food processing plant

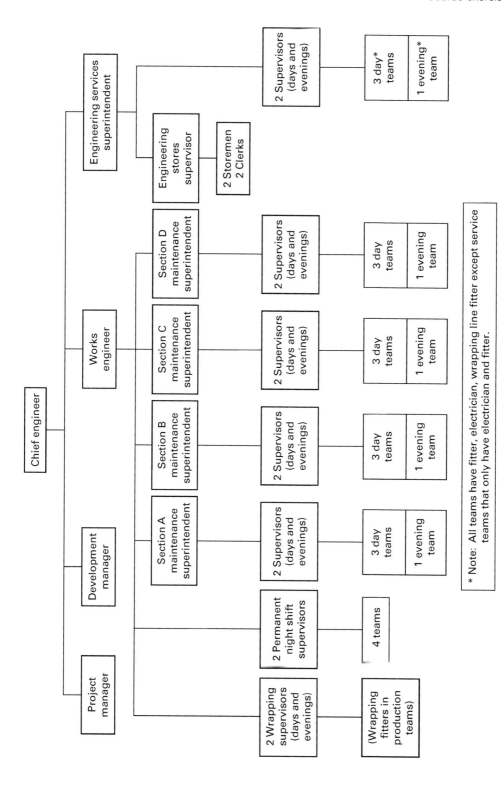

Figure 14.8 Maintenance administrative structure

* Note: All teams have fitter, electrician, wrapping line fitter except service teams that only have electrician and fitter.

There is no maintenance control, i.e. no plant failure or repair information is collected, stored or analyzed. Most documentation is carried out using hard paper systems, with the exception of Section C where a simple, single-user, microcomputer-based preventive maintenance program (with spares lists) is used.

The type and quality of the maintenance life plan varies between the five groups, from a stated fixed-time inspection policy in group C to operate-to-failure (plus lubrication) in group A. Group C declared their approach to maintaining the plant to be as follows:

- Carry out an effective corrective policy, plus daily inspections, from Monday to Friday.
- Inspect at weekends and repair as necessary in order to keep the plant going throughout the following week.
- Carry out other fixed-time work at weekends, or during the annual plant shutdown, or by exploiting spare plant.

14.2.3 The problem

The company has been very profitable and highly unionized. Little organizational change has taken place for some 15 years. Senior management are aware that they have fallen behind benchmark standards and are prepared for change.

Senior management are concerned at the low level of production line availability and the associated high-maintenance costs. In particular, they feel that the maintenance trade-force is far from fully utilized during the weekday production shifts. Figure 14.9 shows the result of a *work sampling* exercise, recently commissioned, which confirms this view (the corresponding graph for electricians shows a similar overstaffing). They also believe that the maintenance strategy is purely reactive and that even in Section C the stated preventive work is not being carried out at weekends because of the pressure of the unplanned corrective work. In addition, they are deeply concerned about the lack of co-operation between production and maintenance in each of the plant sections. They consider that there is no sense of plant ownership at shop floor level.

Questions

Senior management have asked you to consider the problem and to provide them with an approach for improving the situation.

Your answer should include the following:
(a) (i) A list of what you consider to be the main problem areas.
    (ii) An explanation to senior management on your view of the current situation at the plant with regards to maintenance, and the likely outcome if the problems are not overcome. In addition, outline the strategic approach you would advise them to follow to improve the situation in the short term.
(b) Provide an outline of a modified organization to enable the strategic approach outlined in (a)ii to be carried out. Your outline of a modified organization should include:
    (i) A proposed maintenance resource structure. This should take into consideration the information presented in Figure 14.9 and the need to provide resources to carry out an increased level of catch-up work/planned work. The overall size of the workforce must not increase. Contract labor can be used in the short term.

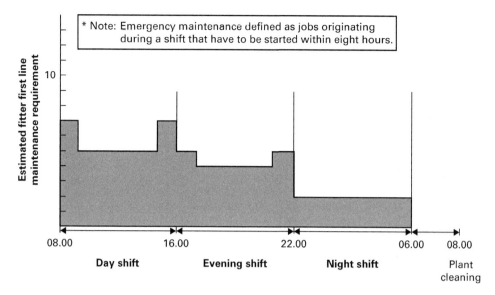

Figure 14.9 First-line fitter workload

    (ii) A proposed administrative structure that shows the main changes that you intend to make to both the maintenance and production departments. These changes should tie up with the resource structure proposals of (b)i.
(c) Provide management with a vision of the longer-term organization they require to come up to international benchmark levels.

Exercise Guideline Solutions

E14.1   (a) The list should be comprehensive, in line with the grid concept, but not a straight copy of Figure 5.11.

     (b) The grid is based on the proportions of time that the supervisor spends in each of the categories – the total must come to 100%.

     (c) In general, the grid will show that the UT + UP duties are much less time consuming than the DT + DP duties.

     (d) In general the grid will show that the balance between the UT + DT and UP + DP duties will depend on the supervisors discipline, i.e. in the case of the instrument supervisor the center of gravity of the grid will be toward the UT + DT tasks; in the case of the services supervisor toward the UP + DP tasks.

     (e) If the supervisor is to successfully carry out his upward-facing duties he needs to be integrative and compliant. In order to successfully carry out his downward-facing duties he needs to be self-assertive, a leader, and needs to have the ability to initiate ideas.

  (f & g) The list should show a reduction in the DT duties as a consequence of having a planning officer (the duties having been transferred). Although the list of DP and UP duties may remain about the same, the time allocated to these will show a large increase as a result of the increased span of control. The center of gravity of the grid will therefore have moved toward the DP category of duties.

(h)   (i) Provision of effective maintenance documentation and information systems.
   (ii) Provision of technical back-up by engineering staff.
   (iii) Recruitment of competent artisans.
   (iv) Provision of plant-specific training for the artisans.
   (v) Promotion of, and training for, inter-trade flexibility.

(i)   The following duties could be:
   (i) Transferred to SET in the short term:
   - UT   Advising on design-out maintenance problems.
       Involvement in setting up the SET objectives.
       Involvement in improving the maintenance-information systems.
   - UP   Involvement in changing working conditions.
   - DT   Assisting in the revision of preventive-maintenance procedures.
       Assisting in the setting of standard job procedures.
       Monitoring work output and performance levels.
       Monitoring work quality and safety issues.
   - DP   Job allocation.
       Motivation of team to achieve targets and objectives.
       Monitoring of team members' progress and problems.

   (ii) Considered for transfer to the SETs after a period of about 12 months of SET operation:
   - UT   The use of condition monitoring equipment.
       Assisting in the revision of maintenance schedules.
   - UP   Influencing personnel policies for artisans and apprentices.
       Involvement in training procedures for the SET members.
   - DT   Establishing job methods and work standards.
       Involvement in the setting of improved team targets.

   (iii) (Four examples of those) considered as lying outside the boundaries of the SETs responsibilities:
   - UT   Co-operating with other departments on technical matters.
   - UP   Influencing personnel policy on pay, promotions and discipline.
   - DT   Organizing on-site contractors.
   - DP   Disciplining individuals in accordance with agreed procedures (?).

   Most of the supervisors' duties listing in Figure 5.11 (and in your own listing) will continue to be relevant and will have to be carried out either by the SETs or by some other member of the management.

(j) The job descriptions are as follows:
   (i) *Maintenance manager.*
   - The clarification of business and departmental maintenance objectives and their transmission to the SETs.
   - The development of a participative leadership style and increased delegation of decision-making to the SETs.

- The convening of a SETs implementation steering committee, which will include the maintenance manager.
  (ii) *Supervisor*:
  - Improvement of their knowledge of how multi-skilled SETs should function. Amendment of their leadership style to complement the operation of SETs. Development of their skills in management of change.
  - Involving them in advising the steering committee on the implementation and operation of SETs.
  (iii) *Artisans*:
  - Development of necessary add-on skills for multi-skilled operation.
  - Setting up procedures for maintenance/production shift workers to take part in joint problem-solving activities.
  - Promotion of shop floor understanding of the reasons for organizational change.
(k) The maintenance supervisors are the key to the successful implementation of the SETs. It is important that they are involved in this at an early stage, *viz.*:
  - advising senior management on the duties of the SETs,
  - assisting in programming the transfer of their own duties to the SETs,
  - assisting in selling the concept to the SETs.
  The SETs must have a clear understanding of the boundaries of their responsibilities. The supervisor must take a flexible approach to his traditional duties, helping the SETs when needed but otherwise standing back. During the transition stage he should act as facilitator, trainer and advisor to one or more of the SETs.
(l) As a technician advisor or a planner, giving technical and planning support to one or more of the SETs.

E14.2   (a) (i)   Main problem areas:
  - Low availability of equipment coupled with high-maintenance cost, which is caused by:
    - Low utilization of trade-force through mismatch of first-line workload to first-line resources.
    - Poor inter-trade flexibility.
    - Poor operator–maintainer flexibility.
    - Poor training.
    - Strict trade demarcation.
    - Poor work planning systems coupled with a reactive workload caused by poor preventive maintenance.
  - Low availability caused by:
    - Little or no preventive maintenance.
    - Low-quality corrective work caused by lack of ownership at trade-force level.
    - Poor documentation and history.
    - Polarization between production and maintenance.
    - No attempt to build teams or introduce the ideas of self-empowerment.
  (ii) The condition of the plant has been allowed to get out of control because in most areas there are no life plans other than operate-to-failure. Where there is a stated preventive strategy, e.g. in group C, it

is not being carried out because of the dominance of high-priority corrective work. This situation has resulted in the organization evolving to cope with reactive maintenance; i.e. it has become a reactive rather than a pro-active organization. In such situations it is difficult to achieve high levels of labor efficiency. These problems are further compounded by such factors as inflexibility and poor work planning.

To improve the situation, two main tasks need to be accomplished.

- Improving the condition of the plant via an injection of corrective maintenance resources. This will certainly require assistance from contractors and the equipment manufacturer.
- It will then be necessary to hold the condition at the improved level by adopting a new life plan for the units and an appropriate maintenance schedule for the plant. Resources are therefore required, at engineer and supervisor level, to design and implement the necessary life plans, procedures and systems, and at trade-force level to carry out the necessary preventive-maintenance tasks. This can be accomplished only by organizational change. It is clear that if the mismatch between the first-line workload and the shift resources were to be corrected then resources would be released for a planned maintenance group. Similarly, a reorganization of the administrative structure to match international benchmark levels should release the necessary engineers and supervisors to inject the planning input.

(b)   (i) *A modified resource structure.* The information given in Figure 14.9 shows that it is important to retain some form of shift cover. It is also important, however, to match the shift resource to the workload shown. Figure 14.10 shows a modified resource structure where the shift resource has been kept decentralized (i.e. equipment-specialized) because of the need to build production–maintenance teams and because of the specialized nature of the work. There are therefore five fitters on each main shift. The overload on days can cascade to the second line 'day resource'. A similar approach is used in the case of the electricians and wrapping fitters.

The centralized night shift teams have been retained but reduced to two teams to match the workload. The reduction in the shift resource allows the creation of second-line day-shift teams to handle the second-line work (mainly planned maintenance). In addition, a permanent weekend group has been established, made up of two teams working 2 × 12 hour shifts (with overtime allowance, this provides a full week's work). These second-line teams are centralized and work throughout the plant by job priority. The annual shutdown resource is also centralized and made up of the internal resource plus contract labor as necessary.

(ii) The main move (see Figure 14.11) has been to create process orientated manufacturing units – to which the shift maintenance teams report – in each plant section. The manufacturing superintendents and supervisors would include in their number some of the previous maintenance staff. The release of several maintenance superintendents and supervisors has provided supervisors for the second-line crews and for the creation of a maintenance planning and support section reporting to the works engineer.

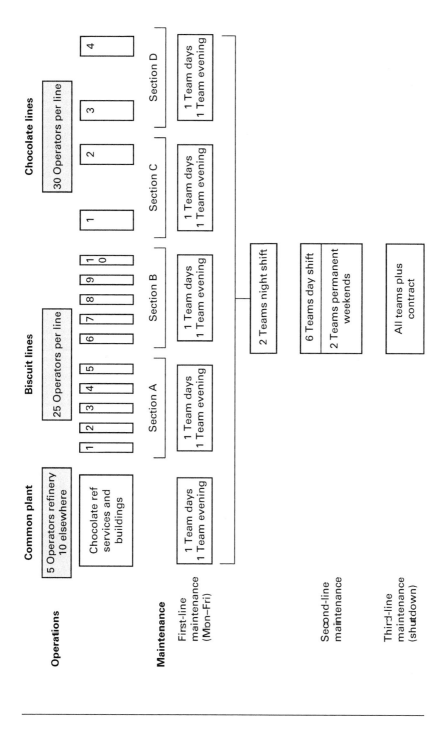

Figure 14.10 Revised resource structure for food processing plant

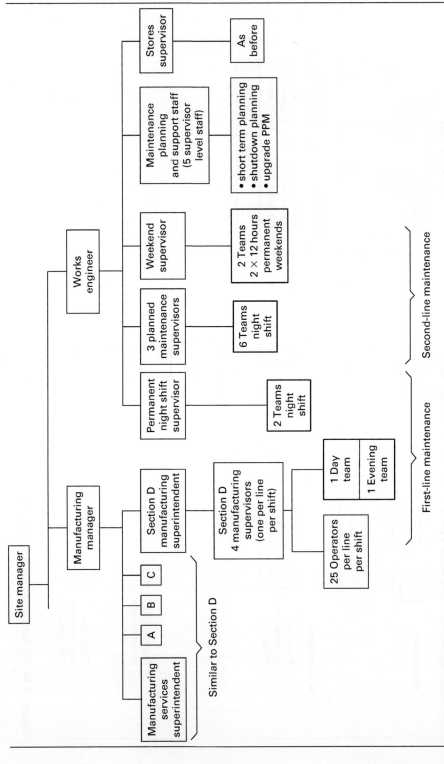

Figure 14.11 Revised administrative structure for food processing plant

(c) The changes proposed in (b) are all short term, i.e. they can be carried out without extensive training and via negotiation with the trade unions.

With time further major improvements can be made to allow the company to come up to international benchmark levels. These changes would include:

- Improved inter-trade flexibility.
- Improved operator–maintenance flexibility.
- Introduction of self-empowered plant-oriented teams.
- Identification of non-core work to be carried out by contractor or company – contractor alliance.

Index

Accountability, 95
Activity sampling, 84
Administrative structure, 15–16, 30
 design or modification, 107–108
 organization vision, 27
 principal functions, 90
Agricultural chemical plant:
 Fertec A, overview, 220–222
 maintenance audit, 219 et seq
 maintenance organization:
  administrative structure, 236 et seq
  resource structure, 232–236
 maintenance strategy:
  ammonia plant, 224 et seq
  plant-operating characteristics, 224
 objectives:
  comments, 222–224
Alliances, 145
Alternative maintenance strategy, for
  continuous operation, 22–23
Aluminum rolling mill:
 background, 175–177
 life plans and preventive schedules,
  177–178
 maintenance systems, 181–182
 observations and recommendations,
  182–183
 operating characteristics and objectives, 177
 overview, 178–180
Attitude, 119
Autonomous teams, 114, 135, 255

BCM, see Business-centered maintenance
Behavioral characteristics, 114 et seq
 group, 120–122
 individual, 115–119
Bottling plant:
 background, 170–171
 maintenance strategy and organization,
  171–173
 organizational change, 173–174
 short-term actions, 174
Business objectives, 4, 24
Business-centered maintenance (BCM),
  1 et seq, 23 et seq
 alternative strategy, 22
 application of, 5–7

 audit, 7 et seq
 maintenance organization, 3 et seq
 methodology, 5
 organizational change, 23
 strategic thought process, 23–24

Cario:
 characteristic teams, 213–214
Case studies:
 agricultural chemical plant:
  Fertec A overview, 220–222
  maintenance organization, 232 et seq
  maintenance strategy, 224 et seq
  objectives, 222–224
 colliery, reorganization:
  COALCOM, 186 et seq
  progress visit and consultancy, 196 et seq
 do's and don'ts:
  Cario, 213–214
  comments, 215–216
  Fertec B, 210–213, 214–215
 moving with times:
  CMG audit, 156–161
  observations, 164–166
  setting up alliance, 162–164
 organizational change, caution:
  aluminum rolling mill, 175 et seq
  bottling plant, 170–175
Chain of command, 95
Chemtow Ltd, 154
 business units, 155
COALCOM, maintenance consultancy (1994):
 background, 186–187
 equipment and operating characteristics,
  187–189
 life plans and preventive schedule, 189–191
 maintenance organization:
  administrative structure, 193–195
  resource structure, 191–193
 maintenance systems, 196
 production and objectives, 189
 recommendations, 196–201
Collateral, 96
Colliery, reorganization:
 COALCOM (1994), 186 et seq
 progress visit and consultancy (1997),
  201 et seq

Company–contractor alliance, 123, 146, 162
Continuous improvement, 116, 135, 256,
    260, 261
Contract labors, 68–71
Contracting, 145
Contractors:
    benefits and problems, 69
Core work, 68
Course exercises:
    FPP, maintenance reorganization, 274 et seq
    maintenance supervisor:
        self-empowered work teams, 272–274
        supervisor's role, 270–272
Culture, 120

Decision model, 67
    resource structure, 67
Demarcation, 132
Departmentalization, 106
Design:
    administrative structure, 107–108
    resource structure, 67
        design-making areas, 69–71
Downsizing, *see* Slimming structure

Emergency maintenance, 42, 43–44, 45
Engineer and supervisor, 104
Envy, 119
Equipment ownership, 115–116
Esprit de corps, 120
European applications:
    non-Japanese companies, 256 et seq

Fertec A, 220 et seq
    overview, 220
Fertec B:
    characteristic teams, 210–213
    improving team operations, 214–215
First-line work, 11, 12
    forecasting, 47
    mapping, 43–45
Food processing plant, maintenance
        department:
    audit of, 7 et seq
    audit summary, 21
    control system, 18–19
    documentation, 19–21
    life plans, 8–11
    objectives, 7–8
    organization:
        administrative structure, 15–16

resource structure, 13–15
    preventive schedule, 8–11
    work planning, 16–18
    workload, 11–13
Food processing plant, maintenance
        reorganization:
    background, 274–276
    maintenance strategy, 276–280
    problem, 280–287
Functional organization, 129

Goodwill, 116

Horizontal polarization, 99, 120, 124
Horizontal skilling, 142
Human factors:
    auditing maintenance management, 124–125
    definition, 112
    human relations approach, 113–114

Inter-plant flexibility, 74, 75, 234

Japanese Institute of Plant Engineering (JIPE),
        249, 253, 257
Jealousy, 119
Job description, 97

Kaizen, 116, 256, 260, 261
Key decision-making areas:
    resource structuring, 68 et seq
Key human factors, 115

Labor flexibility, 73
Line authority, 95
Logistics, 64, 79

Maintenance:
    costing system, 19
    objectives, 7–8
Maintenance administrative structure:
    characteristics:
        engineer and supervisor, 104
        maintenance–engineering interface,
            97–99
        maintenance–production interface,
            99–103
        overhaul administration, 104–106
        spare parts management, 103
        vertical polarization, 103
    modeling, 90–91
    traditional views, 91–97

Maintenance auditing, 7 et seq
Maintenance management:
    auditing, 124–125
    behavioral characteristics:
        group, 120–123
        individual, 115–119
    human factors, 111 et seq
    human relations approach, 113–114
    outsourcing alliances, effect, 123
Maintenance organization:
    administrative structure, 15, 16, 30
    design:
        influencing factors, 33 et seq
    modeling, 31–33
    outline, 29 et seq
    primary task, 30
Maintenance organization, trends:
    centralized resource structures, 129–133
    contracting, 145–146
    flexible working practices, 133–135
    outsourcing, 145–146
    plant manufacturing units, 136–139
    SEPOTs, 142–145
    slimming structure, 139–142
    traditional, organizations, 128–129
Maintenance policy, 251–252, 255
Maintenance resource structure:
    decision-making areas:
        contract labor, 68–71
        logistics, 79
        non-daywork maintenance, 75–76
        plant specialization, 74
        resources locations, 78
        trade-force composition, 71–73
        trade-force location, 74–75
        trade-force sizing, 77–78
    decision model:
        design or modification, 67
    mapping, 58–59
    resource characteristics:
        information, 64–67
        manpower, 63
        spare parts, 63–64
        tools, 64
    systematic procedure:
        existing structure, 81–82
        new plant, 79–81
Maintenance supervisor:
    changing role:
        downsizing exercise, 270–272
        traditional organization, 270

Maintenance teams, do's and don'ts:
    Cario:
        team characteristics, 213–214
    Fertec B:
        improving team operation, 214–215
        team characteristics, 210–213
    general comments, 215–216
Maintenance–engineering interface, 97–99
Maintenance–production interface, 99–103
Management theories, 112
Manufacturing units, 100, 103, 136–138
Mapping resource structure, 58–62
Matrix organizational structure, 97, 100, 238
Morale, 117–118
Motivation, 117
Moving with times:
    background, 154–156
    CMG audit, 156–161
    observations, 164–167
    setting up alliance, 162–164
Mutual recognition units (MRUs), 100

Non-core work, 68, 69, 70, 81
Non-daywork maintenance cover, 75–76

Organization:
    change, 35, 36
    elements, 30
Organizational change, caution:
    aluminum rolling mill, 175 et seq
        characteristics and objectives, 177
        maintenance systems, 181–182
        observations, 182–183
        overview, 178–180
        plans and schedules, 177–178
    bottling plant, 170 et seq
        organization and maintenance, 171–173
        short-term actions, 174
        way forward, 173–174
Organogram, 15, 90
Outsourcing, 145
    alliances, 123
Overall equipment effectiveness, 253
Overhaul administration, 104–106

Parochialism, 119
Participative management, 114
Plant custodian, 132
Plant layout, 58
Plant reliability control (PRC), 181–182
Plant specialization, 74

Prejudice, 119
Preventive maintenance, 9
Pride, 119
Production plan, 10
Progress visit and consultancy (1997):
    life plans and preventive schedule, 204
    organization, 201–204
    recommendations, 204–206
Protectionism, 118
Pyramid of personnel, 31

Queuing theory model, 77

Resentment, 118
Resistance to change, 119
Resource characteristics:
    information, 64–67
    manpower, 63
    spare parts, 63–64
    tools, 64
Resource locations, 78
Resource smoothing, 13
Resource structure, 13–15

Second-line work, 11, 12
    forecasting, 47–48
    mapping, 45–46
Self-empowered plant-oriented teams
        (SEPOT), 74, 100, 142–145
    characteristics, 144
Self-empowered teams, 100, 104, 122
Shift working flexibility, 74, 75, 76
Slimming structure, 139–142
Span of control, 95
Spare parts management, 103
Staff, 96
    inventory, 237
Star configuration, 144
STAR team, 144
Station workload:
    categorization, 42
Strategic thought process, 23–24
Supervisor's role:
    after downsizing exercise, 270–272
    traditional organization, 270
Synergy, 31

Systematic procedure:
    existing resource structure, 81–82
    new plant, 79–81

Team characteristics:
    Cario, 213–214
    Fertec B, 310–213
Third-line work, 12, 13
    forecasting, 48
    mapping, 46
Total productive maintenance (TPM):
    definitions, 248–249
    early case study, 249–253
    European applications:
        non-Japanese companies, 256 et seq
    fundamentals, 253–256
Trade consolidation, 73, 133
Trade-force:
    composition, 68–73
    formulation, 80
    location, 74–75
    sizing, 77–78

Unity of command, 96

Vertical polarization, 103, 122
Vertical skilling, 142

Work control system, 17–18
Work planning system, 31
Workload, 11
    case studies:
        agricultural chemicals, 50–51
        alumina refining, 51–52
        ammonia plant, 49
        chemical plant, 49
    categorization, 11–13, 40–43
    forecasting, 46 et seq
        first-line, 47
        second-line, 47–48
        third-line, 48
    mapping:
        first-line, 43–45
        second-line, 45–46
        third-line, 46

Printed and bound by CPI Group (UK) Ltd, Croydon, CR0 4YY

08/05/2025

01864813-0003